SHADOWS ON THE KLAMATH

A Woman in the Woods

Louise Wagenknecht

Oregon State University Press   Corvallis

Library of Congress Cataloging-in-Publication Data

Names: Wagenknecht, Louise, 1949- author.
Title: Shadows on the Klamath : a woman in the woods / Louise Wagenknecht.
Description: Corvallis : Oregon State University Press, 2021. | Includes
  bibliographical references.
Identifiers: LCCN 2021047558 | ISBN 9780870711565 (trade paperback) |
  ISBN 9780870711572 (ebook)
Subjects: LCSH: Wagenknecht, Louise, 1949- | United States. Forest Service—
  Officials and employees—Biography. | Forest rangers—Montana—Glacier
  National Park—Biography. | Klamath National Forest (Calif. and Or.)—
  History.
Classification: LCC SD129.W335 A3 2021 | DDC 634.9092 [B]—dc23/
  eng/20211015
LC record available at https://lccn.loc.gov/2021047558

♾ This paper meets the requirements of ANSI/NISO Z39.48-1992
(Permanence of Paper).

First published in 2021 by Oregon State University Press
Printed in the United States of America

Oregon State University Press
121 The Valley Library
Corvallis OR 97331-4501
541-737-3166 • fax 541-737-3170
www.osupress.oregonstate.edu

To the memory of Jon Silvius, who saw it coming.

If you bring forth what is within you, what is within you will save you.
If you do not bring forth what is within you,
what is within you will destroy you.

— The Gospel of Thomas

Contents

Acknowledgments

For invaluable feedback on the manuscript in various stages of composition and completion, many thanks to Russell Rowland, Mary Emerick, and Susan Marsh. Your eyes and advice made this a much better book.

To all the wonderful people working at and with Oregon State University Press: Kim Hogeland, Micki Reaman, Marty Brown, Thomas Booth, Martyn Schmoll, and Laurel Anderton—many thanks and genuflections to you all. Go Beavers!

For all the people on the Klamath National Forest who were kind and patient to a very flawed individual, you are loved and remembered. You made—and some of you still make—that wild piece of California a better place.

Concerning names: There are some names in here. Most that belong to living people have been changed.

Part I

CHAPTER I

Line and Staff

Looking up the South Fork of Indian Creek toward Preston Peak, highest peak on the Klamath National Forest.

"You are not," the man in the green uniform shouted at me, *"doing a good job!"* Dick Leslie's palm slapped the blond wood of the lunchroom table. I flinched, and my leg hit the table leg and jiggled the coffee cups. My boss's eyes were angry behind their bifocals. My pen, poised above a yellow legal pad, stopped in midsentence. I had seen that look before, at age five, when my grandfather caught my sister and me trying to roll cigarettes with his tobacco and papers.

All four of us sitting around the table had flinched at his yell, and we stared at him, frozen. When he spoke again, his eyes dropped to his own notebook, and I actually wrote down his words in a shaky hand, unable to break the habit of obsessive note-taking.

Handle telephone switchboard badly.

Erasures on letters.

Follow official Ten Code!

I was so puzzled by the last item that I barely registered Maude and Ann and Joan jumping in to stick up for me. She's very prompt, they said, and she has a very positive attitude, and she's never been late or absent, and ...

As they spoke, Dick continued to stare down at the notebook beneath his hands, not meeting their eyes. When they paused for breath, Dick looked up again and saw tears running down my cheeks. "Stop crying!" he said, his voice rising to a shout again, but I could neither stop them nor trust myself to speak. Dick stood up and left the room.

"That was a scurvy thing to do in front of people," Joan said to me as we walked back down the hall to our desks. She patted me on the shoulder. "I'm pulling for you," she added.

"Thanks," I said, grabbing a Kleenex out of the tissue box. I picked up my bag lunch and fled outside to the side lawn to meditate on my sins under the blue sky of a fine warm day in late April 1974. I was almost twenty-five years old, had been working for the Klamath National Forest for five months, and had never felt like such a failure.

I had grown up in a Forest Service family, babysat the children of district rangers, and seen sweating forest supervisors guzzle beer at August cookouts. I knew from an early age that the honchos put their pants on one leg at a time, just like everybody else. But Dick had brought home to me in a brutal way that familiarity with those men, and with the Klamath National Forest in general, wasn't all that helpful now that I was an adult working for the outfit. I hadn't yet learned the wisdom of feigning more awe than I felt. A few months ago, I had been ecstatic just at the thought of going home to the dark tangle of the Klamath Mountains, far to the north of the sweltering Central Valley town where I found a postcollege job in a county clerk's office.

So when the Klamath National Forest, in its wisdom, offered me a clerical job in the very place where I grew up, the last thing on my mind was that old enmities might lurk beneath the cordial surface of people I had known since high school. My stepfather's eight-year history on the Klamath had made him enemies as well as friends. But I didn't think about that as I packed my Volkswagen and headed north to Happy Camp late in 1973. I felt only the joy of coming home and gave not a thought to who I'd be working for.

Dick Leslie was a pear-shaped man in late middle age. He lived in Seiad Valley, twenty miles up the Klamath River from Happy Camp, with his wife, Mabel, who looked after their rental properties. Dick was the administrative officer for the Happy Camp Ranger District, a comfortable fit for a man who had put in twenty years of staff work in the army. He drew a military pension as well as his Forest Service salary—double-dippers, we called them. Like other military retirees in small western towns, he was prosperous and comfortable.

Both of Dick's careers had involved supervising office staff made up of women. In Happy Camp, this consisted of Maude Ellis, veteran district clerk; Ann Wasson, timber clerk; Joan Richardson, personnel clerk; and two other clerk/typists besides me. I doubled as the receptionist, Karen worked in the mailroom, and Judy was on loan to the presale foresters, where she was learning to draw maps and put together timber sale prospectuses and contract packages. In effect, she was no longer part of Dick's little kingdom, and in another year the foresters would steal her from him by rewriting her job description to make her a forestry technician.

Maude didn't seem overjoyed about Judy's escape from the typing pool, but then Maude was sixty, with twenty-five years on the Klamath, and held the highest rank among the clerks: General Service (GS)-5, at about $9,000 a year. She would go no higher and looked forward to retirement. Ann and Joan were GS-4s, Ann of about Maude's vintage, Joan slightly younger. The rest of us were GS-3s in our twenties, outranking only seasonal field workers on the socioeconomic scale.

I thought about my sister, a navy yeoman who worked across the Potomac from Washington, DC. The best place for a civilian government employee, she told me, was the Pentagon, where even file clerks were GS-11s. But in the Forest Service, clerks had very little promotion potential. Ann was essentially an accountant and would have been paid accordingly had she worked for the part of the government in charge of killing foreigners. But since her husband's business was in Happy Camp, she would never move.

Perhaps, I thought, our lowly status grated on Dick, not because he cared about our welfare but because our status affected his. The oldest line officer on the district—much older than his boss, the GS-12 district ranger—he had nevertheless topped out at GS-9. As a department head, he was nominally equal to other department heads, but they were all GS-11s. Dick was acutely aware that all those other guys ran departments overwhelmingly staffed by men, and that he would have merited a higher pay grade had that been true for him. And it wasn't just a matter of pride: government pensions were based on the highest three-year salary average, so his eventual retirement package would be slimmer because of our lower paychecks. Perhaps this was enough to make anyone cranky, but at the moment, Dick's uneven disposition was focused on me.

I wasn't the world's greatest receptionist, and I knew it, but Maude seemed to think I was learning fast, for she had given me a glowing report on my three-month evaluation back in February. Her review came as a relief, for I knew my limitations. In those days—long before receptionists came to be called "frontliners" in Forest Service-speak—the agency typically reserved the position for the last-hired woman, when what was needed was a grizzled veteran prepared to deal with whatever weirdness came in the front door. I did have some advantages: I knew the landscape, and where the best camping and fishing places were, and how much snow was on top of the Grayback Road to Oregon. I knew how to schmooze with loggers. My screw-ups invariably involved other agency people. In addition to making dozens of verbal faux pas, especially on the telephone, I couldn't seem to nail down the smooth fictions with which gatekeepers shield their bosses from unwelcome visitors. I tended to forget names and procedural details and couldn't seem to think on my feet. I was, however, very good at reading the weather station in the lower parking lot every morning—a task I enjoyed because the rain gauges, thermometers, scales, and fuel moisture sticks were never unhappy to see me.

At first, I rarely knew who was in or out of the office, which frequently got me into trouble until one of the senior foresters took pity on me and installed a sign-in/sign-out chalkboard on the wall of the hall behind my desk. The district ranger didn't want to be "in" to anyone short of his boss, the forest supervisor, but since he neglected to tell me this in words of one syllable, I jauntily waved logging contractors down the hall to his office whenever they showed up. Then I wondered why he glared at me later when I passed him in the hall.

I didn't want to irritate the line and staff officers, but I couldn't seem to help myself. Since spelling and grammar were two of my strong points, I felt confident enough to correct some errors in a sale administrator's letter. Dwayne stomped up to my desk, threw down the offending missive, and demanded that I change it back.

"Oh, just type it the way he has it," Joan said, rolling her eyes at Dwayne's retreating back. "Except for the spelling, of course. He'll be back tomorrow with more changes anyway."

Joan was a retired stockbroker from Chicago who lived with two other women on a mining claim downriver. She knew all about giving the customer what he thought he wanted. "I learned never to make assumptions about how rich someone was by how they dressed," she told me once. "One time I met with a customer that the other brokers walked away from because he wore a threadbare suit. I found out he was a millionaire, and I got his whole account."

Most of the men in the building, however, seemed happy that I could decipher their scrawls and produce some kind of typed letter by the next day. I could read bad handwriting and was rather proud of that ability. So I didn't worry much about Dwayne. And as I passed down the halls distributing telephone messages, as I devoured pamphlets on tree diseases in the lunchroom and asked questions about what I read, as I filed new directives in the rows of loose-leaf Forest Service manuals and handbooks on the shelves, I thought of a career plan.

But any such plan required that I keep my current job for at least a year, to reach the relative security of "career conditional" status. And as I gnawed on my lunch, the morning's department meeting haunted me.

Among my few consolations was that Dick's list of my errors wasn't longer. Either he wanted his lunch or he didn't know about some of them: the time I forgot to take in the flag; the time I left my electric typewriter on overnight, covered but warm and humming; the myriad errors I made on the forms that summarized the monthly vehicle use reports. Mistakes and omissions were constantly pointed out to me by kindly coworkers, but I could always manage to make one more that nobody had thought of yet. When Joan promised to teach me to make out the biweekly time sheets, as though this were some sort of reward, my hands started shaking.

Out on the lawn, under the swelling lilacs, I resolved to do better. Taking the blame for anything—up to and including the breakup of the Beatles—had long been my fallback position, something I was raised to do. But when Dick criticized my radio technique, I was stumped. What the hell was he talking about?

In these latter days, the Forest Service has given up on the Ten Code in favor of normal speech on the radio. Even the multiagency Incident Command System no longer uses it. The truth is that very few people ever took the time to memorize the numbered codes or use them properly. Many vehicles had a typed copy—yellowed by sun and spilled coffee and almost illegible—taped to the dashboard, but few ever referred to it. Field-going people often said, "What's your twenty?" when the correct phrase was "10-20?" meaning "What's your location?" The code was supposed to make it easier to understand a message even with a bad radio connection, but only lookouts and older fire people knew it well. Although I was instructed to use it always, my efforts were often followed by dead air until I translated the message into English.

The Ten Code was lengthy, but what I didn't realize until I cornered a friendly fire person the next day was that the typed list affixed to the radio set on my desk had been tampered with long ago. Some wag who thought that ninety-nine numbers were not enough had added a 10-100 and a 10-101. What they stood for I no longer remember, but at the time they seemed sensible. This evidently horrified some radio eavesdropper out at dispatch in Yreka, who ratted me out to Dick about using the unofficial codes. I never found out who lengthened the original list.

Now I sifted through a mental file labeled "Leslie, Dick," and a couple of memories fell out. I remembered a look on my stepfather's face, quickly suppressed, when I told him who I'd be working for in my new job. Dick had worked on the Seiad Ranger District in the 1960s, when Dad did. Evenings in late fall were burning nights, when all the district men turned out to set recent clear-cuts alight and burn off the slash in preparation for the next spring's planting. Burning at night took advantage of higher humidity, but darkness brought danger, too. One night, as Dick ferried loads of diesel fuel for the drip torches, his truck engine overheated and caught fire on the road above the burn.

He tried to douse the flames with what he thought was water, but the liquid was flammable, and he panicked, grabbed a shovel, and hurled dirt onto the engine block. When the firing boss—Dad—appeared, he chewed Dick out for not using the fire extinguisher behind the seat. After that, Dad didn't have much use for Dick, and Dick must not have liked Dad much. When Dick looked at me, I thought, he remembered.

On that happy note I went back inside, picturing Dick and his gray comb-over in that awkward situation. But my future with the Forest Service hung on this man's opinion. Unless I had a good rating at year's end, I could be let go for any reason—or for no reason at all.

My research had found a way to take me from an office to a field position, but only if I still had a job in November.

In the meantime, I commuted the twenty miles to work from Seiad—where I rented a trailer—with three men, one of them the district silviculturist, Doug Miller. When I told him I wanted to work in his department someday, he neither laughed nor patronized me but instead asked what I had taken in college. "Check out the X-118s," he said. So by the time Joan sat down with me to fill out the training plan required of all employees, I had some ideas.

"What are your career goals?" she asked.

"I want to be a forestry technician and work in reforestation—silviculture," I said. "I took enough science and agriculture courses in college to qualify in the 462 series." I handed her the list of those courses, stapled to a copy of the X-118s—the civil service list of courses and unit requirements for entry-level field positions.

She nodded and took it, and I watched as she wrote in my training plan's comment section: "This would be putting Equal Opportunity into practice."

"Hang in there a few more months," she said, looking at me over her reading glasses. "Once you're on permanent, we'll get this done."

Not long after that training plan was copied and hole-punched and entered in my brown personnel file, however, Dick yelled at me again. This time he took the precaution of first herding me into the ranger's empty office and closing the door. We sat on opposite sides of the oceanic meeting table, constructed from a single thick slice of old-growth Douglas-fir and varnished to a glossy sheen. The morning sun bounced off the slick surface. Again, his voice rose to a shout at the end of sentences; again, tears rolled down my cheeks of their own accord. *Why is that?* I wondered, but I ignored them, stared back into his wrathful eyes, and hated him. I took no notes this time. After he ran down, he stood up, ordered me to "get control of yourself before you go back to your desk," and slammed the door behind him.

Alone, I watched the dust motes float above the table in a beam of sunshine and thought of lemon slushes at the Frosty downtown, in the days when the world was simple. I wandered around the room, read Richard Henry's framed diploma, glanced at the contents of his bookcase, ate a mint out of a glass bowl, and blew my nose on a handful of his Kleenex. I stood behind the vast desk and stared out the window at the Douglas-firs that loomed over the tire shop across the highway. They swayed in the wind that tonight would bring one more storm in from the west. Behind them, the pointed peaks and sharp ridges marched away forever, and the dark spiky forest covered them all.

Everything was out there, everything in the world, if I could only hang on long enough to get there.

CHAPTER 2

Silviculls

"I don't think you know what you're getting into," Maude said as she processed the paperwork to transform me from a GS-3 clerk/typist to a GS-3 forestry aide. This was rare in 1975. Why would a woman with a permanent Forest Service clerical job want to work in the woods instead of a nice comfortable office?

"The new two-oh stuff is in for the outplant site," Doug Miller said when I reported to his cluttered office that afternoon. "Need to get it all planted as quick as we can, so just show up here tomorrow morning with the rest of the gang. Wear rubber boots and gloves."

I knew in a general sort of way what went on at the outplant site. On that flat piece of ground high above the East Fork of Indian Creek, deep red soil made a good growing medium for various species of five-needled pines, part of a decades-long battle to save one of the state's iconic conifer species.

Sheltered from the worst effects of the ice ages, the Klamath Mountains had nurtured the southernmost stands of Alaska yellow cedar, as well as the northernmost of Baker cypress, and were the sole habitat for the shrubby Sadler oak. Many other species found refuge here: black oak, white oak, tan oak, live oak, ponderosa pine, and the vanilla-scented Jeffrey pine adapted to serpentine soils. In addition, Douglas-fir, white fir, red fir, and fire-dependent knobcone pine mingled with madrone, chinquapin, fox pine, mountain hemlock, Brewer spruce with its drooping branches, Pacific yew, incense cedar, Port Orford cedar, and the towering sugar pine, *Pinus lambertiana.*

Sugar pine was not a dominant species. It grew scattered over the midelevations on well-drained soils near ridges. Its orange bark glowed on wet days. Old-growth sugar pine was virtually knot-free for the first three logs up and made wide, light boards that took nails easily and resisted splitting even when thinly sawed. Once valuable for making boxes, it was still unsurpassed for interior trim. Tourists loved its massive cones, and squirrels and humans alike noshed on its tasty seeds.

The price of sugar pine stumpage was often manipulated in Forest Service timber auctions, as I learned one morning when Ann sent me upstairs to the big meeting room, where bidders had gathered to duel for a timber sale on Thompson Ridge. "All you have to do," she said, "is write down the bids on these forms after Judy writes them on the blackboard." I trudged upstairs with a clipboard and pencil. The room was full of local loggers whom I knew by face and voice and reputation, and a few foresters from Oregon mills as far away as Roseburg.

Bidding went by species: so much per thousand board feet for Douglas-fir, for ponderosa pine, sugar pine, and white fir. The logs would eventually be measured by a Forest Service scaler either at the mill or at a scaling shack beside the highway as they came out of the woods. Most of the sale's timber was Douglas-fir, followed by ponderosa pine, with lesser amounts of sugar pine and white fir, each estimated by a Forest Service timber cruise. Now and then one of the very foresters who had done the cruise found a reason to hang out in the kitchenette, grab some coffee, snag a doughnut, and listen.

The highest overall bidder was the biggest mill in Happy Camp. When I gave the final figures to Ann, she clicked her tongue. I waited for her to elaborate, but she had her head buried in the file cabinets again.

"You know what's going on here, don't you?" said Dad when I asked him about it that weekend. I shook my head.

"The mill won the auction because they bid four hundred dollars a thousand for the sugar pine, right?"

"Right," I said. "But the highest bids for Douglas-fir were only twenty dollars a thousand. Is sugar pine really that valuable?"

"Well, it's valuable, sure, and the sugar pine up on Thompson Ridge is nice stuff, very big," Dad said. "But look at the amounts. The mill is offering to pay four hundred dollars per thousand for the sugar pine that the Forest Service cruise says is up there. That's an awful lot of money if the cruise is right. But it isn't."

"The cruise is wrong?" I said.

"The cruise is wrong. There isn't nearly as much sugar pine up there as the cruise says, and the mill's forester knows that, because he's probably cruised it himself and gotten different results. Since the mill only has to pay for the timber they actually cut, they bid high just to get the sale, knowing that it won't cost them nearly that much."

I nodded. "Whenever you see a bid like that on a single species," he said, "you know the bidder doesn't agree with the government's cruise."

I remembered sundry looks and laughs and raised eyebrows at the auction, and snippets of conversation later in the halls. More was involved here than numbers on a blackboard.

Regardless of price, sugar pine was a dying species. As roads advanced into the ancient forest, followed by clear-cuts replanted with Douglas-fir and ponderosa pine seedlings, the population of mature sugar pines shrank. No one planted sugar pine, for almost all the young trees were doomed. Around the feet of the old trees, young ones still grew a few feet tall, but then came a "flag"—a branch with dead, red needles—and the next year the entire tree was dead, killed by *Cronartium ribicola*, white pine blister rust.

Most mature sugar pines were protected from the rust (fungus) spores by their great height and thick bark, but over and over, starting in the 1920s, almost all seedlings succumbed to the introduced disease.

When the Civilian Conservation Corps came to Happy Camp in the 1930s, crews went into the woods with grub hoes to dig out the alternate hosts of the rust—gooseberry and currant bushes (*Ribes* spp.). This kept the young men busy, but the rust kept spreading, blown by the wind over the ridges from Oregon.

In the 1960s, foresters noticed that a few old sugar pines produced seedlings that didn't die. They collected seed from the parent trees and sent them to Forest Service nurseries. An outplant site was established on the Happy Camp District, and when the seeds sent to the nurseries grew into two-year-old stock, they were transplanted here, with *Ribes* bushes between the rows to provide a source of infection. Again, most of the young trees died, but some lived. When they grew tall enough, their cones were pollinated by hand. The work was often frustrating; trees from apparently resistant stock might survive a dry spring, then succumb during a wet one. Doug headed up the program, but Dean ran the site, cruising around on a military surplus "mule" with his long brown ponytail blowing behind him.

The next morning I ate cereal to the sound of rain drumming on the carport roof and a silent lack of enthusiasm from the man I lived with. I packed a lunch, filled a thermos with hot tea, and knocked a dead spider out of my green rubber fishing boots. I wore long underwear beneath my jeans, and a thick sweater under a hooded sweatshirt, and I grabbed a pair of rubber gloves from under the sink to go with my leather woodcutting gloves.

The storm door banged behind Chuck, and I consumed another cup of tea, a piece of toast, the morning news on Chuck's tiny television, and a three-day-old Wall Street Journal. Chuck and I had been living together in his house on Indian Creek since the previous autumn. Cohabitation was new to me, but I was learning that unrestricted sex went only so far in ensuring indulgence toward a housemate, especially after a few months. Dating keeps everyone polite, but there's nothing like sharing a bathroom to bring a person down to earth.

The office parking lot was dark and wet in the February gloom. I walked down the hall to Doug Miller's office. In the adjoining offices, a dozen or so people milled around, searching for truck keys, pouring coffee, banging in and out of restrooms, striding up and down the hall. Paul, the rotund department head, glared at everyone from his office door, daring us to hang out one more minute than absolutely necessary. Oscar tossed me a set of truck keys. "Don't have my government license yet," I said, looking at them.

"Well, you can warm up the engine, can't you?" he said. I headed out the back door and down the steps to the lower parking lot. The number on the key ring matched the number on the door of a one-ton Ford flatbed truck with slatted wooden panels. I hauled myself into the dusty cab and stretched my feet toward the pedals. By the time I figured out how to move the seat forward, Oscar and Doug were already headed down the steps. I cranked the engine, stuck the stick in neutral, and stomped the emergency brake, which slid greasily forward all the way to the firewall. "Gotta grab my stuff," I said to the two men as I ran back up the steps and in the back door. I snatched my backpack from the floor near Oscar's desk and was out the door again.

Oscar drove. Doug balanced a cup of coffee on his knee and

consulted a clipboard jammed with papers. I sat beside the window and looked out at the rain, then glanced in the rearview mirror at the green van and two more green pickups following us. We wound our way through downtown Happy Camp to the "lower station," which had once been the main district office and compound. It still housed the barracks, a couple of government houses, the gas and diesel pumps, the fire warehouse, and the fire control offices. As the vehicles behind us stopped at the fuel pumps, Oscar backed our truck up to the tree cooler, unlocked it, and shoved the heavy steel door aside on its tracks. Doug stepped inside and consulted the clipboard.

The slatted wooden shelves inside the cold, dank cooler held brown paper bags about three feet square, sewn at the top and filled with layers of tree seedlings tied in bundles of fifty. But today Doug pointed to some flats of seedlings sprouting from white plastic cones. We laid them end to end in the truck bed until it was a mass of feathery green fronds.

We drove up Indian Creek and turned off on East Fork Road. We climbed through switchback after switchback up to the outplant site, seventy acres of rare flat ground.

I wondered why no one had ever homesteaded this place where deep red soil practically begged to be plowed and planted. A pipeline from a nearby stream provided a nice head of water to run the sprinklers.

"Better park here," Doug said. "It's pretty slick down in the rows."

Dean pulled up behind us on his olive-drab table-on-wheels as we opened and closed the gate in the high mesh fence. Oscar crawled up in the truck bed and handed down the flats to us. We placed them on the mule and followed it down through the rows of pine trees as the rain fell harder. Fog shrouded the drainage, tendrils of white creeping up every draw. I slid suddenly in my rubber boots, which had little tread, and sat down abruptly, spraining my wrist as I caught myself. I looked down at the ground, wondering why I had fallen, and saw nodules of red stone, worn by eons of time and weather into tiny ball bearings.

Behind us, three other vehicles arrived and disgorged the silviculture crew, including the department's only woman professional. Deborah, a recent graduate of Humboldt State, was sturdy, with wavy black hair growing low on her forehead. She barely noticed me when

I dropped the mail off in the office she shared with Oscar; now she threw me a what-the-hell-are-you-doing-here look. Sisterhood might be powerful, but I didn't feel its presence here.

What was here was gasoline-powered augers that appeared from the back of the van and were hauled down to the ends of the rows. Engines revved up, and their operators braced their feet and began to drill holes into the soil. Over the roar of engines, Oscar demonstrated how to plant a tree: kneel down, lift a tree from a flat, squeeze the plastic cone to release the planting soil and roots, pull the tree out, dangle the roots down the hole, hold the tree with the left hand as the right hand shoves soil back into the hole and compresses it with a fist to eliminate air pockets. Make sure the tree is straight, neither too high nor too low, and give a little tug on the stem. Stand up and move on to the next hole, four feet away.

Two hours later, my thighs were screaming and my jeans were soaked with red mud. At lunchtime as we sat steaming in the vehicles, eating sandwiches, I was grateful for the warmth when I spilled tea on my knees. I looked around at my fellow workers. Most wore rubber overalls and lace-up rubber boots. A row of rubber gloves bled mud onto the truck hood.

Out of the corner of my eye, I caught Deborah looking at my sandwich. "What's that?"

I had made the bread myself; these slices came from the middle of the loaf and overflowed my hands.

"Liverwurst and sweet pickles, with mayonnaise," I said. "I'm the only one who likes it. I made tuna fish for Chuck."

"Why can't he make his own lunch?" she said. I dropped my eyes, ashamed, but of what I hardly knew. That I didn't have a forestry degree? That I had made lunch for someone else? That I shaved my legs?

Deborah got out of the truck and strode toward the taller trees that screened our view of the fence. I turned around and looked at the three young men in the back seat. One of them shrugged. "Don't mind her," he said.

After lunch, I discarded my torn rubber gloves, rinsed out the leather ones under a hydrant, and pulled them back onto my hands.

Doug looked over at me and laughed for the fiftieth time that day.

"I have never seen anybody so covered in mud!"

"Yeah, Doug, we get it," Oscar said as he gassed up his auger. "She's muddy."

By three o'clock, I could avoid violent shivering only by constant movement. But Doug was firm that all these trees had to be planted today, so we emptied all the flats, jammed the white cones together so that they formed a series of limber white rods, and tossed them back into the truck bed. I leaned against the truck and watched steam rising from my soaked pant legs. A hard hat protected my sweat-soaked scalp, but my ears were freezing.

Back in the truck cab, my pant seat left a dark clay stain on the Naugahyde, which camouflaged the arrival of my period. Back at the office, I trudged up the steps and into the hall, grinning despite my aching muscles. At least I wouldn't have to worry about forgetting a tampon.

As I came in the back door that evening, Chuck looked at me over the newspaper and through the smoke of his pipe. I undressed in the laundry room and shoved all my clothes into the washer. I took a very long, very hot shower, which didn't quite erase the East Fork clay stain from my thighs. I dished up a bowl of stew from the slow cooker and thought of telling Chuck about my day, but the newspaper blocked my view. He had grown used to a woman who arrived home from work before he did and had the fire built and the table set and supper ready to dish up. That woman was gone, and he didn't seem to want to talk to her replacement.

Doug's haste to get the sugar pines into the ground arose from the need to have all hands on deck for "force-account" planting—work done by Forest Service employees, not contractors. Two years before, the seven-hundred-acre Wingate Fire had burned through a stand of timber above the mouth of Clear Creek, and most of it still needed replanting. In preparation, I walked down to Hooley's dry goods store and bought a pair of rubber lace-up boots and a set of green rain gear the exact shade of fresh cow manure.

At Wingate the next day, I carried a rubberized tree bag buckled around my waist, filled with bundles of two-year-old Douglas-fir and ponderosa pine seedlings, lifted out of their storage bags and their

Burning thinning piles on a damp fall day, about 1976.

bare roots dunked into a slurry of vermiculite and water. Each of us carried a hoedad, a modified grub hoe with a flat foot-long blade and a sharpened back edge that allowed us to prepare a planting spot by scraping away grass and duff. The planter plunged the blade into the soil and popped the handle forward, opening a hole just the right size for slipping the roots of a seedling into the ground. Walt Robinson, still climbing hills like a teenager at fifty-five, showed me how.

"Be sure the roots are straight—if they're bent, it's a 'J-root' and they won't be able to turn down and reach for water. They may live a year or two, but then they'll die." He demonstrated, slinging the hoedad blade one-handed into the soil, pulling a seedling from his bag—"do it quick, so the roots don't dry out"—slipping it into the hole, then using the blade to tamp it in securely. A quick stomp with his boot, and then he slid eight feet downslope to do it all again.

Our crew lined out on the road above the area to be planted, eight feet apart, then dropped down the slope, each planter keeping an eye on those to his left and right. When we eventually hit the unburned timber at the bottom of the fire scar, we "bumped over" and began to plant uphill toward the road again.

We moved through a carpet of deerbrush (*Ceanothus integerrimus*).

The seeds lay dormant for decades beneath a canopy of trees. Fire opened them, and many thousands sprang to life on every acre. Miner's lettuce, sweet and crunchy, was coming up, too, and I pulled off a stem to chew. Soon, shooting stars, brodiaea, fritillaries, yellow violets, and coralroot would follow in a procession of color, until the heat of summer wilted them just as the deerbrush started to bloom.

"Take a break!" Al Durazo shouted. Al usually worked in the timber sale preparation department, marking trees with blue paint for harvest. We sat down, and packs of cigarettes or round tins of snoose appeared. Most of the planters wore red or yellow multipocketed vests in which they stored candy, cookies, cough drops, and tobacco. The vests came from the fire warehouse, and I made a mental note to get one for myself.

I looked down toward the river and saw, floating below us atop the fog, a pair of ravens. They circled, croaking, as they headed uphill toward us. "Damn things," Al said.

"Why?" I asked.

"Man, leave your backpack in the back of the truck, and you'll see why. They'll tear your pack plumb apart to get at your lunch."

The ravens did seem to be taking quite an interest in the trucks and vans parked up on the road. But after a few dives and circles, they headed back toward the river. I was glad to see them, for in my years growing up on the Klamath, eagles, ospreys, and ravens were rare. Scientists said DDT had thinned their eggshells so that the eggs shattered during incubation. I suspected that the pioneer habit of shooting anything that moved might have had something to do with it. Target shooters at the Happy Camp dump picked off crows and ravens whenever they could. But now, ospreys were once again colonizing snags overlooking the river, and even bald eagle sightings were no longer remarkable.

"Huginn and Muninn," I said.

"What?" said Joe, between draws on a Camel.

"Odin's ravens," I said. He still looked blank. "In Old Norse mythology, there's these two ravens that belong to the god Odin. They fly over the world and come back and tell him things."

"Cool," Joe said. "How the *hell* do you know that?"

"Read it somewhere," I said, remembering high school study

hall, where I combed the encyclopedias for bits of Scandinavian mythology.

"You should be a teacher," Jim's quiet voice said from my other side. I shook my head.

"Hard to find a teaching job right now," I said.

"You're right about that," Joe said. "I'm certified to teach math, but there's no teaching jobs on the West Coast unless you want to go to East LA."

I hummed assent. I was glad to hear another education graduate utter the stock excuse I had been using on my parents for the past year. If teaching jobs ever did open up, I would have to think of something else.

I checked the number of seedlings left in my bag. I didn't know how many trees I could plant in a morning, and Walt suggested that I take 200—four bundles of 50 each, half Douglas-fir and half ponderosa pine. I estimated that I had planted almost 100, which I thought pretty good for a beginner, but Joe and Jim had started out with 250, and their bags now sagged empty on their hips. They volunteered to hike up to the trucks and fetch more trees for everyone.

We spent a month planting Wingate. Every day we hiked farther and farther down the hill, until at last we carried one full bag on each hip and hauled our water and lunches with us.

One day, we stopped for lunch on a bench below a steep hillside. I sat down on a smooth, knee-high stone the size of an ottoman. Several similar stones were scattered around the bench. The ground here was littered with smaller river cobbles, smooth from the action of water, in a place they did not belong, far from any stream. Strands of red flagging hung all around the bench.

"You know what you're looking at?" Oscar said. I wasn't sure, but something clicked.

"Archaeological site?"

"Yup, this is an old Karuk village."

"You mean somebody hauled these rocks all the way up here from the river? Why?"

"To have something to sit on, of course," Oscar said. "And all these other rocks are cooking stones and sweathouse rocks or parts of hearths. All hauled up from the river."

Later, the Klamath National Forest's archaeologist told me that all previously known Karuk village sites were near the Klamath River or its major tributaries. This was different: perhaps a seasonal camp used for hunting or acorn gathering, perhaps with religious significance. Clear Creek was nearby, where the World Renewal ceremonies took place every August, and the medicine man walked a route that recapitulated the creation of the world. Perhaps these rocks had been here long before the mid-nineteenth century. We didn't plant trees inside the flagged area, but already the brush was growing high enough to hide the stones, and in a few years they would be invisible.

That first month of planting toughened me. New calluses protected my hands, although I woke up every morning with my fingers curled into numb, then aching, claws. The blisters on my feet healed. As the weather dried, I bought a pair of West Coast boots, not to be compared with made-to-measure White's, but still a good boot, and when well greased with Sno-Seal, waterproof for at least a few hours. I wore two pairs of socks, a good brand of rubberized gloves, "stagged-off" (hems or cuffs removed) trousers with suspenders, and a mattress-ticking pullover shirt. When it rained, I had my rubber pants with more suspenders and matching coat, and the raindrops fell in friendly fashion on my brimmed hard hat. My planting rate climbed to five hundred a day, which kept me up with the rest of the crew. I didn't fall behind. I could do this.

CHAPTER 3

Strangers in the Forest

Oscar sat across from me in the silviculture crew room and fiddled with a clear plastic tube he had pulled from a desk drawer. He upended it on the desk blotter, and something pale and slender slid out. He carried it over to the windowsill and set it down with exaggerated courtesy. "Don't tell Doug about this," he said.

I rose from behind the other desk and walked over to look at the object: a core of wood from the center of a tree, the result of using a tool called an increment borer on a living conifer. The core was about eight inches long and delicate; Oscar's touch had broken it in two. I counted the widely spaced rings, which indicated a fast-growing tree, caused by wet years, good soil, and little competition. "Okay, but don't let him see you doing that," I said, wondering why Oscar even needed a plastic tube.

"Oh, there's lots more in here," he said, continuing to rummage in the center drawer of the desk. "He's probably forgotten about these since he moved upstairs. Ha!" He held up a map tack—the kind with a cylindrical plastic head—between thumb and forefinger. He dropped it into the plastic tube. "Well, looky here," he said, "it fits."

He held one end of the tube to his mouth, faced the bulletin board behind my head, and blew. The tack thudded into the corkboard and stuck there. "Oh, yeah . . . ," said Oscar, and I knew he had found a way to relieve the tedium of a January day in the office.

For the rest of the month, Oscar ambushed various members of the (male) work force as they exited the men's room around the corner from his office. In this new year of 1976, it killed some time as he waited for February and the start of contract planting season.

Typical clear-cut on
the Happy Camp
District in the 1970s.

By the early 1960s, nursery technology had made artificial forest
regeneration possible on a large scale, and foresters rationalized the
layout of larger and larger clear-cuts. On our district, fifteen hundred
acres of last year's clear-cuts had to be planted before the winter and
spring rains stopped and the summer drought began. This required
large crews of efficient tree planters willing to work long hours on
steep slopes. Enter labor contractors with experience in California's
industrial agriculture, and laborers from Mexico.

Even as Oscar engaged in running map-tack battles with the
foresters upstairs, the Klamath's contracting officer, Gil Davies, sat
across a table in Yreka with contractors' representatives and read them
the boilerplate about not hiring illegal aliens. "All our guys have green
cards," the reps said. Nods, smiles, handshakes, and two weeks later,
the work began.

At five o'clock in the morning on a cold and rainy February day, I
pulled into the office parking lot, sleepwalked my way down to the
trucks, warmed up #1626, picked up Oscar and Gary in front of the
office, and drove down to the tree cooler. We picked out the trees we'd
need for the day, carried the bags out of the cooler, and stacked them

in the pickup bed. We snapped open outdated foil fire shelters and spread them over the bags, weighing the whole pile down with heavy rubber tubs. We filled the two milk cans beside the tailgate with water from a hose, stuffed a couple of sacks of vermiculite in beside them, and roared back up to the station.

Beneath the sulfurous glow of the parking lot lights, two dark vans appeared; faces peered at us from foggy windows. They followed us as we pulled back onto the highway.

An hour later, we stopped at a wide spot on a muddy logging road and looked down on the clear-cut, scraped clean by logging and charred by broadcast burning: Swillup A.

Logging on an industrial scale began on the Happy Camp District in the early 1950s, and as one old logger remembered, "It was all selective Cat logging up until 1954." The first logging roads ascended main drainages such as Indian Creek and Elk Creek and were built close to the creeks to minimize the amount of earth moving. Trees were cut in narrow units of ten or fifteen acres, called strip cuts. After slash burning, seeds from surrounding old growth colonized the bare soil. The next crop of trees got a good start and grew fast.

But the roads didn't stop. They spread out into the secondary drainages, then climbed toward the main ridges. The road into the Swillup Sale followed the route of the old Kelsey Trail, a pack train route from Arcata on the coast to the interior mining camps. Before white miners descended on the Klamath country in 1850, the ridgelines belonged to migrating elk and the Karuk people.

As the roads advanced, the strip cuts grew longer and wider and became block cuts. By the early 1960s, with Forest Service nurseries propagating ever-greater numbers of seedlings, silviculturists grew confident that they could grow enough stock to replant the larger block cuts: clear-cuts, some called them; even-aged management, others said. Forty-acre cuts became sixty-acre cuts. And why not? One big cut was more efficient than several small ones.

On ground too steep to log with Caterpillar tractors, high-lead logging with cable systems and spar trees appeared. Men who had used that system in Oregon now worked on the Klamath, and local logging contractors were quick to learn techniques that allowed logging on the steepest ground. By the 1970s, skyline logging and helicopter logging appeared, and the Klamath was where foresters came to cut their professional teeth on a variety of logging systems. Cutting trees and replanting them depended on a series of complicated steps, of which logging was the simplest.

I stepped out of the truck and looked over the edge of the road. A thousand feet of 60 percent slope fell away beneath my feet, bordered by dark palisades of uncut trees, like doorways to dim cathedrals where sunshine is a brief visitor. Rain drummed on my hard hat. Mist cloaked the bottom reaches of the clear-cut.

When I turned around, the green pickup was surrounded by twenty men. Gary, his brown beard beaded with raindrops, sliced open the bags of trees that Oscar tossed from the truck. I climbed up on the tailgate, knocked the lid off the milk can with a hoedad, poured water into the black rubber tub on the ground, and sent a stream of vermiculite after it. Gary stirred the mess with a stick, and the planters gathered around to slosh the roots of their tree bundles in the slurry before stuffing them in their bags. Gary joshed with the planters in broken Spanish, inserting his favorite word—"cabrón!"—every so often for emphasis. They grinned and tried out their English on him.

The planters were from southern Mexico, and the contractor who cut their paychecks was famous for employing those we unabashedly called wetbacks. Chico and Jose, the two foremen, had known Oscar for years, having worked in the States for decades. They were dressed much as we were—hard hats, green rain gear, waterproof boots and gloves. They leaned on their hoedads and grinned at their charges. The latter were remarkable for their youth, thinness, inadequate clothing, and almost giddy cheerfulness. They wore a medley of tennis shoes, cowboy boots, polyester shirts, corduroy trousers, out-at-the-elbows jackets, ragged sweatshirts, and baseball caps. Most had no gloves. The thermometer stood at thirty-five degrees and the rain came down at a steady inch-a-day clip, and there is nothing colder. I looked at the brown work-roughened hands and bony wrists protruding from too-short sleeves and shivered for them.

Rubberized bags cinched to their waists, the planters gathered around to receive instructions from the foremen. Each bag held about five hundred trees, and some planters carried two bags so as to have extra to share out. Jose pulled a seedling from a bag and demonstrated proper planting technique in the loose soil of the road shoulder. "Ocho a ocho," he said, moving to plant another one eight feet away. Everyone nodded, and then the crew spread out and dropped as one over the edge, working their way into the clear-cut, searching for good planting spots among the blackened debris left by the fall slash burning. With the sides of their hoedads, they scraped out a clear spot about two feet square, buried the blade in the bare soil, then popped the handle up sharply to break out a space for the tree roots. Reaching into the bag, they deftly slipped the tree into place, lifted the blade clear, and tamped the soil in around the roots. A tug on the stem to make sure the tree was firmly seated, and the planter was gone again, sliding downhill to search for the next spot.

We inspectors watched for planters taking shortcuts, such as carrying trees in hands or even teeth. This dried out the delicate root hairs. Oscar slid down beside me. "Watch for anybody stashing trees under a rock or a log," he said. "They get paid by the tree."

He warned me about root pruners, who surreptitiously sliced roots across the back blade of the hoedad, shortening them so the trees would be easier to plant. We watched the planters move down the slope, Gary and I looking for Oscar's signal to "throw a plot." He tossed a fence spike adorned with a piece of orange flagging over his shoulder, and we converged on it. The landing point was the center of a circular plot with a sixteen-foot radius, and I stood at the center holding a tape measure clipped to a belt loop while Gary circled the perimeter and dropped pieces of tape to mark the circumference.

We counted the number of planted trees in the plot, neither too many nor too few, and looked for those planted too deeply or not deeply enough. We dug up a small percentage of the trees, scraping in downhill from the planting spot, nudging the soil away from the roots with a jealously guarded mechanical pencil. If the taproot dove straight down, with no bending sideways or upward—the dreaded L-root or J-root—the tree was well planted and had as good a chance as any at survival. I found that I liked digging up trees; as I reclined with my head close to the ground, my hard hat deflected the rain from the hole and brought a brief illusion of warmth and shelter as I peered into a smaller world. I flicked aside shining grains of quartz in the soil as I followed the path of the roots, themselves intruders among the burrows of centipedes and millipedes. It was like solving a puzzle.

Chico and Jose stood just outside the plot and waited. As Oscar flipped up the cover of his small steel clipboard and began to fill out the inspection form, they watched as he scribbled.

Oscar looked up. "Two errors!" he called out. "One J-root and one too high!" He pointed at the offending trees, and Chico chased after the culprits and pointed out the error of their ways. When he finished, the boys were no longer smiling. They ducked their heads and planted even faster to catch up with the rest of the crew.

Chico hiked across the slope and stood near us. He shook his head. "That one should know better," he said. "He's my cousin."

"How old is he?" Gary asked.

"Fourteen, I think," Chico said without embarrassment. He yelled something down the hill at the boy, who replied, "No, fifteen."

The crew took a short break at the bottom of the unit while a few at a time disappeared into the timber. Break over, they spread out again and began planting uphill. We threw a few more plots, but all passed easily. "I think they've got the idea," Oscar said and tossed me the clipboard. By the time we dragged ourselves back up to the road, Chico and Jose were there ahead of us and had built an enormous fire on the roadbed. As the fire burned down to coals, frying pans appeared from the vans, and the crew warmed tortillas, heated beans, and fried meat. Peppers and salsa, sodas, cookies, and cupcakes appeared and disappeared as the planters laughed and talked in the rain, or took turns sitting in the vans to get a little less wet.

Inside the Forest Service truck, I took off my raincoat. My long underwear was soaked with sweat. We ate sandwiches and drank tea or coffee from our thermoses. Gary and I talked about books and movies. Oscar dozed behind the wheel, leaning against the door.

And that was our day for the next two months.

From Swillup to Fortune Cookie to Hardscrabble to Frying Pan, the cleverly named and incredibly steep timber sales flowed beneath the hoedads in an endless succession of dark and rainy winter days. Unless the planters ran out of groceries, there were no days off. I took to leaving wads of cash along with my car keys on Chuck's desk with notes: "Please put gas in the VW, almost out." "Please deposit my check and get me some quarters for the Coke machine." We left before anything was open and came back after everything except the bars and liquor store was closed. No cashless gas pumps existed then. Chuck did his own laundry, and we ate sandwiches and scrambled eggs for supper. "How much overtime are you getting?" he asked me now and then, in an effort to find an upside to my neglect of the housework.

One day Bill, one of the silviculturists, came out to Swillup in his own truck, a brown utility job that made him look like an out-of-work plumber. We saw him coming from far off, driving slowly, his Irish setter galloping ahead of him. The planters looked up and I heard someone say, "Inmigración." They didn't wait for more but dropped their tools as one and raced for the timber. Chico and Jose shook their heads and began plodding up toward the road.

Bill stepped out of his truck, preceded by several empty beer cans, as the foremen came puffing over the lip of the road. They looked at Bill's wild red beard, red nose, and red dog and began to laugh.

"Your truck," they gasped. "Same color as the Border Patrol trucks—you scared them pretty good!" And they turned to shout downhill.

The real raid came some days later, by night, as the crew snored in their beds in a by-the-week motel in Happy Camp. Only Chico and Jose were left in town as the INS vans drove away upriver. For the next couple of weeks, Gary and Oscar and I slept in, caught up on paperwork, cleaned out the tree cooler, did laundry, went to the bank, ate pizza for lunch, and started the prework for the herbicide spraying projects. We also tried to figure out what to do with the eighty thousand seedlings that had arrived in a refrigerated truck from the Forest Service nursery in McKinleyville. We stacked them up in the nice clean cooler and periodically checked with Chico and Jose on when the crew would return. The contractor would pick them up once they made it to Southern California, but getting back across the border took time. In those days it was much easier to go to and from Mexico, but the lost boys were only human and visited their families before attempting the return trip.

On the crew's first day back, with grins all around, we pulled trees from the cooler and met them out in the woods. Now clad in good boots, with gloves and hard hats and jackets and rain gear, they planted like fiends. Taking no chances, Chico and Jose camped them out in the woods near our job sites. In a manic succession of fourteen-hour days, seven days a week, they moved faster even as time ran short. Day by day the weather grew hotter, and soon the spring planting window would end. On April 28, a marathon day that lasted until eight o'clock in the evening, they planted over ninety acres and twenty-three thousand trees. Oscar looked at the weather forecast for the next week, shook his head, shook hands with Chico and Jose, and called the game.

The next week, Gary and I loaded the leftover trees onto the stakeside truck and drove them up to the airport. We piled the bags high on the edge of the tarmac, poured diesel on them, and set them alight on one of the last cool spring mornings.

CHAPTER 4

All the Waters Run South

"What street is this?" Chuck leaned toward the windshield of the red Volkswagen sedan and squinted into the gloom beyond.

"If you don't know, I sure don't," I said, feeling crabby. Long Beach was Chuck's hometown, not mine, and trying to navigate in any strange city was harder after dark, especially in a pea soup fog. The sunny day had given way to a night full of mist so thick that visibility was reduced to a few feet in this part of the Los Angeles Basin. At least we weren't on the freeway.

"Get out and see if you can read that sign," Chuck said, and I stepped out and groped my way over to the sidewalk and peered up. In the glow cast by the headlights, I could just make out the street name. "Oh good," Chuck said. "Just two more blocks."

We crept onward and finally reached the sanctuary of Ebell Street, a cul-de-sac lined with houses built in the late 1940s, where Chuck's parents still lived. Here Chuck and his younger brother and sister had grown up and lived and played in a neighborhood where everyone had kids and looked out for everyone else. It felt claustrophobic to me, and perhaps to Chuck, too, for he had been a Boy Scout and reveled in camping trips to the mountains and deserts. And when the time came for college, he had gone as far north as he could get and still be in California: Humboldt State College and its forestry school.

I was relieved to arrive anywhere that offered a promise of lying flat in a dark room, for my head screamed with another migraine. And nobody would be getting up early in the morning. It was the second day of 1976, and I had been married for a week.

Spending my honeymoon in my mother-in-law's house was a good indication that my new husband was one of the cheapest men ever to walk the face of the earth. But I had been raised by cheap people myself—my parents said it would cost too much for them to attend the wedding—so I didn't think much about it. My sister and her husband made the trip up from San Diego, a gesture that touched me, for I truly had been too poor to attend Liz's wedding two years before. But my parents' absence seemed to worry Chuck's mother.

"Do your parents approve of your marriage?" Beatrice asked me in her oddly formal way a couple of days after we arrived in Long Beach. She drew out the word "approve" and inserted half a question mark, and later I realized that her hawklike focus as she waited for an answer concealed a tenuous hope that the whole thing might still be called off.

"Oh, yes," I said brightly. "They're fine with it. They just can't afford the trip, is all."

Neither of my parents had expressed much of an opinion on the subject. Mother seemed relieved that I would no longer be living in sin, while Dad just grunted and said "congratulations" in a flat tone.

Dad's relationship with Chuck, while outwardly cordial, had never been warm. Shortly after we began sleeping together late in the fall of 1974, I brought Chuck along on a family hunt up on Grider Ridge. During one of Dad's convoluted deer drives, Chuck walked too fast and spooked a buck that Dad believed he would have been able to shoot. As Dad said to me later, "If your MAAAN didn't have such long legs, I would have been able to get a shot at it." His eyes flashed at the drawn-out word, and I knew he found this lapse in hunter etiquette difficult to forgive. Not for the first time, I thought about the advantages of being an orphan. They didn't have to worry about introducing their boyfriends to their parents.

On our drive down to Southern California, Chuck and I stopped overnight in Sacramento, where we stayed with my college friend Joan and her husband. Joan and I met in a horse husbandry class at Chico State, and for about a year after graduation, we shared a house near Woodland. Joan worked for a savings and loan company, and I landed a job in the county clerk's office. Joan's parents were rich in a quiet way. Her father owned an almond orchard and some real estate and played golf. They gave their children not just material goods, but the easy assurance that they would always live in comfort.

On Saturday nights Joan and her friend Becky cruised the talent at a country-and-western dance club near Sacramento. Joan knew it was time to find a mate. I was a romantic who stayed home on Saturday nights to watch *The Mary Tyler Moore Show*. My one love affair had ended three years ago, and I did not want another.

Joan married Rick, a nice man who worked for a door manufacturer. As we walked her dogs around her tidy residential neighborhood while the men got acquainted over a beer, she homed in, in her blunt way, on the differences between our marriages.

"Of course, I was really in love with *my* husband when we got married," she said, and when I hastily said that I also loved Chuck, she looked at me with a raised eyebrow. She had outed me. In the many letters Joan and I had exchanged since I moved to Happy Camp—we seldom spoke by phone—I never said that I loved Chuck, just told her the facts: that we had moved in together, that we were getting married, that being married would save us money, that we'd be coming south in December and would marry in Las Vegas. In short, I had—as I did with my parents and everyone else—been careful to leave emotion completely out of the story. And now, on the eve of the great event, I felt a hot flush of shame and fear cover my face. Why had I agreed to marry this guy, anyway?

I totted up the reasons: he was tall and good looking, he was smart and had a good job. He drank little, and although he enjoyed playing poker and blackjack—the latter especially at casinos, where he liked to think he could beat the house—he was a Capricorn, and careful with money. He knew when to quit. And he had pursued me, a nearly novel event in my life, and I allowed myself to be reeled in. I realized the advantages: he had a pickup truck and let me use it to haul hay for my two horses; I didn't have to pay rent or utilities; he was hardworking and handy around the house. In short, he was the dream catch for many a Happy Camp girl. But just now as I walked with Joan, I let myself wonder why I was doing this and could come up with no better reasons than that he had asked me and that we seemed to get along together. I didn't even have the excuse of many a young woman that he looked like a man who could support children. I had never wanted children, and he had never brought up the subject.

He proposed in the kitchen as I prepared to do the supper dishes, in the same casual way he might have proposed a trip to Tahoe over the weekend. "We should get married," he said.

"I'll think about it," I said absently and only later remembered that Chuck's most serious ideas often came out of the blue like this, on the spur of the moment. That was how he asked me to move in with him—not with a question, but a declaration. As he dropped me off at my trailer in Seiad Valley one Sunday afternoon, he kissed me and said, "Next week, you're moving in with me."

This astonished me, for we had just returned from a trip to Eureka and Arcata, where we took in a forestry class reunion picnic and softball game. When I walloped a nice triple, he seemed embarrassed rather than proud. We stayed overnight with some old friends of his in Eureka, where I further embarrassed him by accidentally tipping over a lamp during some rather vigorous late-night sex. We went to see *Five Easy Pieces* with his friends, and I saw in myself the double of Jack Nicholson's kind but ditsy girlfriend, abandoned at the end. Chuck's going to dump me, I thought. On the long, long drive back upriver to Happy Camp, he was silent, and I grew certain of it. The immeasurably sad voice of Jim Croce, condemned to intone forever about time in a bottle on the eight-track player, didn't help my mood, either. So when his move-in-with-me declaration came, I just nodded, surprised and numb.

It took him another year to propose, and in the meantime he didn't even hint about marriage. So, with my hands buried in suds, I begged for time. The next morning, we climbed into his truck for the drive to work, and as we parked in front of the office, I started talking about some social engagement coming up. Chuck looked at me with sad eyes. "How can you talk about that," he said, "when you don't even want to marry me?" I felt like a heel.

"That's not true," I said and put my hand over his atop the gear shift knob. "I'll marry you anytime you like." And I kissed him on the lips, and as we walked across the parking lot, he was smiling.

As I lay down on the bed in Beatrice's guest room and slapped a cold wet washcloth over my throbbing forehead on that foggy night in Long Beach, I thought about childhood dreams in which I walked through darkness and fog and ran screaming into the night, only to feel the ground disappear beneath my feet and feel myself fall as I told myself to wake up. Which I always did, of course. I pressed the cold terry cloth down harder on my forehead. Just let me wake up back home, I thought.

A few days later, we left Long Beach, and as we crested the Grapevine and exited the Los Angeles Basin, I blew out a great sigh of relief. The past two weeks hadn't been enjoyable except for visits to Chuck's aunt Margaret over in Sierra Madre. Margaret's cool dim Craftsman house, full of bookcases, with an enormous avocado tree looming over the backyard, was the only place I felt even slightly relaxed. Although Chuck liked his aunt, she also lived about a mile from the end point of the Pasadena Rose Parade, and on New Year's Day we walked in the brilliant winter sunshine to see the end of that event. It was odd to see the exhausted band members, their instruments silent, straggle across the line like marathoners, but I liked seeing the mounted groups and the Budweiser Clydesdales. Still, Chuck had seen many Rose Parades, and he didn't want to stay long.

Chuck heard the sigh and launched into a vituperative condemnation of the fact that I obviously hadn't had any fun on this trip, that I hadn't appreciated anything he or his family had done for me, and that he didn't want to take me anywhere ever again. He was right. I hadn't enjoyed the lecture he gave me about forgetting to wipe down the glass shower doors in his parents' bathroom (I had never stayed in a house with glass shower doors before and didn't know I was supposed to). I hadn't enjoyed watching his father bribe the maître d' to get us better seats at the *Lido de Paris* floor show in Las Vegas. I hadn't enjoyed being so close to so many bare breasts. The San Diego Zoo was fun, but not the visit to the XXX movie theater with Chuck and Liz and Ed that evening. The jungle cruise at Disneyland was mildly amusing, but to get there we drove past fields of strawberries encircled ever more tightly by housing developments, which made me sad. I hadn't enjoyed the wedding in the county courthouse, or the way our twelfth-floor hotel room swayed when a nuclear bomb detonated underground in the nearby desert. I hadn't enjoyed listening to Chuck's sister-in-law throw an amazing tantrum in the hotel dining room when the Keno runner failed to turn in her ticket and she turned out to have the winning numbers. I hadn't enjoyed playing Keno myself just to have a place to sit down while Chuck played blackjack for hours on end. At least I could read while I sat at one of the tiny desks. In those days, Las Vegas was devoid of the family entertainment that has kept it alive ever since. I did enjoy one of my wedding gifts, my very own copy of *Joy of Cooking*, and now, as Chuck berated me, I pretended to study it. Not take me anywhere ever again? You promise? Every mile brought me closer to home, and if Chuck continued to act like this once we got there, I would just file for divorce. I had worked in a county clerk's office and knew exactly the forms I would need.

By the time we arrived back on Indian Creek, we were both tired and Chuck had mellowed out. I settled into the winter routine of cooking and cleaning, and Chuck went to work and seemed disinclined to bring up my faults when he got home. I put my divorce plans on hold at least until spring, and by early summer I was out tending the garden and Chuck was full of plans for remodeling the bathroom. And then the god of hydraulics made our differences recede into unimportance.

Chuck's house sat on a flat shelf of greenish-gray rock that stretched for a narrow quarter of a mile between Indian Creek Road and Indian Creek itself. The rock shelf had, over the centuries, become clothed with soil and vegetation, but we knew what the underlying rock looked like, because over those same centuries Indian Creek had carved a twenty-foot gorge into it, flush up against the mountainside. People built houses along the flat after World War II to shelter the newly arrived loggers and mill workers who could afford the tiny squares of land.

The houses were eclectic in design and built according to the whims of the carpenters, and most had been thrown up without benefit of county building codes and inspectors. When you live seventy miles from the county seat, such things happen. Fifteen years ago, the house that would become Chuck's held a certain fascination for me because of its wild experiments with paint. The girl who lived there shrugged when I asked her about it; they were renters, and the paint job had nothing to do with them. The front of the house was neatly slathered in pink, but just past the side door, the color trailed off in ragged stripes, then resumed in virulent green for a few feet before giving up entirely and revealing naked lumber. Whether the local hardware store had run out of those colors, or the painter out of money or ambition, the experiment ended. Chuck scratched his head about it, but his first priorities were a new roof and a carport, so he ignored it for the time being.

Another noticeable feature of Poverty Flat, as the impromptu subdivision was called, was that all the domestic wells were laid out in a more or less straight line. The symmetry of those well locations didn't strike me until our own water problems began the summer after we were married.

Our next-door neighbor knocked on the door one Sunday afternoon to announce that both his family and his renter's family were out of water. Chuck and I gave him blank looks, but then Chuck's eyes widened as he realized what Steve was telling him. Chuck's well was (a) providing water to two other families, and (b) not working at the moment.

I stepped to the kitchen sink and turned on the tap, which spit out a mixture of rusty water and air, then went quiet. "Could be the pump," I said as Chuck and Steve exited to look at the well. They pried off the lid and peered down inside. "There's water here," Chuck said.

"Turn on the tap again!" Chuck shouted at me. I did, to no effect.

"Pump's quit," we all said, with some relief. Pumps could be fixed.

Soon after, Steve and his wife, Susan, sat sipping iced tea with us while their three-year-old pounded his sticky palms on the glass top of the coffee table. Susan explained how our problem had come to be their problem, too. Her parents had built their two-story dwelling—the oldest house on the Flat—after hand digging the original well, the one that sat just outside our kitchen window.

"But why did they dig it so far from the house site?" Chuck asked.

"It was in the middle of the goat pasture then," Susan said. "One of the goats broke its leg trying to get to water down at the creek, so they wanted to put in a water supply up here. When they built the house, it just seemed easier to pipe it over rather than dig another well."

When another family bought the goat pasture from Susan's parents and built the house in which we sat, the one well came to serve both houses. Still later, Steve bought a mobile home, installed it on the south side of his property, rented it out, and extended the pipeline once more. In this drought year, the water level sometimes fell so low that we had to stop watering the lawn.

Drought wasn't the immediate problem now, but we had barely even had a winter, and scarcely any snow fell in the high country. In February, the silviculture crew planted trees near the top of Grider Ridge. We looked up at the Siskiyou Divide across the Klamath River and saw the Red Buttes and Kangaroo Mountain standing bare and rosy in the thin morning sunlight. Our one serious snowfall, toward the end of February, was cause for rejoicing.

After Steve and Susan and the toddler left, I wiped the coffee table with Windex while Chuck slumped in his recliner and muttered about the hard labor he'd put into that well. He had torn down the old wooden well house, deepened the well by digging out several feet of sediment, constructed a sturdy wooden platform to support the well pump, built a neat cylindrical wall of creek cobbles and concrete around the well, and capped it with a round steel lid, salvaged from somewhere, that fit neatly into the lip of the concrete.

Steve soon returned with his toolbox, and while the men lifted the well pump off its platform and examined it on the lawn, I looked up and down the Flat, and that's when I noticed that the locations of all the wells in the neighborhood formed a rough line. The old bachelor who lived just up the road from us had fenced off his acre and a half last year, then acquired a few goats and turned them loose on the blackberry vines around his unpainted cabin. Before long, their browsing uncovered the carcasses of several vintage cars and a small building that turned out to be his well house.

I knew that anybody willing to brave the black widow spiders could have peered into a well about eight feet deep, its bottom containing about two feet of clear water, constantly replenished by groundwater flowing over the gravel. And if it seemed amazing that such shallow pools could supply the dozen or so houses up and down the Flat, I had watched ours in operation once and seen how it worked with all the outside faucets turned on. As the pump hummed, the water level dropped, until you saw fresh water pouring in from the upstream side. Turn the faucets off, and the water level rose again.

While Chuck and Steve sucked on beers and fiddled with the pump, I peered into the well. Sure enough, the water had risen again, and a pair of water skippers cruised around the surface. I went inside to watch *60 Minutes*. I was familiar enough with mechanical disasters by now to know that nothing good could come of me watching them. If they wanted help, they would yell.

The end result of all this was a new pump—stainless steel and submersible—and the realization that not only would our neighbors not help us pay for it, they also wouldn't start paying us for their water supply. A lengthy phone call from Chuck to an old college buddy who now worked for a state agency brought the unwelcome news that if we started billing the neighbors for water, we then became a utility and would have to guarantee the purity of the product. "You'd have to have the water tested every month," Old Buddy said, "and if there's contamination, you'd have to put in a chlorinator."

"What if we don't charge anything for it?"

"Then it's voluntary on their part, and you don't owe them any guarantees."

With the pump fixed and the water supply, if used cautiously, assured, I stopped thinking about the underlying geology of the place. We had a fenced garden plot full of fine brown topsoil that we thought went deep—I had never hit rock or even subsoil when digging there. And in the spirit of not borrowing trouble, we didn't think about that thriving patch of Himalayan blackberries directly between our house and Steve and Susan's, until the day the toilet backed up.

The very first house that my parents rented on Indian Creek, back in 1962, had an outhouse as well as indoor plumbing, and now I sorely missed it. Chuck's first reaction to the outage was to progress from plunger to plumber's snake, but when I heard Susan's tentative knock on the back door, I knew this was bigger than both of us. Chuck put on gloves, found the pruning shears, and started cutting blackberry canes. I followed him with the shovel and scraped away at the ground until we found what we were looking for: a row of rotted boards atop the septic tank. Steve took the shovel from me and pried them up, to reveal a pool of gray water on which floated turds, toilet paper, and used condoms. Susan remembered she had something on the stove and did not return. Well, at least the condoms weren't ours: I was on the pill.

Art Tisdale, septic tank specialist, soon arrived and pumped the contents of the tank into his tanker truck. He also informed us that (a) our tank was, thank God, a good concrete one, and (b) this one had never had a proper leach field dug, only a too-short galvanized pipe that stretched out across the backyard toward the creek.

Chuck got out several stakes and a ball of twine and lined out a route for a leach field according to Art's directions, and he and Steve commenced digging. Art had recommended digging the trench four feet deep, but at three feet down the boys ran into an immovable object: the same solid greenish bedrock that walled in the roaring waters of Indian Creek. They dug as deeply as they could, working their way in the general direction of the creek. Days later, Art's dump truck brought in a load of gravel, which Chuck transported one wheelbarrow load at a time to line the bottom of the trench. Steve and Chuck laid perforated PVC pipe the length of the trench, atop the gravel, and made sure it was securely attached to the tank. We knew, and Art knew, that the bedrock simply acted as a conduit for the liquids to run over the bedrock shelf, spill over its lip, and trickle down into the creek. We would all just pretend it wasn't happening.

CHAPTER 5
Herbicides

The 1976 planting season was over, and the summer seasonals due to show up soon, when Paul shifted our department into high gear. He brought in an old fire hand as crew boss—Dick Priddy's years of experience and solid protruding gut would presumably inspire confidence in a large crew. Several crew members, I was pleased to note, were women. "Well, what are you gonna do?" I heard an old sale administrator say. "The forestry schools are full of 'em these days."

If the seedlings we planted survived their first few years, they grew up beside hardwood sprouts and brush seedlings, which soon outpaced them. How could we even the odds? In the 1950s, herbicides emerged as a possibility. The first efforts involved backpack sprayers and herbicides mixed with diesel. But backpack spraying was slow. A loaded pack weighed fifty pounds, and carrying the sloshing liquid was hazardous. Workers fell and injured their backs and knees; the backpacks often leaked, soaking shirts and pants.

In the 1960s and 1970s, helicopters proved a much more effective delivery system. With tanks and spray booms, helicopter spraying was not only faster but cost only twenty-five dollars an acre. The herbicides consisted of chemicals that had been used—quite recently—to discourage the rain forests of Vietnam: 2,4-D and 2,4,5-T. Mix them together and you had Agent Orange.

True, the Forest Service used much milder concentrations than the military, applied them only once or twice in a generation, and did not mix the two, but the realization that the Forest Service was spraying diluted war weaponry onto the people's forests was not exactly a public relations coup.

Robert, the newest and most intellectual forester in the silviculture

Helicopter spraying
herbicide on tree
plantation, early 1980s.

department, addressed the issue on all our minds one morning. Before
he got his master's degree in forestry, he was an army intelligence
officer, and he was still a major in the reserves. He lived in hope that
Soviet tanks would thunder out of Poland for his entertainment and
possible promotion. He spent several years in Germany preparing for
that, but fate sent him to Vietnam, where he stepped off a plane into
the confusion of the Tet Offensive. "They lost my luggage," he told us,
aggrieved.

"You see," he said now, between handfuls of popcorn from the
store across the street, "the army didn't want to just knock the brush
back for a few years, like we do here. They wanted to kill everything
on the Laotian and Cambodian borders, but it was triple-canopy
jungle. So they needed a lot of herbicide, and fast, and they hit it
over and over again with really heavy concentrations, not the three
pounds per acre we use. And when you use that much herbicide, you
don't buy it just from Dow Chemical. You take the lowest bidder,
which turns out to be some fly-by-night chemical company from
lower Louisiana, so instead of having a couple parts per million of
dioxin in the 2,4,5-T, you have thousands. And since dioxin is both
toxic and teratogenic . . ." He paused, looked out the window, and
took a thoughtful swig of V8.

Heads nodded around the room. We had read the literature. The herbicides 2,4-D and 2,4,5-T had been exhaustively tested. You could practically drink the stuff. In fact, one patient with an intractable fungus infection had been fed heavy doses of 2,4,5-T in the hope that it would help him (it didn't). It wasn't particularly toxic to birds; chickens, for instance, could be fed very large doses without noticeable harm. It was more toxic to fish.

"Did it work?" someone asked.

Robert shrugged. "Not really. They never could quite kill that last third of the canopy. But it did encourage the Viet Cong to leave and go to Cambodia. So Nixon invaded Cambodia."

"Ah," we said.

To Robert and Doug, herbicides were just a way to solve a problem. They saw those artificial plant hormones as a benign tool that attacked broad-leaved plants by fooling their upper branches into growing themselves to death. The resulting topkill knocked back their growth for a few years. The chemical molecules bonded to whatever they landed on, so they didn't move down into the soil and they broke down under sunlight in a few days. But the beauty part, as Doug said, was that conifers were largely immune to their effects once their annual growth spurt was over and the new needles had hardened off in early summer, especially if water and not diesel was used as a carrier.

The optimal result was a plantation of happy Douglas-firs and ponderosa pines poking their heads through a sea of wilted brush.

In deference to the herbicides' toxicity to fish, we flagged out buffer zones around creeks so the helicopter pilots—capable of laying down a swath of spray with great precision—could avoid them. Rhodamine dye in the spray mix, and strips of photo-sensitive paper on the buffer boundaries, provided a check on their accuracy. Water samples taken downstream at intervals were sent out to labs to be tested.

But someone had to hike along those buffer strips, tie flagging at the buffer boundaries, and place the squares of paper on the boundary lines. These jobs fell to the silviculture crew. Some of us also had to be out on the ground when the helicopter flew, to measure wind speed— no spraying if it rose above ten miles an hour—watch the helicopter, and later pick up those squares of paper.

Once, spray units were chosen by driving around and eyeballing clear-cuts, but when the district hired Robert and the equally wonky Bert, things changed. Robert and Bert were tech savvy and willing to try new things. Since no one knew exactly how many conifer seedlings per acre survived or how many stems of brush or hardwoods competed with them, they set out to learn, helped by a new tool: Hewlett-Packard's handheld programmable calculators—really the first small computers. By walking a grid pattern across the landscape, taking plots, and later running the numbers through the calculators, we could rank units by any number of measurements.

With the silviculture crew as a work force, Robert and Bert refined their system again and again as the crew thrashed its way through brush and over steep terrain in straight lines, frequently checked by compass. Our field tools were decidedly low tech: a six-foot-long staff and a printed form clasped to a small steel clipboard. Eventually we got it down to a science. Number of trees, number of shrubs, number of hardwoods, species, how tall, how fast growing. We learned to offset around rattlesnakes, hornet nests, and head-high charred logs, and even how to cheat a little and still be pretty accurate.

This led to days like this:

November 4, 1976

Arriving at the bottom of the infamous 90-acre Block M, we bombed Priddy's hard hat with rocks and listened to Bert explain, for the benefit of the new people, his plot-taking system. This took until 11:50, at which time we broke for lunch. Finally we drove up to the TOP of the monster block in 2 pickups, bailed over the side, and Bert measured off a chain on the contour and had us all pace it. Went over some logs and was hard walking. Then Bert headed across the block, sighting on a distant object, but not before a lot of questions as to plot-taking and a lively argument as to how big the block was. Bert said 60, I said it was more like 90 according to the old sale map. So Bert walked back up to the road (no easy feat) to see if the aerial photo was there. Presently he yelled at Ingram, "Where is it?" "It's on the dashboard, uh . . . unless it's on my clipboard," herewith taking his clipboard out from under his arm and opening it. "Here it is!" he exclaimed happily. "I didn't know it was there," he said, as a stream of vituperation floated down to us. We cracked up. "I should keep a

better diary," I said in Joe's direction. "No one would believe it." "Sell
it to Jack Anderson for an exposé," he said. So we went down the
mountain, eventually splitting into twos and threes to take plots. I let
Marla do it since she'd never done it before. We got back down to the
lower road finally, sent three guys back up in the crummy to get the
trucks, and Bert expounded on age determination of trees until we
reminded him it was 3:30. Got back at 4:45.

Back in the office, Robert and Bert programmed the HP-40s
with equations, input the numbers, hit the calculate key, and came
up with figures that enabled them to prioritize any treatments: this
unit needed replanting, this one should be sprayed next year, this one
could be thinned in three years if it kept growing at the same rate.
If someone demanded justification as to why these units should be
sprayed, Robert and Bert were ready.

Once they had picked out the units they wanted to manipulate, the
next step was mapping them. This was accomplished by teams of two
people working with a Redy-Mapper, a portable plane table about a
foot square on which a unit map could be traced. By walking around
the unit with a steel tape measure marked out in "chains"—a surveying
unit of sixty-six feet—and taking compass and clinometer readings
every chain or two (depending on how far the couple could see), we
could achieve an accurate measurement of shape and acreage. Often,
however, underground ore bodies threw off the compass readings, so
the map drawing wouldn't close. If the error was sufficiently great, the
team marched around the unit again, this time with both the front
and rear person taking compass readings and splitting the difference.
All this was accomplished on slopes so steep that sometimes the only
way to navigate them was to cling to branches.

Preparation wasn't even the hardest part of a spray project. New
people had come to live on the river in the past few years, young people
who wanted to escape cities and chemicals and contamination and all
unnatural things. On the Salmon River, a commune on the old Black
Bear Mine property attracted a community of newcomers whose
unconventionality in matters of hair, dress, and lifestyle attracted
much comment and censure. The Happy Camp Ranger District
had its share of the counterculture, too, and some of them worked

on the district. They, too, lived in the forest and were not shy about challenging the Forest Service's logging and silvicultural practices. Some shook their heads and declared they didn't want to work around herbicides. Forty miles downriver, the community of Orleans had been worried by accounts of miscarriages and birth defects. Were they connected to the use of herbicides by the Six Rivers National Forest? Some thought they were. I was skeptical. How could our herbicide spraying, which used small amounts of herbicide every twenty-five years or so, possibly have such effects, when corn farmers used the stuff every year, and in far heavier doses? I knew how careful we were on the Klamath. Was the Six Cricks any less so?

These questions evidently preyed on the district ranger's mind, too, for one day he announced at a staff meeting that henceforth no women of childbearing age would be allowed to work on spray projects when the helicopters were actually flying, or walk through the sprayed areas afterward.

Paul announced the new policy just as we staggered in from the field one day, after flagging out creeks and draws in the Phillips Gulch area west of town. My assignment had included the north side of a unit covered in tan-oak sprouts higher than my head. I stood on the road looking up as Dick pointed out my assignment on the map. The road bank was vertical and fifteen feet high, and I had to walk a hundred yards down the road before I found a place to crawl up and make my way over to the edge of the old clear-cut.

Somehow, until that day, I hadn't known about the tiny scales, like dust, that covered the thick oblong leaves of young tan-oak trees. As I crawled through the thousand stems per acre that choked the place, snatching at their branches for support, scales cascaded down on my hard hat and poured onto my shirt and into the sweaty crevice between my breasts, where they lodged between skin and bra. They invaded my eyes, nose, mouth, and throat. I knelt in the duff and retched, tears pouring so that I could barely see. I pulled a handkerchief out of my pocket, also full of the yellow dust. I tried to rinse it out in the trickle of water in the draw, with little success. It took me hours to flag out both sides of the draw, with more sneezing and hacking and blindness. By the time we all got back to the office, I was not in a good mood.

As Paul declared the Will of the Ranger, I stared up at him and felt fury. To suffer all that and not see the payoff, to not be allowed to see the helicopter unload its pink swirls of death on our enemy, the brush? This was profoundly unfair.

The rest of the crew, though, took it well. Some were uneasy about the chemical to begin with and had friends who spoke out against spraying. Also, spray projects meant getting up at four o'clock in the morning for a week, which nobody liked despite the overtime pay. We started early because the herbicide volatilized and drifted once the temperature rose above eighty degrees. But now I forgot how much I hated an early alarm clock. Last year, I had struggled just to get here and be accepted into the department, to be allowed to plant trees in the rain. I didn't want to be excluded now.

I flagged out streams the following week with ill humor. As our crew went on to other projects, the contract bids started coming in.

One day, as Dick lined out Jim, Gary, and me to survey one of the old Fortune Cookie clear-cuts, I sensed a shuffling of feet. "You know," Jim said, "they just sprayed that unit with atrazine and dalapon." A backpack project, it was designed to kill grass on the relatively flat area. Jim and Gary clattered back up the steps to the office. When they came back, they said, "Paul says if it bothers us we shouldn't go."

Dick scratched his head, his plans for the day scotched, but finally announced that we could get some chainsaws and go up Kemper Gulch to an area where some hardwoods needed felling.

By the time we arrived, it was raining, a rare event for the time of year. We killed some time eating lunch, then Dick and I worked above the road and Gary and Jim below. I had never felled trees this large before, so Dick coached me, and I managed to fell some tan oaks about a foot in diameter without mishap. We worked our way uphill, me lugging the Homelite. When Dick offered to show me how to fell an uphill-leaning black oak, I handed him the saw with relief and was delighted when the trunk tipped the wrong way and trapped the saw blade. This sort of thing could, it seemed, happen even to veterans. Dick held up the tree from below and told me to yank on the saw. "And that," he said as we both sat down for a breather, "is what not to do."

By the end of the day, my arms were trembling and the pie wedges of the undercuts were getting harder and harder to carve out; the saw chewed at them from the sides for what seemed like forever before I could make the final back cut and send the tree falling downhill. As we hiked back down to the truck, we were soaked through.

The next day, Bill had some information on atrazine and dalapon for Jim and Gary's benefit, showing that they weren't much more toxic than table salt and weren't absorbed through the skin. The pamphlets seemed to reassure them, but Bill told them we could wait until Monday to survey the Fortune Cookie unit.

Jim chuckled. "What a group!" he said, looking at me. "You're complaining because they won't let you work around this stuff, and us babies are complaining because we *can*."

The next day, late in the afternoon, as I crunched numbers on an HP-40, I turned to see Oscar and Ken, a GS-9 from upstairs in sale prep, standing in the doorway. "What?" I said.

"Do you want to file a complaint about Dick Henry excluding women from the spray projects?" Oscar said.

"Yeah, sure," I said. My eyes shifted back and forth between the two of them. I remembered now: Ken was the union rep.

"We'll back you up on it," Ken said. "We don't think it's fair, either."

"Go see Joan and file an informal complaint," Oscar said. "She'll walk you through the paperwork."

Joan pulled forms from her desk drawers and explained to me the difference between informal and formal discrimination complaints. The object of an informal complaint was to find a solution to the problem. If that didn't work, it could go formal. In my case, informal meant a tense meeting with Ranger Henry a few days later. He ushered Joan and me into his office. "So that you won't think I'm a male chauvinist pig," he said, "I've asked Joan to come in."

From the expression on Joan's face, that ship had already sailed, but in the end he offered no compromises. He told me instead that although he thought herbicides were perfectly safe, himself, he didn't want the Forest Service to be sued. I had written down a few talking points, which I gripped in a sweaty hand, and in a shaky voice managed to paraphrase some of them. The policy set women apart from the rest of the department, I said. To be banned from certain areas of the district was embarrassing. And shouldn't we be warning members of the community not to go there, either? If I couldn't get experience on spray projects, it might mean not being considered for promotions later on. Also, the policy applied only to the Happy Camp District, not the rest of the Klamath.

He shook his head and laughed. "Well, life isn't fair, and anyway, experience is overrated. Heck, I signed off on all kinds of road location work down in the Sierras, but I never actually went out and did any of it myself."

And that, I thought, explains a lot. "But I still don't think it's a fair policy," I said. "And don't you think that not letting women work on herbicide projects will just confirm public suspicion that the stuff isn't safe?"

Richard Henry's scalp turned bright red beneath his buzz cut, and the flush spread down his ample neck.

"That may be," he said. "But you should remember that you're in the job you're in because I signed off on it. And another thing: I'll certainly think twice now about hiring another woman professional in the silviculture department, now that Deborah's left."

That brought Joan's head up. She shifted in her chair. Way to impress the Federal Women's Program representative, I thought. Belatedly, he seemed to realize that this had been a tactical error. He cleared his throat.

"Well, do you want to take this complaint further?" he said.

"I'll have to, now," I said. The ranger opened his mouth, shut it, and then stood up.

As Joan and I walked back down the hall, she muttered, "Welcome to the Forest Service, ladies."

The next couple of weeks were uncomfortable. Both the ranger and Paul looked over my head when I passed them in the hall. When I broke the news to Chuck at home, his face turned red and his mouth closed in a thin line. "Oh, boy," he said.

The next day he closeted himself with the ranger and assured him that all this was coming out of my own head and that he, Chuck, had nothing to do with it—nada, nothing—and that he really didn't even want me to work now that we were married.

"Why did you tell him that?" I asked.

"Because I have a career here, even if you don't," he said.

"I do too have a career," I said, realizing even as I said them that the words sounded kind of whiny.

"No, you don't. You have a job. And maybe," he added, "if you went over to have coffee with Nancy Henry once in a while, I wouldn't have had to have that conversation with her husband."

I stared at him, and he threw up his hands and went outside.

I wondered, not for the first time, why I was here, in this house, and gave myself the same answer I always did: because Chuck had asked me to live with him, and then asked me to marry him, and so I had done both, because at the time I thought, why not? I couldn't afford to live on my salary and rent my own place, too. When I rented a trailer in Seiad Valley and commuted to Happy Camp, even though I carpooled with four other employees, at one point I was so broke that I borrowed five dollars to buy a fifty-pound sack of potatoes, on which I lived most of the winter. When Chuck asked me to move in with him the next fall, it seemed only logical. But the bargain had its limits.

On April 20, just as I was about to walk into Joan's office and tell her to take the horrid thing formal, the ranger caved. He called me into his office just as I was leaving for the field. "The policy has been rescinded," he said. "Is that all you wanted?"

"Yes," I said, gobsmacked by this sudden turn of events. "That was it."

As I walked across the parking lot that evening, I saw Oscar walking toward the back door. I trotted to catch up with him. "Did you hear?" I said. "They rescinded the herbicide policy."

I hadn't exactly expected a clap on the back or a hearty word of congratulation, but Oscar didn't even crack a smile. He just nodded, said "I heard," and kept walking. I stood still and watched him enter the side door of the office. I wondered what he was thinking and suddenly knew that for him, this wasn't about me at all. Oscar hadn't wanted Ranger Henry to cave—at least, not yet. He wanted testimony and witness statements. He wanted things to get messy for Richard Henry—so messy that the forest supervisor would, to avoid public airing of dirty agency laundry, send the man down the road.

Now the forest supervisor had nipped that situation in the bud by telling the ranger what I had tried to tell him. So I won my case, but Henry was still here, which meant that Oscar had just lost his.

I knew little about Oscar. He had been a door gunner on a helicopter gunship in Vietnam. He collected old clocks. His practical jokes were legendary. He lived in the bunkhouse during the week and his mother's house in Scott Valley on weekends. He hated Dick Henry, and this made us allies for a time. But with that over, he remained an enigma, like every man I had ever known.

CHAPTER 6

Alice

On an autumn afternoon in 1977 I ran down an office hallway, skidded around a corner, and swung myself past the threshold of Jeff's office, clinging to the door frame. "I just heard the new district ranger's from the Modoc," I said.

Jeff's mouth split in a grin. "And . . . ?" he said.

"And you used to work there. So spill: What's he like?"

Jeff leaned back in his chair and arched his arms over his head in a stretch of pure satisfaction. "George," he said, "is a hundred and eighty degrees from Dick Henry," he assured me, and I let out a breath of relief. Since the news that Henry was on his way to Arizona, the hall talk had been of little else than his possible replacements. "George was raised on the Modoc," Jeff continued, "but he did a stint down on the Salmon River, too, so he knows the Klamath."

I rotated my hand, encouraging him to continue. "Married, no kids, heck of a nice guy. His wife's a trip. You'll see," he said, and I left, feeling giddy. The district could use a break, I thought. For myself, I was happy with my job and a recent promotion to GS-4 forestry technician. Paul seemed to have put the whole herbicide kerfuffle behind him and had even made a point of including me—and himself—in a work party to hand spray a steep clear-cut above a piece of private property, rather than include it in a helicopter contract. This might have been a bit of payback on his part; he smirked slightly as he announced the makeup of the work party. "*You want to do this shit so bad, you can just come along on this little project.*"

So we filled our backpack sprayers with the smelly pink liquid and descended into the brush. I was the only woman present, but as I watched Paul's face get redder as the day went along, I realized that

51

I was in pretty good shape compared to some of the party. But, office belly or no, neither Paul nor anyone else complained. The private property below us, along China Creek, was an old homestead with an apple orchard, owned by a strange little man whose face resembled his pet Chihuahua's, and who often wrote letters protesting spray projects. Now and then, despite my field-going position, I was sometimes drafted to type up Paul's handwritten letters to Mr. Chance. "Dear Mr. Chance," one of them began, "You are without a doubt the biggest son of a bitch I have ever met. You have your head so far up your ass you will never again see the light of day." And I typed it up exactly that way and returned it to Paul, who lined out the too-frank passages and replaced them with proper bureaucratic prose.

George arrived on the district early in the winter, and he and his wife moved into one of the two Forest Service houses across the river on Curly Jack Road. In his late thirties, with dark hair and eyes, an Abe Lincoln beard, and a slow voice that always seemed about to break into a chuckle, he put us at ease immediately. "He knows his stuff," Chuck said of his comments on timber sales.

I was laid off early in November, not unusual for my thirteen-and-thirteen appointment. The Forest Service guaranteed me at least six months (thirteen pay periods) of work each year, but anything more depended on the budget. So right after we finished burning the thinning slash piles along the logging roads, I became a winter housewife. I got up with Chuck, made his breakfast, waved goodbye to him from the kitchen doorway, then turned off the porch light, lay down on the couch, pulled the afghan over my head, and fell asleep to the drone of the Today show. For the rest of the day, I cleaned, cooked, fed the fire in the Franklin stove, walked the dogs, read my way through the branch library's collection of Georgette Heyer novels, caught up on soap operas on Chuck's six-inch Sony TV, and scribbled away in a spiral notebook on the world's most derivative Regency romance. For days at a time, I forgot that my stepfather was dying out in Montague, seventy miles away.

Mother kept me posted by telephone on his decline. He was in the hospital now, on an IV to control his seizures from the brain tumor; for all practical purposes he was in a coma. She drove in to see him every day, but after months of nursing him at home, at least she now had some rest. Before that, Chuck and I drove up the river every Saturday; I helped Mother shop and do housework while Chuck sat with Dad. I was happy not to bother Chuck with this anymore.

A few days before Christmas, Dad stopped breathing, and late in the evening Mother called to tell us. I hung up, told Chuck the news, and sat down again with my book. After a few minutes, I looked up to find him staring at me. "What?" I said.

He shook his head. "Nothing," he said. "You okay?"

"Fine," I said. "Mother's going in to the Forest Service tomorrow to tell them she's ready to come back to work."

Chuck shook his head again. "You're kidding."

I shrugged. "Well, there's not going to be a funeral, so there's nothing to do at home, and neither Tom nor Liz can be here, so . . ."

"Okay," he said, still frowning a little. "It just seems kind of . . . odd."

"Yes," I said. "Yes, it is."

In January, with his odd mother-in-law working and his odd wife not, Chuck once more encouraged me to visit the new ranger's wife and strike up an acquaintance. This did seem interesting—Jeff's description of Alice as "a trip" made her sound approachable, at least. And I was curious about their house—I hadn't been inside it since my parents had lived in the house next door.

When I was a sophomore in college, Dad, a sale administrator on the Seiad District, was offered a promotion to move back to Happy Camp and become the timber management officer there. He and Mother and Tom lived in one of two Forest Service houses across the river from Happy Camp, on Curly Jack Road. I associated those houses with the onset of Dad's illness in the summer of 1969, when I looked after my little brother while Mother was in Medford with Dad during his surgery and radiation treatments.

That summer, Liz worked as a stock girl in Doc Hall's grocery store six days a week. During the long hot afternoons of August and early September, I taught myself to sew. Sometimes I bought more fabric or patterns at Evans Mercantile or stocked up on P. G. Wodehouse novels at the library. Both distracted me from the looming disaster of Dad's cancer and the unremitting pain of a totally unsuitable love affair into which I had tumbled earlier in the year while working at a summer camp in the Sierras. After three years of college, which netted me exactly one date, I fell hard for a Nevada cowboy with a sketchy past who was almost certainly lying about being thirty-nine. But there's nothing like the smell of horse manure to spark a love affair, so I wrote him long letters in care of a bar in Fallon. I wanted, very much, to be neither worried nor in love, but both were like tumors in my gut that no operation could remove.

My sister, more practical, contented herself with slipping out the back door after dark to meet one of the seasonal Forest Service employees who was repainting the government houses that summer. Another worry: but Liz only shrugged. "He uses protection," she said.

"Condoms break sometimes," I said and wondered what Jeeves would have done.

So I didn't have especially happy memories of those houses, but curiosity about the mysterious Alice encouraged me to shower, put on a skirt, wrap up a plate of cookies, and drive the two miles downtown and across the river on a gray day between rainstorms.

I pulled into their driveway and parked in front of a long shiny silver car, of a make I didn't recognize. The hood was up, and someone's jeans-clad butt and legs stuck out of it.

"Hi," I said, and a head of red hair popped up. "Oh, hi there," its owner said, sliding out of the engine compartment and wiping her hands on a rag before shaking mine. We introduced ourselves and looked at the mammoth engine.

"It's a Jaguar," Alice said, and when I did not reply, explained further. "I've had it for years, but never in this wet of a climate, and I think there's condensation on the heads. Anyway, when it's damp the engine doesn't want to turn over." She looked up at the gunmetal sky. "And it's always damp."

My knowledge of mechanics was pretty much limited to changing tires and checking oil levels, so I nodded and made sympathetic noises. "Well, c'mon in," she said, and I followed her through the back door and into the laundry room. Alice tossed the rag into the laundry room sink and led me into the kitchen. I put down the cookies and Alice made coffee, and for the rest of the afternoon we told each other edited versions of our lives.

Compared to me, Alice was a marvel of sophistication. Raised in

Sacramento, she was a computer programmer on one of the air force bases, and when she quit to marry George, she far outranked him on the GS scale, the Department of Defense being more generous than the Forest Service. Her childhood summers were spent on Coffee Creek, a tributary of the Trinity River, where her father had a mining claim. There she met Ethel Steele, who ran a dude ranch nearby and had grazing allotments on the national forest. Ethel was like a second mother to her, and she learned to ride while helping Ethel wrangle dudes and cattle in the Trinity Alps. Ethel was raised one drainage over on a fork of the Salmon River, in a family of mixed Karuk and white heritage. One of her aunts, Hallie Daggett, was the Forest Service's first woman lookout in 1910. Ethel lived on a ranch near Redding now, with her second husband, but she still brought her cattle up to Coffee Creek every summer and pastured some of them on another grazing allotment near Mount Eddy. She had sold the dude ranch. Alice didn't have horses herself, but she followed Ethel's cattle into the mountains, riding a couple of Ethel's dependable mules.

George and Alice met one summer when George visited the dude ranch; six months later they were married and living on the Forest Service compound at Sawyers Bar, one of the most isolated stations in California.

As we sipped coffee and ate cookies, Alice wondered aloud what she would find to do in Happy Camp when she wasn't helping Ethel move cattle in the summer. She did a lot of leatherwork and liked to refinish old pieces of furniture. She also liked to dig up the dumps of old mining cabins to find antique bottles and especially Chinese relics. "Do you know of any around here?" she asked. I rummaged in my mental Rolodex and came up with nothing, although I knew that the Chinese miners who had worked in these mountains in the last century had left many sites that hadn't been discovered yet. I thought of old mining ditches I had seen on aerial photographs or stumbled across at the bottom of clear-cuts; ditches that wound for miles up most of the major drainages, most dug by Chinese companies. "I think I know where to start looking," I said.

"I have a lot of old iron and furniture—stoves and stuff that I've found over the years," she said. "I'll show them to you later."

I looked more closely at her. Her face had wrinkled early—she was forty-two then, thirteen years my senior—and her blue eyes sat deep in slightly slanted lids. She resembled the English actress Glenda Jackson.

"I think," I said, "that I know where there might be some old cabins. Although I'm sure a lot of them have already been dug."

"You'd be surprised," Alice said. "Sometimes people look at an old Chinese chimney and they think it's just a pile of rocks. They don't know what they're looking at."

Alice took me out into the backyard, which was littered with antique stove parts, and after peering into the shed at her furniture projects, we said a shivery goodbye as it grew dark, the rain pelted down harder than ever, and George pulled into the driveway. I waved at them and left with a head stuffed full of anecdotes and a promise to be available for expeditions into the surrounding country in search of treasure.

"How did you like Alice?" Chuck asked me later.

"She seems nice," I said. "I think I'll take her up Elk Creek next week, show her around a little bit."

Chuck grinned and stuck his pipe back into his mouth. "Sounds good," he said.

We did drive up Elk Creek, on one of those sunny winter days that made you think spring was very close. We trudged around some flats near the road, then explored the old homestead where Oscar and I— on one of our odder assignments together—had torched a sturdy old cabin two winters ago. While I kept one eye on the fire, Oscar began to dig up the cabin's dump.

I was nervous about this, knowing that digging up a dump on the national forest was technically pot hunting and therefore illegal. And here we were, right next to the main Elk Creek road where someone could drive by any minute. Oscar didn't seem to care. He didn't want to burn down the cabin at all. When ordered to do it, he would, but there had better not be any complaining about how he spent his time while we waited for the flames to die down. After a while, I caught the spirit and began to dig into the soft, root-infested dirt myself. I was picking my way around and through the mother of all condensed milk can collections when I heard Oscar say "Huh!" in a self-satisfied way as he held up an enameled disk with two sets of numbers marching around its rim.

"What's that?" I asked, and he turned it toward me.

"Schoolhouse clock," he said. "It tells the time and the day of the week and the date, all three."

"Wow," I said. "How do you know it came from a schoolhouse?"

"Oh, I've seen them before," he said, and then I remembered that he collected clocks.

"So, this was a schoolhouse?" I asked, cocking an elbow at the flaming mass of logs and shingles.

"I don't think so," he said, squinting through the smoke. "Just someone's house. It's probably from the Depression times—they used concrete for the chinking."

"But it's on national forest land."

One side of Oscar's mouth rose in a twitch. "Mining claim," he said. "And no one cared, in those days. To work a claim, you had to live pretty close."

Now, as Alice and I drove by the desolate spot, I pointed toward it and told her about digging up the dump with Oscar. She shook her head at the lost opportunity and launched into a condemnation of the Forest Service policy of destroying old cabins on the national forests. "They're afraid of hippies and recreational miners moving in," she said, "but these are historic places. Couldn't they just leave them alone? I was raised in a mining claim cabin. It's gone now, too," she added. "Daddy never patented the claim."

As we drove on, we stopped to scope out every flat spot and each pile of rocks. We stopped to walk through a grove of moss-covered oaks and I heard a Steller's jay squawk almost at my feet. I looked down and saw his wings flap, but he couldn't fly with one leg caught in a trap. Above his head swung a lump of meat that had served as bait. He was angry, and when I reached out to him, his black beak stabbed at me. I took off my jacket and threw it over him to pin down his wings. Alice and I peeled the fabric back to expose the bird's leg. The jaws had closed around his lower leg and crushed the bone. I could see it hanging by a single thread of tendon. We looked at it and agreed that the leg was a goner. Alice pulled a Swiss Army knife from her pants pocket and used the little scissors to snip the remnant of tissue. We lifted him free and I pinned his wings to his body while we peered at the amputation. It wasn't bleeding, so I set him on the ground and we stepped back. He swayed, fluttered, then took wing and flew up into the oak above our heads.

"Let's get rid of this damn thing," Alice said, and I pulled up the stake and carried the whole thing across the road and tossed it into the creek.

We drove back down Elk Creek and stopped near the Five Mile Bridge. I pointed out a tiny meadow, tucked like a vest pocket between the road and the timber, across the road from Oscar's burned cabin. The previous summer, during an archaeological field trip, Jim Rock, the forest archaeologist, had used the spot to point out some features of prehistoric sites. I told Alice what I could remember, aware that I was probably teaching my grandmother to suck eggs. I pointed to the ditch bank between the meadow and the road. "See the black soil here?" I knelt down. "Lots of organic material. And lots of charcoal."

"Not to mention obsidian chips." Alice held a flake of volcanic glass up to the sky, then dropped it. "I don't like digging in Indian sites," she said. "I know other people do it, but I just don't think it's good luck for me. I'll pick up an arrowhead if it's on top of the ground, but that's it. Maybe I'm part Indian, somewhere way back. And I know Jim Rock really doesn't like that sort of thing."

"You know Jim?" I asked.

"Oh, yes, for years and years, since I was down on the Salmon River." She looked at me. "He really doesn't mind if I look for old Chinese cabin sites and can and bottle dumps," she assured me. "He just says he wants to know exactly where they are, so he can put it on his maps. And he'll ask me about how old I think it is. All the artifacts from the post-1850 sites are the same for any given period of time: they all ate the same canned and bottled food and it was all manufactured stuff that was packed in anyway."

I thought of the glass-fronted cabinets in Alice's living room, full of pottery and glass artifacts found while digging up cabin sites in the Sawyers Bar and Forks of Salmon area. But however much she was willing to rationalize her hobby, I knew it wasn't legal. So did Jim, of course. But Alice gave him information on locations, and he saw no reason to get in a fight with a line officer's wife over technicalities.

Over the next few weeks, Alice and I drove up all the main drainages around Happy Camp, and as we drove, we talked. She seemed to like to hear me talk about books I had read, but any list of her favorites would have been short, for she told me early on that except for binging on Gothic romances from the general store when she lived in Sawyers Bar, she had read only two books in her life, Sammy Davis Jr.'s *Yes I Can* and George R. Stewart's *Earth Abides*. She loaned me her copies and I read them both and thought she could have done worse. "I don't have patience to read now," she said. "Too much to do." And she certainly had that.

Sometimes we located a cabin site. The first time we dug into the ruins of an actual Chinese cabin, going by nothing more than Alice's eye for a pile of stones, was a revelation. We found flattened opium tins, and a few of the two-inch-long green glass vials that once held herbal medicines.

"I found an opium pipe once," Alice said as she knelt in her trench and scraped delicately at the brown earth with a bent fork. "But usually you don't find them. When they left, they took all their valuables along."

It was almost dark when I got back from that dig. Chuck looked at my muddy knees and stained hands and his eyes narrowed. "You two," he said, "have been pot hunting."

"Uh-huh," I said. "Me and Alice."

"You know that's illegal," he said. "You could get in trouble."

I tried to look innocent. "Alice's been doing it for years," I said. "Jim Rock knows she does it."

"Doesn't make it right," Chuck said. "And somebody else might report you."

I lifted my shoulders and slunk off toward the bathroom. As I scrubbed my hands and changed into dry sweatpants, I knew he was right. But I had made a friend, a friend who did things that were fun, and who seemed to like me, and who had never been angry with me. And that was something so rare in my life that it was worth a few risks.

CHAPTER 7

Put Me In, Coach

*You may glory in a team triumphant,
but you fall in love with a team in defeat.*
—Roger Kahn

*I spent the first eleven years of my conscious life in a minuscule company-*owned lumber town, and I tend to think I remember everything about it, but not long ago I saw a photograph taken in 1954 from Watertank Hill above Hilt. The town's elementary school is the focus, but the camera looks beyond it to Bailey Hill. In between is a fenced baseball diamond.

I was five then and old enough to notice a weathered fence with a scoreboard attached, but I don't remember it. It was certainly gone four years later when we moved to a house overlooking the diamond. The roofed grandstand was still there then, for sometimes I walked to it and sat looking out at remnants of baselines and a barely discernible pimple where the pitchers once stood. I felt the presence of those long-ago contests. The town's semipro team had folded several years before as its players acquired wives and families and cars. Now the field was decorated with three painted steel drums, around which a neighbor girl sometimes raced her horse, practicing for the barrel racing at the county fair.

One length of fencing remained—just a couple of posts joined by boards, halfway up the slope of the loaf-shaped hill that paralleled the old first base line. A mere sketch of a fence, it certainly posed no barrier to the range cattle that wandered Hilt's streets in the spring. Thanks to that photo, I now know what it was. But who builds a foul-line fence on the slope of a hill, knowing that the first baseman must navigate that slope to chase a foul? The flat where the diamond was built was big enough to avoid it. Perhaps someone got a kick out of seeing a visiting player leap over rocks and gopher holes to nab a high one.

When I sat in the grandstand and channeled the ghosts of baseball past, I already knew how to use a bat, thanks to a potholed dirt playground across the alley from my grandmother's house. Home plate was a round chunk of concrete, a remnant of a vanished tennis court. A few feet behind the plate, the back wall of one of Hilt's communal garages made a handy backstop. Sometimes the ball shot through a gap in the wall and into the scary underbelly of the building. Then we waited while an older, braver kid ran to the end of the garage and scuttled through a larger opening to retrieve the ball. We played "pinky," where catching a fly ball entitled you to take the batter's place, or work-ups when we had enough players to cover the bases.

Little League arrived in Hilt in the late 1950s, bringing a new diamond near the railroad tracks, but only for boys. Softball leagues for girls were still unknown, so the games at school were all I had. The school yard boasted two softball fields, each with a wooden backstop. Here, we practiced for interschool softball games, and I remember May mornings of pellucid sunlight, and Mr. Rhodes hitting fungoes out to a team clad in dresses and sweaters, corduroys and plaid shirts, wearing mitts too big for our hands. My sister and I owned identical Roberto Clemente models from the Sears catalog. At night we rubbed linseed oil into the pockets and tied them around softballs after a game of catch in the alley.

On Saturdays we watched the Game of the Week at Grandmother's house, while Grandfather sat on the couch and smoked cigarettes behind a newspaper. He was a Yankees fan, so we learned to love Mantle and Berra and Kubek and Maris.

I collected baseball cards, traded for the players I didn't have, kept the cards in my jewelry box, and took them out for inspection several times a week.

We moved to Happy Camp just as the Yankees slid into their long exile from greatness, and for a while we left baseball behind. We weren't allowed to waste perfectly good Saturdays watching baseball, so I saw only brief snatches of the World Series during high school lunch hours, when the football coach brought a portable television into a classroom. In those days, the series played out in the daytime, as God intended. Our own television died in 1964 and was not replaced. So I missed the next few years of baseball, except for a few weeks in summer when we visited our grandparents, who now wallowed in cable television heaven in the Sacramento Valley.

But in New York, a new team called the Mets were so creatively bad that multitudes of new fans loved them for it. Sometimes on a summer visit, I read about them in the newspapers, while Grandfather listened to a San Francisco Giants game on the radio, attentive to every play. For him, the Giants' move to San Francisco was but a moment ago. He told me about the Seals, the old Pacific Coast league team in San Francisco, where Joe DiMaggio played. Grandfather, I realized, was from the Cretaceous.

When my college dormitory got cable TV, along with *Bowling for Dollars* and *Dark Shadows*, there were baseball games. I walked out to the college fields and saw the Chico Wildcats do battle with other college teams. Once I watched the JV baseball squad take on College of the Siskiyous, which boasted several Hilt boys on its roster, and I was back in seventh grade, yelling "hey batter" as Mike or Doug stepped up to the plate.

Just before the World Series, a banner proclaiming "Go Mets— Flip the Birds" appeared in the high windows of the new dorm across the parking lot. I found a paperback edition of Jimmy Breslin's *Can't Anybody Here Play This Game?* and read it obsessively as the Mets, the despised Mets, with their roster of young and unstoppable players, won the World Series. They were my team now.

I was just recovering from their loss in the 1973 fall classic when I joined the Forest Service and moved, once more, to Happy Camp. But in my absence something wonderful had happened: slow-pitch softball. For grown-ups. Of both sexes. In the spring of 1974, I started playing ball again and didn't stop for fifteen years. And then in the fall and winter of 1975, I discovered the Red Sox.

Three generations in the past, my paternal grandmother's family lived in Red Sox Nation; had been there, in fact, since about 1630. But I didn't know that then. Perhaps my subscription to *Yankee*, or all those years of looking at calendars featuring flame-colored Vermont hillsides, was trying to tell me something, but my actual career as a Sox fangirl began with a single event seen on a six-inch black-and-white Sony television: game six of the World Series, and Carlton Fisk jumping, waving his arms, sending his strength out toward a flying white sphere and pleading with it to go fair, fair, fair.

Books have been written about that game, but my joy at what I had just seen—and what *had* I seen, anyway, besides the very best game of my life?—was short-lived. When I bounced into the office the next day, full of wonder at what I was convinced was a prelude to final victory, I was brought down to earth by Charlie Ellis, a lumbering engineer on the brink of retirement who shook his head when I blurted out the good news that, of course, he already knew.

"Oh, no, they'll lose the seventh game," he said.

"What? Why?"

"Because that's what they do." His jowls shook and his sad eyes drew down with the weight of a history I didn't understand. He sipped at his mug of coffee and walked down the hall, leaving me puzzled and deflated. I went home that afternoon thinking that he couldn't be right, he just couldn't.

After the seventh game, I came to work a chastened woman. I didn't want Charlie to tell me "Told you so," and he didn't. He walked up to my desk and placed a book on it: *The Third Fireside Book of Baseball*.

"Read the piece by Roger Angell on the Sox," he said. I did, over lunch, and a shock of recognition went through me. Somehow I knew these guys, this great team with a history of blowing it at the last possible moment.

Over the course of that long winter, Chuck brought me more books and introduced me to the canon of baseball writers: Roger Angell, Jim Brosnan, Roger Kahn, Ring Lardner, Ed Linn, George Plimpton, Grantland Rice. He told me stories about Ted Williams. He owned a first edition of Ted's book on hitting—had even seen him play at Fenway Park. I read *The Boys of Summer* and picked up on the elegiac mood engendered by baseball. I had felt it myself, long before I knew the word for it, as I sat on splintered gray seats and looked out from cool shade onto a deserted ballpark. Something remained, even then, of the magic of bats and balls and gloves, something that time and decay couldn't erase.

By spring I was hooked, and the new year of 1976 marked the beginning of either heaven or hell, depending on where you stood on free agency. Whatever happened, winters promised to be more interesting for fans, thanks to endless speculation about who was going where. And with spring came softball.

Most of the major businesses in Happy Camp sponsored teams. The Forest Service had a couple, made up of those who showed up for practice. Since pitching for slow-pitch required not brute strength but a looping underhand arm motion, some of our best pitchers were women. No bunting was allowed, no sliding, and there were only seven innings. Wally Sutcliffe, recently retired from the Forest Service and a walking rule book, stood behind the plate to call balls and strikes.

A couple of years on and softball, too, would feel the effects of what we called the Class of '78. The place crawled with young, athletic, at-loose-ends-after-quitting-time men and women who didn't mind practicing on Wednesday evenings and showing up for games on Fridays and Saturdays, so finding players was easy. The difficulty was corralling someone who wanted to manage: to write out the lineups and work a rotation and pull someone out of the game in the third inning. That was harder, and in the summer of 1978 that role on my team fell to Matt, a young eastern transplant.

He was a good batting and fielding coach, especially for those of us unsure of our talents. "Don't use a heavy bat," he told me. "Use a light one, and don't try to wallop the ball. Just meet it."

At first I thought he told me this because I was a girl and he didn't think I could handle a heavier bat. But I followed his advice and was surprised to find that I could get the bat around faster that way and meet the ball cleanly. I drove it just as far—if not farther—into the outfield. "Told ya," he grinned as I arrived back in the dugout after hitting a double and being driven in by the next batter.

Matt ran with his knees bent in a strange stiff way, as though he sat on a unicycle, the result of a motorbike accident years before. But he reached long fly balls in the outfield and then threw runners out, and he thought deep thoughts about who should bat cleanup.

When an all–Forest Service tournament was scheduled out in Scott Valley, Matt gazed at all of us in the dugout and told us that he wanted everyone to show up in Fort Jones that Saturday, as though there was some doubt on the subject. Not showing up never occurred to me. Besides, I could take Chuck's pickup and drive out to the Griswold ranch to buy a ton of hay during the lunch break.

In Fort Jones, the perfectly calm sunny day that showed off the bright green grass, the baselines freshly marked with lime, the bases swept clean, seemed to portend nothing but good. And everyone had shown up: everyone, including young men who hadn't bothered to come to most of the practices. As the games wore on, it grew apparent to me that size and strength and beer-fueled enthusiasm outpaced perfect attendance when it came to deciding who should play. Surely, I thought as I loaded hay, Matt will put me in this afternoon.

But I never appeared on the lineup card, although now and then Matt cast a despairing glance down the bench at his leftovers: the faithful, the short, the—let's face it—female. I was an outfielder, and although short, I could hit the cutoff man. Also, I didn't fall to the ground moaning when an errant line drive bounced up and hit me in the crotch, as I had seen big strong men do.

At least our manager did us the honor of looking guilty about it, but he also wanted to win, and as he looked out at our opponents— strong of arm and full of testosterone—he made his decisions. Doubtless he was influenced by the knowledge that he would have a fight on his hands if he took his star performers out for the sake of mere inclusiveness. As the sun drew closer to the mountains in the west, I glared at him as we lost our last game anyway and everyone headed for the parking lot.

Two hours later, I peeled myself off the hot upholstery and dragged my dejected spirit into Chuck's house. "How did it go?" he asked, and without warning to him or myself, I burst into tears and flung myself onto his chest.

"I've been to every practice," I sobbed, "and I stayed out there all day today, and they never once put me in!"

Chuck patted my back and for once refrained from saying something like I told you softball's a waste of time or you could have been doing something productive instead. The voice in my head said it for me, and I didn't need anyone else chiming in. He led me over to the refrigerator, pulled out a beer and opened it for me, then led me to the couch. After a while I went back out to the truck and drove up to Doc Hall's barn and unloaded the hay. Then I felt better.

But on Monday the grudge remained, so I found an excuse to march upstairs to sale prep, stand in Matt's doorway, and fix him with a caustic glare. "Thanks for nothin', Coach," I said. At that point I didn't care about his reaction, but he surprised me by tipping his head back and covering his face with his hands. "I'm sorry, I'm sorry," he said from beneath his palms. "I'm never going to do that again."

"Not put all your players in?" I said.

He lowered his hands and looked at me. "That, too," he said. "But mainly not get talked into being manager again. All those guys show up, and none of them listen to me. Should have stuck with the people who came to practice, if we were just going to lose anyway."

It wasn't much of an apology, but my resentment melted and Fort Jones receded into the unimportant past. "Well, the town tournament's coming up in a couple weeks," I said. "See you at practice." And I headed back downstairs, already looking forward to both.

CHAPTER 8

The Class of '78

By 1978, I felt like an old hand on the Happy Camp District, surrounded by kids just out of college. In the spring of that year, a substantial jump in the Klamath National Forest's budget brought in a crowd of newbies: permanents, seasonals, or term appointments, but all young and eager.

Anytime I wanted to feel like an ingenue again, however, all I had to do was look at Bert. Over forty and going gray at the temples, he often got sidetracked on his way to the woods and spent the whole day in the office, still wearing his hard hat and vest, the latter crammed with Rite in the Rain notebook, compass, clinometer, increment borer, rolls of flagging, and diameter tape measure, with his lunch and a full canteen riding in the pouch in back. One day he paused by my desk, suited up as usual, and observed, "I'm getting disgusted with the new sixty percent clear-cut policy on the Klamath."

I looked up from sorting a pile of stand record cards and nodded as he continued. "It's going to cause us problems, you wait and see," he said. "I saw it happen on the Bitterroot. I almost hope all the RARE II stuff goes into wilderness, otherwise we'll start overcutting those lands to make up for lost time."

We both looked at a map on the wall with the RARE II roadless areas delineated. Anyone could see where the existing logging roads ended, and where they must go next.

I had only a hazy idea where the Bitterroot was, but I associated it with a scandal about clear-cutting and terracing. Bert had told me about a report written by Arnold Bolle of the University of Montana, which deplored the terracing of clear-cuts and made a hair-raising prediction: "The management sequence of clearcutting–terracing–

planting cannot be justified as an investment for producing timber on the Bitterroot National Forest," Bolle wrote. "We doubt that the Bitterroot can continue to produce timber at the present harvest level."

The Bitterroot had logged off some lodgepole pine stands, terraced the steep hillsides, and replanted them to ponderosa pine. I had never seen a lodgepole pine, but Bert—who until a couple of years ago had worked in the northern Rocky Mountains—told me that like the seeds of our own knobcone pine, the seeds of lodgepole pine lay dormant until stimulated by fire to sprout. Lodgepole pine was worth little in the commercial lumber market—"they mainly use it for log houses and posts and poles and firewood"—and the Forest Service liked the idea of replacing it with more valuable sawtimber species.

I remembered something I'd seen here. "So how did the ponderosa do?"

Bert blew out his lips in disdain. "It was all off-site stuff," he said. "From lower elevations. A lot of it didn't survive."

I told him about the terracing high up in the Walker Creek drainage in the early 1960s, which hadn't worked out well, either.

Our district had many understocked clear-cuts. Based on their ages, they should have grown tall enough to be thinned soon. Hitting them with a dose of 2,4,5-T from a helicopter to knock the brush and hardwoods back for a few years would have only a small payoff. But we had enough timber stand improvement money to do it.

We had money—and halls full of twenty-somethings—because of RARE II, the second stage of the gigantic Roadless Area Review and Evaluation process. Although the final RARE II environmental impact statement wouldn't be released until 1979, the issue of what to do with roadless areas—landscapes of five thousand acres or more without roads—had simmered for decades.

Six years before the Wilderness Act of 1964, the Forest Service had designated fourteen million acres of the national forests as "wilderness," "wild," or "primitive" areas, where neither roads nor timber sales were planned. Most were either above timberline or in such remote and rugged country that roads were impractical. On the Klamath, the Marble Mountains Primitive Area fell into this category. Lobbying for formal unroaded classifications grew over the years as more and more conservationists came to distrust the Forest Service's assurances that the agency could protect ecosystems as well as produce wood products. By the 1960s, the Forest Service road network had grown to thousands of miles, with plans for thousands more, and the agency didn't like the idea of a law to constrain its decisions.

But the Wilderness Act was welcomed by the Wilderness Society, the Sierra Club, the California Native Plant Society, and newer, bolder conservation organizations happy to be called environmentalists. And by the 1970s, laws such as the National Environmental Policy Act (NEPA) gave these groups a legal lift.

NEPA was about disclosure rather than protection, but it had that effect. Although drastic things could be done to a landscape, their effects now had to be disclosed to the public. So land management agencies had to hire specialists to write about soil erosion and water pollution and the effects of projects on plants and animals. The Forest Service hired landscape architects to give advice on how to minimize the visual impacts of clear-cuts. Still, when it came to environmental assessments (EAs) and environmental impact statements (EISs), the Forest Service tried to make them short and get them over with so as to get on with its real mission: cutting timber. Conservation groups knew this and felt that only a firm zoning law like the Wilderness Act could permanently protect land from roads and logging.

At first, the Wilderness Act protected only eight million acres out of fourteen million acres of de facto wilderness. Conservation groups were disappointed, but the act did contain a mechanism for creating new wilderness areas, and they were prepared to bide their time.

The Forest Service was not. After 1964, roadbuilding and logging accelerated on the national forests as the long-planned system of roads climbed higher and higher into remote drainages. Nobody talked about what the leadership already knew: the Wilderness Act itself gave the Forest Service ten years to decide the fate of the inventoried roadless areas, to determine which ones would remain eligible for wilderness designation.

In 1969, the Forest Service had produced the Douglas-fir Supply Study, revealing that the timber harvest from national forests on the West Coast had peaked and would decline over the rest of the century. Sustained yield, one of the cornerstones of national forest policy, had been exceeded already.

But an even greater threat to long-term logging plans in national forests surfaced in the 1970s: a court challenge to clear-cutting on the Monongahela National Forest in West Virginia. To the dismay of the Forest Service, a federal appeals court ruled that the 1897 Organic Act (the law that essentially established the National Forest System) meant just what it said: clear-cutting on the national forests was not permitted. Go talk to Congress, said the court.

The resulting panic within the Forest Service, the timber industry, and the allies of both in Congress eventually created the 1976 National Forest Management Act (NFMA). The intent of NFMA was to let clear-cutting remain an option, but when combined with NEPA, it became a tool for environmental groups. "If they disclose with NEPA, we can get them on NFMA," one environmental attorney said some years later. "If they're okay with NFMA, they often aren't good on NEPA."

Both sides tested the waters. What did the new law require? Every national forest now had to have a forest plan, updated every decade or so, developed in a process governed by NEPA and additional rules. Every national forest had to maintain viable populations of native wildlife. In practice, however, roadbuilding and clear-cutting went on, along with more paperwork and the hiring of specialists. Opposition to Forest Service actions had once been diffuse and toothless; now it was organized, alert, and had a bite. In an evolutionary dance, both the Forest Service and its opponents changed tactics frequently.

In the late 1970s and early 1980s, the Forest Service planned as though anything outside a wilderness area could be logged, thus ensuring the maintenance and even increase of the annual cut. Meanwhile, faulty assumptions about how fast plantations grew continued to be used, if not entirely believed. The Klamath National Forest used the Scarlett O'Hara method of planning: we'll think about it tomorrow.

During those years, the allowable cut for the national forests rose from 13.6 billion board feet to 21 billion board feet per year. Investments in reforestation and stand improvement were supposed to ensure that every acre that could produce a log would. The mixed-species stands of the Klamath included many broad-leaved trees: oaks, tan oaks, live oaks, madrones, and chinquapins, which could be removed and the acres planted to more valuable conifers. In the late 1970s the wood chip market went sky high, making it economically feasible to cut a tan oak, haul it to town, chip it, and send the chips to the coast in big-bellied chip trucks, even though diesel prices had doubled since 1973.

We started hearing a new word: departure, as in departing from previous levels of timber cutting, beyond prior calculations of sustained yield. Departure meant more money to put up timber sales, which in turn meant more people hired. Politicians hoped to keep lumber prices down in an era of inflation, to encourage housing starts.

The Class of '78 was mostly men with a scattering of women. They were foresters, wildlife biologists, fisheries biologists, soil scientists, geologists, hydrologists. Most were in their mid- to late twenties, from universities stretching from Massachusetts to Utah to Berkeley to Oregon State. The district scattered them among the departments, but most spent at least some time upstairs in sale prep—the labor-intensive effort of marking, cruising, and general preparation of timber sales.

We all spent time together during and after working hours. As a woman, I was no longer a rare bird in a field position. Our silviculture crew was large, diverse, and less tied to old norms. Photos from those days show women and men, dark skin and light, long hair and short, beards and smooth chins.

The higher budgets continued through the Carter administration, but even they could not help the larger lumber markets. In May 1980, I wrote to my brother in the navy about it:

> The mills in Happy Camp are both shut down. The woods are going to be virtually shut down this summer. The lumber market is very bad because the housing market is very bad, and the housing market is very bad because the Federal Reserve finally clamped down. . . . The interest rates rose to twenty percent a couple of months back. They have fallen to about fourteen or fifteen percent now, but as the bank manager told me a few days ago, "We aren't fooling anybody but ourselves. Interest rates are still so high no one can afford to buy a house."

Timber purchasers who bid too much for stumpage in the good times couldn't afford to sell timber in a collapsing market. In an election year, their pleas reached Congress, and buybacks ensued.

The incoming Reagan administration knew it couldn't help the larger lumber markets until interest rates came down, but Reagan's first term brought leaner times for the Forest Service. The new kids learned that what the federal budget gave, it could also take away. In January 1982, the silviculture department lost 68 percent of its budget. All but the bosses were laid off for most of March. Still, judicious hoarding of what were known as K-V funds left us better off than sale prep, which ran out of money entirely. Young foresters who had been preparing timber sales upstairs found themselves cutting brush in old plantations, day after rainy, bone-chilling day, using silviculture money.

The new administration, like its predecessor, wanted more timber, but it offered less money to put up timber sales. Meanwhile, the overall economy remained in recession.

One lunch break, as I sat at Bill Jones's desk reading the papers piled high in his in-box ("Go ahead," he said one day when he caught me at it. "Lord knows I don't want to."), I came upon a Western Timber Association newsletter that yelled at the Forest Service for adhering to the sustained yield part of the Multiple Use–Sustained Yield Act. "Stop putting up sales when times are bad," he said. That makes sense, I thought. The Forest Service often offered sales where no private company in its right mind would think of building roads and cutting trees, but the Forest Service still acted as if demand for timber was inflexible. But interest rates were high, the housing market was dead, and oil prices had doubled. Something had to give.

For the most part, though, we didn't question our agency's mission—me least of all, for I had grown up with it. I might have been more skeptical had I known that Max Peterson, then chief of the Forest Service, had recently received a memo from his boss that by 2030 the actual annual cut on the national forests would be twenty billion board feet. Twenty years later, safely retired, the man we called Fat Max scoffed that "anybody could have calculated on the back of an envelope" that this was impossible. But in 1982 he had the good sense not to mention that to the undersecretary of agriculture.

Logging required roads, and most roads in the national forests were financed using an accounting device called purchaser road credits. For each mile of logging road built to government specifications by a timber purchaser, an amount was credited against the price paid for stumpage. Quite often this meant that nothing was actually paid for the timber. On its books, the Forest Service amortized these roads over many decades. Profit or loss, for the Forest Service, was immaterial; what mattered to Congress was board feet sold and cut. Our funding was tied to volume removed, and what mattered to a district ranger, what he was graded on, was "getting out the cut."

If the Klamath National Forest didn't meet its timber sale targets, it received less money the following year. Unsold timber meant cuts in next year's budget. This disappointed men like Senator McClure of Idaho, the committee chair who held the forest roads budget in his hands. So influential was McClure that when he retired, decades later, we said, "There goes the roads budget." And we were right: his successor had nothing like his power.

Most wildlife biologists and other specialists felt an attachment to their resource but soon learned that most of their time and budget supported timber sales. The more cynical learned to behave accordingly. Those who wouldn't play ball soon found themselves out of sync with their bosses.

Once the Forest Service got used to dealing with NEPA and NFMA, it saw a path to continued logging, based on elaborate calculations of future growth in plantations. These were often fictional, but they justified the allowable cuts. The timber yield model developed by the Forest Service in California tended to overestimate growth rates and made our cutting rates seem sustainable. Later, a computer program called FORPLAN (or FOREPLAY, as we termed it) accepted as fact other things not strictly true on the ground. And while allowable sale quantity (ASQ) represented a theoretical upper limit on the yearly cut, it soon became an expected output for all years. Since nonexistent trees can't be cut, some people noticed this. In 1991, for instance, the Kootenai National Forest in northwestern Montana asked to lower its ASQ by 30 percent in deference to those missing trees.

Our silviculture department often struggled to find funds to meet our targets. But we did have access to K-V funds, named for the

Knutson-Vandenberg Act of 1930, which set aside money from timber sale receipts for reforestation and stand improvement. K-V money, however, could be used only within the boundaries of the timber sales from which the money was originally collected, and then only for ten years after the sale had closed. But since timber sale boundaries often overlapped, we found a loophole.

Bill Jones sent me upstairs to make copies of old timber sale maps. I traced their boundaries onto other maps that displayed all the district's roads and clear-cuts. Later, I rifled the upstairs file cabinets for information on how much K-V money had been collected from each sale, and how much of that money was still left. I sat cross-legged on the floor of the timber records room and combed through manila folders, coming across papers signed by my stepfather, with figures in his precise printing.

Months later, one of the sale prep foresters told me that we were actually breaking the law, since K-V money wasn't automatic but had to be appropriated by Congress. I shrugged: that was far above my pay grade. I merely found the leftover funds; my bosses magically turned them into contracts, plus a slush fund for force-account work. Life was good.

CHAPTER 9

Breaking Up

Chuck's 1972 Ford three-quarter-ton pickup was the pride of his existence, and whenever I saw it, a thrill of transportational concupiscence ran through me. The long bed. The three (count 'em, three!) gas tanks. The toolbox container in a handy-dandy lockable alcove on one slender flank. The eight-track tape player and radio. The leather seats.

If he hadn't owned a truck, would we have gotten together? Probably. I could see what was coming when Chuck found excuses to stop by the office on Saturday afternoons in August when I was still the receptionist. Someone decided that the office should be open on Saturdays during fire season. Sometimes we went out to dinner later. Chuck was tall, with thick dark wavy hair and a beard that hid the absence of a chin. (Never marry a man with a beard unless you know what he looks like without one.) Four years older than me, he had done a hitch in the navy at the height of the Vietnam War. He was educated. He was buying a house. He had a truck, and he seemed charmed to help me haul hay from Scott Valley for my horses. It was a match made in heaven, or what passed for it on the Klamath.

Once we were a couple, and living together in the house we had reroofed together, Chuck trusted me to use the truck, especially when he didn't want to spend a Saturday hauling hay, which turned out to be most of the time. Still, there were limits to that trust. One weekend, after he helped me unload thirty bales that had ridden seventy miles rubbing against the back of the cab, he moistened a finger and rubbed it over the surface.

"It's scratched!" he moaned. "The hay scratched it!"

I crawled up beside him, still holding my set of vicious antique hay hooks. I peered where he pointed, at the tiny whitish lines that marred the green paint job. It seemed to me that they could easily be buffed to invisibility with the next waxing. When I pointed this out, Chuck glared at me and I suddenly felt small and mean and selfish. He was right: it wasn't my truck, and it was bad of me to have injured it.

"It's okay," I said, my hand on his rigid arm. "From now on, I'll keep a piece of canvas in the truck, and we can drape it over the back of the cab while we're loading, then fold it over the hay and tie it down." He shook his head and looked daggers at me, then muttered, "Okay, that would work."

"Well, gotta remember men like their stuff," said Willy Worcester on Monday. For reasons unclear to me, I had stuck my head into the cloud of smoke in his office and spilled the sad story to him. Willy worked in solitary splendor in a storeroom slowly evolving into a computing center, thanks to some programmable office equipment that nobody except Willy seemed able to fix. Something about him drew confidences, in my case helped by the fact that I knew how to pronounce his last name. A fondness for English history and literature came in handy sometimes.

He squinted at me through clouds of cigarette smoke and added, "The thing is, does he like you better than he likes his stuff?" I looked up at the corner of the room, as though I might find the answer there, and shrugged, for this question lurked behind me every day. Did we really love each other, or was this an association of convenience? I suspected the latter, for why else would I hoard rolls of currency in the bottom of the oatmeal container? We weren't married yet, and if he were given a choice between me and the sanctity of Big Green's paint job, I had no doubt that I would come in second.

"It's complicated," I said, echoing a line from one of last winter's soap operas, and scurried down the hall to silviculture, where things were hard and muddy and steep and cold, but blessedly simple.

My truck-driving privileges were not revoked, however, and one cool and cloudy fall day I drove the truck out toward Yreka. As I neared the Ash Creek Bridge, the truck began to sputter and choke, and I managed to guide it to a stop in a turnout. I tried to crank it over, but it was having none of that. I turned the key again and watched the gas gauge creep up to half full. Plenty of gas. I looked in the rearview mirror and assessed my plight. Coming up the straightaway behind me was a possible rescuer—the downriver mail stage. I stepped out and flagged him down. He assisted me with a look under the hood, but neither of us could see anything wrong. He offered to send a tow truck back for me, but faced with a long cold wait, I instead locked the truck, climbed into the stage, and rode with him to Yreka. Chuck was at a meeting at the Klamath headquarters building, and when that adjourned, I filled him in on the situation, then called Dad and begged him for a lift back downriver. "Nothing worse than two tons of metal that won't run," Dad said cheerfully and soon showed up in his white pickup.

Back down the river road the three of us went, crowded into the Chevy LUV. When we reached the turnout where I had left the truck, Chuck took the key from me and tried to start it. Then he climbed out and looked under the driver's seat, and I smacked myself in the forehead. "The gas lever!" I said. "Of course!"

A lever under the seat controlled the gas tank on which the truck ran and could point in one of three directions: straight ahead for the main tank, to the right for the right saddle tank, to the left for the left saddle tank. But only the main tank was connected to the gas gauge. In my eagerness not to be stranded in a dead vehicle, I had neglected to check that lever.

"It was pointing to the left tank," Chuck said. "Try it now." His voice was cold as he handed me the keys. I peeked under the seat myself before I accepted the invitation. Sure enough, with the lever under the seat now pointing forward, the engine turned over like a lamb. Chuck climbed back into Dad's truck and I followed them back to Yreka. Chuck probably wants to cool off a little, I thought, feeling mortified. It had been months since we had used either of the saddle tanks; whenever I used the truck, I habitually used the main tank. Why hadn't Chuck told me he switched them? Because he assumed I would be smart enough to check.

We went to a going-away party for a headquarters employee that night and drank and chatted and laughed with other people and didn't speak to each other more than necessary. We drove back to Happy Camp late that night, still quiet. I admired his restraint: in his place, I wouldn't have resisted the urge to twit me about the whole fiasco.

That night, as Chuck snored in the bedroom, I took out the oatmeal canister and counted out the rolled bills. My five hundred dollars was safe, for Chuck hated oatmeal and never opened the canister. Perhaps, I thought, my days of free rent and utilities are almost over. Chuck wouldn't put up with me for long after this, surely. If worse came to worst, I could move into the Lower Station barracks, but two dogs and a cat would have to move with me, and I didn't see a barracks life working for them.

I dated my oatmeal hoard to a summer day when Chuck drove me and one of the horses to a riding arena forty miles upriver where a trainer was giving—for a fee—lessons in the finer points of horsemanship. On the way back, and quite without warning, Chuck rebuked me for the money spent and how this was going to end up making him poor. I had paid the fee myself, just as I paid for hay and gave Doc Hall ten dollars a month for the use of his barn and field. I said nothing but started making contingency plans.

His proposal of marriage had come as a surprise, and I didn't know why he had done it, until he asked me for a divorce. Looking back on it, I suppose I should have hastened to crank out a couple of kids, so that when they grew into teenagers and wrecked his vehicles, he'd have had someone else to blame. And if he thought horses were going to inhale all his money, he had no clue at all what children would do. He could have saved himself considerable trouble by mentioning kids to me before the wedding; had he done so, I would have said no, thank you, and changed the subject. Roof over my head or no, hay-hauling vehicle or no, it would have given both of us an easy out. As it was, when he finally introduced the subject of offspring three years into the marriage, it was no more welcome to me than it would have been before. After that, I knew he was thinking about his options. He had been divorced once before, and he could do it again.

Even at the best of times, we were ill suited to a permanent life together. He was an orderly Capricorn with a yen for financial success. I was a Gemini who loved books and horses and tackled ten projects at once. If we had worked in the same office in a larger town, he probably wouldn't even have asked me out. Both his first wife and the woman he had lived with for two years before he met me had been tall,

Chuck and horses in one of Doc Hall's fields on Indian Creek in 1977, practicing for his first pack trip. In the background, part of the west side of the 1966 Indian Ridge Burn, fated to burn again.

willowy blonds with good taste in clothes. They knew how to apply makeup and pile their hair into the beehive creations of the day. But such women were in short supply in Happy Camp, and we found each other to be clean, not unattractive, capable of intelligent conversation, and near enough in age, education, and social class to be a reasonable fit, at least at first. He was easily the most handsome man who had ever been interested in me, but I could count those on the fingers of one hand maimed by an industrial accident.

I did grow fond of him, and since he was only twenty-nine when we met, the lure of a relationship with a nice girl in this isolated place was perhaps irresistible. Later, our differences mattered more. He put up with a lot from me, starting with an orphan foal I raised on goat's milk in 1976. Raising the colt led me into goat husbandry, which involved Chuck in several horror stories including a cesarean section in the front yard and a milk goat expiring from ketosis in the carport. He hadn't bargained for any of these things. Still, he liked to take pack trips into the Marble Mountains and up onto the Siskiyou Divide with the horses, so he tolerated them. What he resented was the necessity of dealing with their health and behavioral problems. Horses were cheap to keep in Happy Camp in those days, in monetary terms, but they still had to be cared for every day.

"Chuck and I are the original Felix Unger and Oscar Madison," I wrote to my brother. "I'm Oscar, he's Felix. He has high standards; alas, I don't measure up to them."

I was a homebody with the soul of a European peasant; Chuck worked hard at projects around the house and yard, but for real fun, he wanted to see the bright lights of Reno and Las Vegas. The only trip to Reno I actually enjoyed coincided with an Arabian horse show at the fairgrounds. We saw little of each other that weekend but came home content. The people who raised me didn't consider fun important, but Chuck actually became angry at me if I didn't at least look like I was having a good time on a trip. My idea of a great summer weekend was riding horseback, gardening, watching the ball game, and sitting down with a book in the heat of the afternoon. And as time went on, I looked forward to the times when Chuck got that Reno glint in his eye. Go, go, I thought, and have a good time. Without me, please.

A failing marriage gives both parties some freedom. Alice lent me a ready ear whenever I wanted to talk about it. She had never cared much for Chuck. "After all, he won't even let you have a screen door in the laundry room, or a clothesline," she said. "Isn't it your house, too?"

"Well, not really," I said. "But it doesn't matter. I know what's going to happen. At some point he's going to be ready for a promotion off the Klamath, and when that day comes, I'm just not going to go with him."

But when the promotion came, it was to Oak Knoll, and instead of moving permanently upriver or to Yreka, he decided to purchase a camp trailer, park it near his new district's office, and commute back to Happy Camp on weekends. This gave me four days of solitude every week, and I settled into a routine that consisted of utter relaxation on Monday and growing tension by Thursday afternoon, since Chuck worked four ten-hour days at Oak Knoll. Chuck used the time—inadvertently, at first—to get himself into a situation that forced both his hand and mine. I knew that something was going on at Oak Knoll, and that it involved another woman. And I wished him luck. He was going to need it.

"You know," one of the Oak Knoll foresters said to me, "the trouble with Chuck is he's a crabby perfectionist." I nodded, wondering why I had never put that equation together myself. I heard his words with relief. It wasn't just me, then.

He did scare me a bit in midsummer when he talked about getting a transfer back to Happy Camp. He even spoke to George about it, and I wondered whether his girlfriend had dumped him. A bit embarrassed for him, I told Alice I wished Chuck wouldn't bother George about such things.

"Oh, that stuff just rolls off George's back," Alice said. "People are always hitting him up about jobs. But if it's any consolation," she added, "he wouldn't hire Chuck even if there was a vacancy, which there isn't now. Chuck can't get along with the folks he'd have to work with again."

On an autumn evening in 1980 as I sat doing leatherwork at a card table in the corner of the living room, Chuck rose from his recliner and stood beside me. "Can you stop that for a minute?" he said. At first I thought that the hammer and punch routine was wearing on his nerves. I put down the tools and looked up at him. He took a deep breath and dove in.

"I think we ought to split up," he said. He leaned over as he said this, but for once his great height didn't intimidate me. He seemed to be begging for something he wanted very much.

"I think you're right," I heard myself say, and he inhaled sharply, then smiled at me. He had assembled a series of arguments, but I had rendered them unnecessary. Still, some of them wanted to come out anyway, so he sat down on the couch beside me.

"We just don't get along," he said, "and I think we'd both be happier not being married to each other." I nodded.

"We both want different things," I said, and with that, he looked so happy and relieved that I reached over and put my arms around him and we hugged, for a long time and almost for the last time. That night we made love, cheerfully, and definitely for the very last time. Then I opened up the hide-a-bed in the spare room and slept long and soundly.

Days later, as we sat down at the kitchen table to work out the details and compare lists of property, I told him about the oatmeal canister. Its contents had seen ups and downs—two years into the marriage, we had traveled to San Francisco so that Chuck could see an eye specialist, and I raided it for traveling money. We laughed about that, and he confessed that he had removed our collection of gold coins from the safe deposit box. I would, he assured me, get my half back when the paperwork was done.

"When did you do that?" I asked.

He looked down, his forehead turning red. "Before I asked you for the divorce," he said. "I was afraid you might get mad and take them."

As I digested this latest proof of how little each of us had trusted the other, Chuck said, "Remember when you got stuck in the truck going out to Yreka because you forgot to check the gas lever?"

I nodded. "I'm not likely ever to forget that," I said.

"Well, when I was riding back into town with your dad—which I did just to cool off, so I wouldn't yell at you"—I nodded—"and start a fight, your dad and I started talking. And he told me not to marry you."

"What?"

"He told me not to marry you. Said that you were crazy and always had been, and that I shouldn't tie myself down by marrying you."

The room whirled. "Say that again," I said. "He told you not to marry me?"

"Yes, said that you were nuts, and that I shouldn't marry you."

"What did you think when he said that?"

"Well, it made me kind of mad that he would say that about you, because I don't think you're nuts—eccentric and stubborn, maybe, but not nuts—and I thought, that's not true. And I decided right then that I was going to marry you, because I thought that would make you feel safer and more secure, if we were married instead of just living together." His voice trailed off.

I shook my head, remembering that day. "You should have listened to him," I said. "You should have."

"I'm sorry things didn't work out between us," he told me one evening as he brought some insurance papers to me at my new house.

"Don't worry about it," I said. "Believe me, you're better off without all of my hassle." And he turned to go and drove off toward another wife and, eventually, two children. But for the next thirty-one years, he never forgot to send me a Christmas card.

CHAPTER 10

Out of the Frying Pan

The first six months after the divorce amounted to an orgy of reading, arranging my dwelling any way I liked, spreading my hobbies out on any flat surface, listening to music I liked, and cooking according to my own tastes. I came home directly after work, closed the shutters against the winter night, and hibernated. I slept on the fold-out couch, and when my sheets were in the laundry, in my sleeping bag. For some reason, Chuck had rebelled against the idea of splitting the linens fifty-fifty, so I took with me one set of sheets and pillowcases, plus the towels I had arrived with six years ago.

And sometime in the spring of 1981, in my thirty-second year, I woke to a world of freedom and possibilities.

One of the more mundane of these blessings was cable television, which finally made its way up Indian Creek. I pored over the brochures and chose a package that included TBS—which carried the Atlanta Braves games—and WGN—ditto Harry Carey and the Cubs. I subscribed to *The Sporting News.* Being a fan meant doing the research. Every week, the colorful tabloid arrived in the mail, and I brought it to work with me and let it ride on the dashboard when I drove out to the woods.

"You're the only woman I know who reads this stuff," said a sleepy-eyed tech with a two-day growth of beard. He lived in the barracks during the week and went home to his wife in Scott Valley on weekends. I wondered how well that suited both of them, and whether it was working out better than it had for Chuck and me.

"I aim to please," I said. Would this be another case of a guy regarding me as a walking commissary? I learned early on that carrying a can of snoose and a package of Red Man tobacco in my fire vest made me a more desirable partner for mop-up duty on fires. But Todd's main use for the sports publication was to cover his face when he napped after lunch. For other people, it provided a store of subjects for idle conversation, sorely needed during the rainy months, and especially during planting and when inspecting contractors. Force account, everyone agreed, was the worst, since using our own people meant that we worked in areas where planting had already failed a time or two. For weeks on end, we scrabbled down precipitous slopes in the rain, looking for a place to stick a tree. One perennially favorite location for this was the old Frying Pan Sale on the slopes of knife-edged Frying Pan Ridge, east of Happy Camp and overlooking the river.

The clear-cuts on either side of the ridge weren't marvels of production to begin with; the stumps were not very large and they were widely spaced. The old-growth stands destroyed so we could plant seedlings in the rain had been Douglas-fir mixed with tan oak, growing on thin soil punctuated by rockslides. Poison oak grew everywhere, and in the summer the heat was brutal. We planted in February, hoping that by June the seedlings would put down roots to find moisture. The results from previous years were not encouraging, but since people and money were available, we tried again.

We didn't hurry to finish a unit, for every hour paid the same as every other hour. We tried to run out the clock, for sooner or later—sooner, please God—something else would come along that was more bearable. So—depending on the whims of the day's crew boss—we took half-hour coffee breaks, a full hour for lunch, knocked off early, and took our time driving back to the station. In short, we were dogging it. We cheered when our bosses gave up and contracted the whole sorry mess out. With a couple of stalwarts from the silviculture department and a rotating crew from the Class of '78 to handle inspections, we gave Frying Pan and several other lost causes one more try, this time with the more competent and rapid help of Mexican tree planters.

I sat in green pickup trucks with a rotating cast of men and women and learned more about them, where they came from and where they had gone to school, their favorite sports and how they ended up in Happy Camp. At the start of their careers, they looked on this place not as a permanent home, but a step along the way. Most were a few years younger than me. The couples with whom Chuck and I had socialized tended to be older. Except for softball, I didn't mingle with the Class when I was married. Now I orbited the periphery of their world, tagging along for beer at the pizza parlor, and was sometimes included in party invitations. At first I thought it was politeness, because I happened to be in the van when someone announced a party that weekend, but I seemed to be just as welcome as anyone else. And it was quite a group.

Patty, for instance, had been raised in Beverly Hills, where her father worked as an accountant in the movie industry. She went to high school with the children of movie stars. "Most of them were monsters," she said, her thick eyebrows pulling together in a frown. She went off to college in Berkeley to get away from Southern California and discovered the forestry school, and beyond it a world of rivers and wild redwoods. She never looked back.

Nevertheless, we worried about Patty. I couldn't decide whether she was brave, foolhardy, or just unlucky, for she managed, in the course of only a couple of summers, to be chased up a young fir tree by an angry black bear, to be stung by bald-faced hornets so many times that she came in from the woods one day with an unrecognizable face, and to have her dog bitten by a rattlesnake. After the hornet incident, which happened on a Friday, she went home and passed out for forty-eight hours on her couch, still wearing her field clothes. She eventually fell into a relationship with an older forester in what seemed to the rest of us like the mésalliance of the ages, but it turned out to be a good match. They both loved opera, which helped.

Michael, a bouncy redhead from Michigan, fresh off two years with the Peace Corps in Niger, told stories of almost dying from a kidney infection and nearly marrying a Tuareg girl. He came home with boxes of slides that he showed at parties, for which he wore colorful hand-dyed cotton shirts. He was full of a boundless self-confidence and certainty about forestry practices in this place he had never seen before. He couldn't wait to start cutting down hardwoods.

I caught up with the local news through Gary, who had been here a couple of years longer, and whose irrepressible love for life and food and human contact made me smile as I watched him across a clear-cut, waving his arms and yelling in broken Spanish to the grinning planters. He seemed to regard me as some sort of mother confessor, which surprised me as this was usually Laura's role in our group. One morning, he walked slowly across the parking lot toward me, his back cocked at an odd angle, a brace cinched around his waist. "What the hell did you do?" I asked.

"Tell you on the way up," he said, and so I learned of his torrid affair with the neglected girlfriend of one of the fire gods. The god came home unexpectedly and found Gary and the woman naked. Gary escaped through a window. Clutching his clothes—"Seriously? A window?" I whooped at the cliché—he fled to the home of the friend whose roof he was supposed to be helping to repair, but—and here he blamed his emotional upset—he failed to take enough care on the rooftop, slid off, and wrenched his back.

"Did that teach you anything?" I said, sounding like the schoolmarm I had once trained to be.

"Yeah," he groaned and shifted in the seat as I hit a pothole. "Don't ever do it in the guy's house. And you know the worst part?" he added. "When I got home, my wife had just been to the clinic for that ultrasound thing? She's going to have twins!" He groaned again.

"They know what causes that now," I said.

"I know, I know. But this is gonna be the last. As soon as I can walk straight I'm going to the doc and get snipped. One baby was bad enough, but three?"

Conversations like this made me look forward to working with Joe, a quiet man who always had a book with him, and since his house was on the way up to the ridge, we often stopped to pick him up in the morning. A door flew open and out he dashed with his pack, snatching a cup of coffee, Dagwood-like, from his wife as he went. We talked about Isak Dinesen and exchanged book recommendations. I still have the copy of *Seven Gothic Tales* he gave me.

Then there was Matt, who lived far downriver but was never late to work. Raised in New England, where he played pond hockey, he found our warm wet winters depressing. He actually read the stories in *The Sporting News* over lunch, though, and I learned he had been to Fenway Park. This impressed me more than travels to Africa or living next door to Susan Hayward. Someone I knew had actually seen the Green Monster, and Carlton Fisk. My attitude toward his recent career as a softball manager softened.

Sometimes he shared the front seat with Dave, a wiry Pisces reared on the rivers of Virginia. In a rare example of the Forest Service precisely matching the person to the job, he was about to become the district's first river patrolman. He slept a great deal, probably dreaming of what to name the virgin whitewater rapids of the Klamath.

Over time, many of these youngsters would shuffle and reshuffle into couples, both married and unmarried. I didn't hope or expect, at first, that any of this coupling would involve me. I wasn't eager to jump into a new relationship. I enjoyed my solitary evenings at home. But after a time, it was not so much that I went searching for partners as that a few men started to look at me.

"Well," Laura laughed when I mentioned the number of phone calls I was getting, "there aren't that many eligible single women around here, you know."

She had a point. Many of the new women on the district—Laura among them—had arrived with boyfriends already in tow. I had few illusions about my looks, but I'd certainly never broken any mirrors when I was fixed up a bit. I began to go to parties, to show up for pickup soccer games, to drink beer with the rest of the crowd when someone got a promotion. I enjoyed talking to these new people in my life, outside work as well as in. They weren't people with whom Chuck would have socialized. They smoked weed, played Hacky-Sack, and didn't want to hang out with line officers.

Eventually, I went out on dates that no one wanted to call dates anymore. Whatever they were, I was old enough not to expect an evening, or even sex, to lead to anything more, no matter how entertaining the experience. Permanence wasn't part of the deal in the 1980s. But I knew myself for a hopeless serial monogamist. One man at a time had always been more than enough complication for me.

Some of these encounters turned out to be quite useful: one young man taught me how to install linoleum on the living room floor when I moved into the larger of the two cabins I had inherited from the divorce. Another helped me muscle a stove inside and hook up the stovepipe. A third had a sauna where naked women were always welcome, and a freezer full of ice cream. And if none of us became the love of each other's life, that was fine, for we knew enough not to utter the fatal words, to spring the ultimate trap. When I stopped seeing them, or they me, no one's heart was broken. We were all adults here, and besides, we had to work together. But as I clambered up and down mountains with these new men and women, as I talked to them and laughed with them and learned about their lives and hopes, the feeling that I was fated never to find anyone else to live with or love began to fade. Maybe my life still held surprises. Perhaps there was more to my future than nostalgia and attachment to a place. Perhaps there was someone out there for me, but if so, he'd better show up pretty darn soon, for through all the laughter and the Hacky-Sack circles, through all the games of volleyball on the lawn at someone's party, through all the loping after a soccer ball on summer evenings, through all the optimism about a second chance at life and youth and happiness, in the background lurked the truth that most of these kids were five or six years younger than me, and time was not about to stop or go backward. A window would close on this present sunshine, and soon.

I tried not to think about that, so I almost didn't notice when I started looking forward to working with one person more than any other. How does that happen? How does it happen that the way someone's eyes squeeze shut when he throws back his head and laughs, the way his damp black curls cling to his neck under a hard hat in the rain, the way his green eyes flash with anger or amusement, the way his long fingers hold a thermos, all become lovely, so that we anticipate them and feel our hearts beat a little faster when we know he'll be with us? And how does it happen that even though we enjoy hilarious stories about postcoital pratfalls, or talks about books, or stories about millet mush in Niger or running the Appalachian rapids, it's another that we think about after work, so that one evening as upbeat music is playing on my stereo, I look up from gluing a strut on the *Millennium Falcon*, and it strikes me with the force of a hammer, this feeling. And in the space of three minutes, as the music ends, my foot is well and truly caught in the door, and I slide about the kitchen and even sing a little, making up lyrics to a piece of music that has none, surrendering to the soaring feeling that the world calls being in love.

Perhaps, just perhaps, out of the frying pan of a failed marriage and failed plantations, out of the futility of planting yet more trees to be poured down the rathole of industrial forestry, has come this one amazing thing: a man who works beside me in green rain gear, who lopes across a draw to point out a spot with a badly planted tree, who stands balanced like a lance on a steep slope with the fog-shrouded forest behind him, and makes it all beautiful. I had not the slightest clue what to do about all this, but I did know that nothing would ever be the same.

By the next day, I knew I couldn't look at him, or talk to him, or work with him and still feel at ease, as I used to. I was glad when, soon afterward, sale prep coughed up enough money to bring Matt back on, and he went upstairs again. I didn't know how I could be around him for any length of time now and not have him see in my face what I felt.

I stopped sleeping with my occasional lover, to his bemused puzzlement, and settled in to research All Things Matt. Our paths crossed, in hallways and at the parties that I increasingly attended just because he might be there. Driven by the unfortunate compulsion that drives us to tell someone about these misfortunes, I blurted it all out to Laura, and her gray eyes filled with compassion because she already knew, from the way I looked at him at one of those parties. She tried to warn me that it was already too late. "Do you remember back when Heather hurt her knee and had to wear that brace?" I did.

"Well, one day I asked Matt if he liked any of the girls here"—Laura could get away with asking men things like that—"and he laughed like he does"—I knew exactly how—"and he said, 'I kind of like the gimp.'"

"Oh," I said. And I remembered what I had seen at one larger district party—someone was retiring—at which several of us—Laura, Heather, Helen, Patricia, and I—had all, on a bet, come wearing our best approximations of formals. I had hoped that Matt would look at me, but his eyes followed Heather around the room and lit up in a way that tugged at my heart. I must have known even then that the ship had sailed and the train had left the station. But hope, too cruel to kill outright, threw me a line. "She's going back East to stay with her sister this winter," I said. "Maybe he'll notice me while she's gone." And Laura patted my shoulder.

Part II

CHAPTER 11

Luke Skywalker vs. Darth Plumbing

I just want to turn on the faucet and have water!
I don't want to know where it's coming from!
—Diane Keaton in *Baby Boom*

In Hilt, the company made sure that we all had water. It came out of Hungry Creek, and it was (usually) chlorinated. Sewage was collected into pipes and sent downhill to a pond a mile downwind of town, where it eventually leached into Cottonwood Creek. It wasn't perfect, but it worked. Toilets flushed, bathtubs drained, and we were happy. Nobody ever looked out their front windows to see a four-foot zit swelling beneath the skin of their front lawn, as we did one morning in Seiad when I was in high school.

That was when we learned that our septic tank was a fifty-five-gallon drum with an outflow pipe that leached into some blackberry vines in the ditch above the county road. That was the first time I stuck a shovel into a lawn, not sure of what I would find. But it wouldn't be the last.

When I moved out of Chuck's house and into the smaller of the two rental houses bought from Doc Hall as an investment two years before, the delicate nature of my new water system didn't concern me for a while. I knew about it in an academic sense, but the temporary fix that Chuck had devised with a neighbor, to bring water in the summertime to the well that serviced the property, worked well up to a point. No, the first plumbing challenge I faced was one of outflow.

I had moved into the two-bedroom cabin and rented out the one-bedroom to Dani and his girlfriend. He was the district archaeologist and Marie worked on the river patrol. He was the son of wealthy

Postdivorce digs: the blackberry patch in the foreground, and the flourishing cherry tree, hide a few surprises.

Iranian refugees settled in Southern California—"Tehrangeles," he called it—and I wondered whether he was yet another case of a well-off kid disappointing his parents with an outdoor career. But I had other things to think about, especially after my brother came to stay with me for the summer.

Tom had just gotten out of the navy, which taught him to fix the electronics systems of jet aircraft. I remembered how I felt when home from college and at first just let him sleep. But soon enough, I needed him.

I came home from work one June afternoon to find Tom sitting on the porch sipping a beer. He waved the bottle uphill toward the one-bedroom house. "Trouble in River City," he said.

"What?" I said and rolled my eyes. I felt hot and sticky as I unlaced my boots on the steps and peeled the socks from my feet. I couldn't wait to get into some shorts and drive up the creek to the swimming hole.

"Dani's toilet's stopped up," he said.

"Oh no. Did you take the plunger up there?"

"Yup." He took another sip of beer. "Man, that guy smokes a lot of weed. Smoke just billowed out the door when he opened it up."

"Great." Dani always seemed slightly buzzed and reeked of patchouli, but it was none of my business. "Any luck?"

"No. I think I'm gonna need a snake."

"Can you go down to the hardware store and get one tomorrow?"

"Sure," he said and looked happy to be doing something useful and guy-like.

But the snake didn't work, either. "Guy at the store thinks we need a power snake," he said the next afternoon. "He says Art Tisdale's the only guy around here with one."

"I'll call him later," I said as Tom went inside to get me a beer, and I looked up to see Dani's girlfriend heading up into the timber with a roll of toilet paper. She did not look happy.

I wonder now why I didn't just offer her the use of our bathroom, or rent a port-a-potty from Art. But I didn't think of either, probably because I believed it would all be resolved by tomorrow.

But it wasn't. Art arrived the following morning with the power snake, a dangerous-looking implement rolled up on a round metal contraption, powered by an electric motor. He and Tom stood in Dani's bathroom and nose-dived the snake's head down into the toilet bowl. It went, and it went, and it went. Art watched it go and shook his head. "This isn't right," he said, as the snake continued its journey, until its full length disappeared into the porcelain maw. "Should have hit something by now." He pushed back his cap and scratched his forehead. Tom smacked his own forehead and ran outside, backing up until he could see the vent pipe. "Hey, Art!" he shouted. "It's gone up the vent pipe!"

Art came out and the two men stared up at the impotent snake's head, waving blindly in the summer air. "Let's have some coffee and think about this," Art said, turning off the snake motor and heading for his truck and thermos.

"Sounds like a plan," Tom said and went in the house, returning with a pen, tablet, and cup of coffee. Over the next half hour they scribbled diagrams and tried to figure out what was going on. "You see," Art said, "the old fart who built that house was hell on wheels when it came to concrete, but he didn't know shit about plumbing. He put the vent pipe right there, where the outflow pipe makes a ninety-degree turn at the corner of the house. So when we ran the snake down the toilet, it tended to go up the vent pipe instead of making the turn. Most plumbers, now, they would have put the vent pipe opening on the straightaway, so a snake would go right on past it and head further down the line."

"So what do we do?" Tom asked.

Art lit another cigarette. "Well, we know where the clog isn't. So it's got to be somewhere past that bend. But beyond the bend, you've got solid concrete above the pipe for quite a ways. And we don't even know where the clog is. It might even be closer to the septic tank than to the house. So let's find the septic tank."

He looked at the patch of Himalayan blackberries between the kitchen window of the larger cabin and the driveway. He grabbed a shovel from the back of his truck and swiped the canes aside, moving toward the center of the patch.

"There's at least part of your problem," he announced as he pointed to the glint of gray water nourishing the rich growth.

"Oh my God," Tom said.

"So what's next?" I said that evening as I lay on the couch with a cold wet washcloth over my eyes to try to shut down my migraine. "No, please, no beer. Get me a Coke," I said. "And some aspirin. Or a merciful bullet."

I was not well. That afternoon I had, for the first time in my life, invited a man to a movie, and not just any man, but Matt, and not just any movie, but *Star Wars*, now in a short-term revival at the Craterian Theater in Medford. I didn't know what gave me the courage to march upstairs to Matt's office and ask him, with an Oscar-worthy attempt at nonchalance, if he'd like to go see a movie with me this weekend. And it didn't really matter, for Matt turned me down flat, in a casual no-thanks way, as he picked up his pack and headed for the door. His body language and voice told me that not only did he have no interest in me, but that he hadn't a clue that I had any in him. That ignorance was my only comfort. Deep as my humiliation went, it hadn't touched bottom yet. But I replayed the awful moment over and over, even as I took in what Tom told me and realized the full scope of our plumbing predicament. When he said "backhoe," I wanted to crawl into the very large hole for which I would shortly be paying more than I could afford. I lay in a fetal position and moaned as Tom shook my shoulder to make sure I'd heard him.

"So is he coming tomorrow?"

"No, tomorrow's Saturday, Twinkletoes. He'll be here Monday. But that'll give us time to clear out the blackberry brambles."

"Okay," I said. "I'm going to sleep now."

I woke up at eleven o'clock in the silent dark and for a moment didn't know where I was. Then the cat stirred against my legs, and I came awake to the sure knowledge that my life sucked, I was an idiot, and I was about to lose my renters.

Tom and I went to Medford on Sunday and saw *Star Wars* once more. I didn't tell my brother, as we sat there in the cool darkness, that to me he would always be Luke Skywalker, since that far-off summer of '77 when the two merged in my mind.

I especially loved the scene in which Luke stands on a ridge at sunset (two suns—way cool!) and John Williams's music swells as Luke dreams of places far away from the moisture farm. That year, my brother was on the USS *Constellation*, sailing in circles on the Indian Ocean and wishing vainly for shore leave in Australia. We wrote to each other often, and I told friends about my talented little brother who kept the F-14s flying and made sure the plane that brought the mail was in tip-top shape.

But just now I felt bad for him, back on land and staying with the sister without a clue. He had gone above and beyond Art's instructions to "just clear off the blackberries." Like an archaeologist at an ancient site, he peeled back the grass and leaves and dirt and found the tank, and the inflow pipe from the upper cabin, broken away from the opening. "That explains the gray water," I said.

"Wonder how long it's been that way?" Tom said.

I thought back. "Since one of Chuck's renters parked something heavy right here, I'm betting," I said.

"You could ask Chuck," Tom said, tilting his chin down-creek toward Poverty Flat.

"Not in a million years," I said. His new wife was there, and I was not about to remind Debbie of her beloved's matrimonial past.

Tom's eyes traced the path between the cabin on the hillside and the end of the pipe. "Ohh-kay," he said. "Time for a cup of coffee."

After lunch, we rounded up the Pulaski and Tom started chopping at the ground, following the pipe up toward the other house. He gave up when he hit the compacted soil of the driveway. The temperature was over a hundred degrees now, anyway. We put on our swimsuits and drove up the creek to Laura's place, where we sluiced off the grime in the deep green pool on Indian Creek. Later I spread my towel out on the hot bedrock and told Laura about the septic tank, and about the invitation gone wrong. "Well," she said, "at least he didn't tell you to go to hell or anything."

"But maybe he wouldn't, even if he thought it," I said. "He's very polite."

Laura laughed. "Most of the time, anyway. On the sale prep crew, he has a reputation for getting mad when things go wrong." She paused and stared off across the creek. "I think he likes to get mad, actually," she added. "Makes life seem more exciting."

I thought about Matt and his snapping eyes. "Could be," I said, knowing what she meant, and knowing, as well, that I had the charisma of mayonnaise and that nothing about me had ever excited anyone.

On Monday, Tom and Art and Art's backhoe carved a ditch across the driveway, following the path of the septic pipe. When they stopped for lunch, Art expounded on the problem. "I think maybe it's the way they laid this pipe," he said, taking a bite of sandwich. "The pipeline drops too fast. It's only supposed to drop an inch every ten feet, but this one goes down a lot faster than that."

"And that means . . .?" Tom said.

"That the liquids tend to move down the pipe a lot faster than the solids," Art said, chomping on a pickle. "Over time, that means a lot of solids are stuck up there"—he waved the pickle at the cabin on the hill—"and so they don't make it down here."

"Oh," Tom said.

"It also means," Art added, "that the further up that hill we go, the deeper that pipe's going to be buried."

"Damn," Tom said.

And so it proved. Section by section, the backhoe unearthed the pipeline. The men stopped now and then to break the sections apart and check for clogs. At four o'clock, Art stopped the machine and wiped his forehead. The trench was five feet deep, with the steepest part of the hill still to come.

"I've got another job tomorrow that I've got to get to," Art said. "You might try digging more on your own, but I think the problem's got to be right close to the house."

Tom nodded, sent Art and his truck and trailer and backhoe down the driveway with a wave, and stepped over to the faucet to rinse the sweat off his head. He was met by a sputter of water, a gasp of air, and then nothing.

"Fuuuuuuccckk!" he screamed, stomping toward the well house.

I came home to find my brother looking damp and cool and wearing clean clothes. "You been swimming already?" I asked.

"Nope, just walked up to the barn and lay down in the horse trough," he said. "What the hell is wrong with all the water systems around here?"

I explained. The pump was submersible and was supposed to be near the bottom of a 180-foot well, but the well driller had cased the well down to only 30 feet; no one knew why. In the twenty years since, the uncased portion of the well had collapsed upon itself. The submersible pump hung about 30 feet down, which put it about 15 feet below the water line in winter. But in summer, the water level dropped.

"Let me guess. It's dropped about fifteen feet," Tom said.

"Bingo," I said.

I remembered that I hadn't been sanguine about the prospects when Doc Hall knocked on Chuck's door one evening and offered to sell us the one-acre-with-two-houses that bordered his horse pasture. Doc usually got the better of any real estate deal. But Chuck had the heart of a capitalist as well and was convinced of his own acuity. That didn't matter to the well, though, as we learned the following summer when it went dry. Then we learned about the backup system from Sonny, the next-door neighbor to the south.

Sonny had built a green and pleasant home for his wife and (now grown) children by buying land near the mouth of Slater Creek and diverting its waters before they could reach Indian Creek. He led Chuck on a short walk up the creek and pointed out the concrete dam and diversion pipes, one of which, buried in a shallow trench, headed across his horse pasture toward our rentals. Crossing under Sonny's fence, it continued to the well house, where it dumped water into the well via a length of plastic pipe and a PVC elbow over the top of the well casing.

I took Tom out and showed him the setup, and we both noticed that no water trickled into the well. I explained that the creek had dropped below the intake. Although Sonny would eventually notice this and adjust the dam to bring the water level back up, a bubble would remain in our line, since the pipeline was laid without bleeder valves. The bubble would work its way through the line and the flow would resume, but not for a couple of weeks.

"What do we do in the meantime?" Tom said.

"The water level in the well may rise tonight," I said, "but not enough to take a bath or water the yard. So we go to Plan B."

"What's that?"

"I'll show you tonight, after dark."

By moonlight, we stepped over the strands of barbed wire that divided my property from Doc Hall's and walked up the slope toward the old barn, followed by the horses, who blew softly in hope of apples. I dragged about 150 feet of garden hose behind me. I attached one end to the faucet above the horse trough and had Tom run down and stick the other end into the well casing. When he heard water running into the well, he whistled at me and I kinked the hose, unscrewed it from the faucet, and submerged it in the trough. I laid a finger over the end to make sure the siphon was working, and left the faucet running into the trough a little to compensate for the outflow.

"You've done this before," Tom said, breathing hard from his climb back up the hill.

"No kidding," I said.

"Has he ever caught you?"

"Not yet. I get up before sunrise and shut it off, then drag the hose back down the hill."

"God in heaven, Sister."

Tom looked down at the horse trough, the old claw-footed bathtub in which he had soaked only a couple of hours ago. It was clean because Doc's hired man—he wasn't actually hired, because Doc didn't pay him anything but let him live in a cabin on the large property—scrubbed it out every other day with cleanser and a scrub brush. This water, I told Tom, came from a couple of springs up on the mountainside behind the property, which never failed.

As we walked back across the field, Tom said, "So if that spring is so good, what's that all about?" He pointed to the well-drilling rig that sat in the middle of Doc's hayfield in a pool of gray muck. "That's Doc betting that if he just drills deep enough, there's water down there. Word is he's down four hundred feet now, and all they've hit is a little pocket of salt water." And I told him the story of the wells-all-in-a-row on Poverty Flat. "Around here, if you aren't hitting the old creek bed, you aren't hitting anything, ever."

"Doesn't he know that?"

"Probably, but he's between a rock and a hard place." In past years, I'd irrigated those hayfields for Doc myself in exchange for horse pasture. "Doc had a pump on a platform above Indian Creek, and a pipe that went under the county road," I said, pointing. "And I'd move the Rain Bird pipes every day and then go down and prime the pump and wait and wait and finally get it going if I was lucky. He got the water for free, but it cost him so much in electricity it wasn't worth it. He wanted his pasture to look nice, but he didn't want to pay for it. And now he's paying thousands and thousands for a new well, which the Forest Service geologist says won't pay off because there's no aquifer down there."

Later, as we watched the Cubs lose on WGN, Tom said, "Why not just go over to Sonny's and check on the inflow pipe?"

I shrugged. "I did that last year, before I knew how long it took an air pocket to work through the pipe, and I talked to Sonny about it. We walked up and checked the inflow pipe, and then he asked if he could feel my boobs."

"No way! What did you do?"

"I told him no, that his wife wouldn't like it. And then I found another way."

Tom kept digging uphill all the next day. I came home from work, surveyed the damage, and took him swimming. The next day, he walked around the cabin and looked at the concrete apron that almost surrounded the building. The old man who had built it—several years after the larger house was built—had been a stonemason and concrete artist. He built a cistern on the northwest corner of the cabin. It filled up quite nicely in winter, but an insufficient sealing job caused the water to leak out in summer. On the south side of the cabin, in the shade of the cherry tree, Tom found a gap between the concrete sidewalk and the cabin wall. He got a shovel and started to dig. It's not much of a chance, he thought, but I'll take it.

Two feet down, he struck something: a piece of perforated concrete pipe about three feet long, packed completely full of twisted roots from the cherry tree. The roots were big and fat from their diet of human feces and gray water. Later, we both stared at his find, then went swimming and downtown for a pizza and a pitcher of beer.

When Art appeared again he laughed, scratched his head, and laughed some more. "Who the hell would use a piece of perforated concrete pipe in a septic line? Well, at least this makes the rest easy-peasy. We just hook up a new piece of pipe."

"With a take-out valve in case we ever need to put a snake down there again," Tom added.

"Yup, a take-out valve, and then we pump out the septic tank, which I know no one's ever done, and replace the lower pipe sections, and fill up the trench. No problem!"

"Thank God," Tom muttered. And about the time those chores were finished and Art had left for the last time, that recalcitrant air pocket burped its way down Sonny's water line, and one night as Tom prepared to drag the hoses uphill yet again—his sister gone on a lightning fire—he opened the well-house door and heard the welcome splash of water already pouring into the well. He went inside and went to bed to the sound of the drilling rig in the pasture, as Doc tried to conjure water from the dry Jurassic rock.

CHAPTER 12

We Survived the Five

One hot July day in 1982, as I drove back from scouting out possible camping places for a contract thinning crew, I crested Thompson Ridge at the intersection below Slater Butte Lookout and was smacked in the eyes by a white mushroom cloud on the western horizon. Big already and growing every second, it rose high above the Clear Creek drainage, a cauliflower gone mad.

A "blow-up" on a forest fire is a combination of heat, fuel, and sometimes wind. As the fire gets into an area of heavy fuels, the flames grow taller and smoke climbs high into the atmosphere, until it reaches an elevation at which the particles and water vapor in the smoke form a thunderhead, driven by the same physical realities that bring lightning storms. The column may even generate its own lightning and showers, before the heated gases cool and rush downward again, collapsing the column and sending fire rushing outward in all directions. If the fuel in the area is more or less continuous, this process repeats itself, the fractals reproducing again and again.

I parked the truck, dragged a pair of binoculars from beneath the seat, stepped out, and braced my elbows on the hot green hood. The base of the cloud had turned a dark russet, colored by the combustion of heavy, dry fuels rapidly transforming into gas and ash. Stray bands of smoke spread horizontally as the fire heated adjoining areas and brought them up to kindling temperature.

I didn't bother to get on the radio to report the fire, as I would have done for a thin wisp of smoke. This one was so big that it must already have been seen, and first of all by the lookout in the Slater Butte tower behind me. In the radio-silent hole of Thompson Creek, I hadn't heard the initial excitement, but now as I flipped the radio switch to channel 3 and turned the squelch up to hear the fire traffic, I listened to the sputters and squawks and "10-4s" as the fire people tried to figure out just what they were dealing with. I climbed back into the truck and made all good speed back to the station.

When I first started working "in the field," I wasn't all that enthusiastic about going out on fires. My daily job was exhausting enough that being called out on a lightning fire in the evening and working all night was not attractive. Nor did our bosses in the silviculture department like losing most of their crew during lightning busts—it was hard enough to complete the summer's work as it was. But the forest administrators made it clear that firefighting came first. I soon learned to value the money: I'd been shocked at the difference in my paycheck after my first all-nighter earned me eighteen hours of hazard pay. Now it was a habit to walk down the hall to dispatch and tell them I was available.

"Okay, get your fire pack ready and your Nomex on," Al said from behind the high desk. "We're putting a couple of crews together."

I grabbed a Coke from the machine and headed for my office, where I dragged my fire pack out from under a table and emptied it onto the floor. My old dark green fire pack had given way to the newer-style red canvas pack with zippered pockets, web shoulder straps and carrying handles, and even enough room for a compact sleeping bag. I didn't have one of those, but I did have my stiff yellow fire coat with reflective strips on the back, my fire shelter, a headlamp and extra batteries, a wool hat, leather fire gloves, extra socks, foot powder (military issue, found in the fire warehouse but never used), toothbrush and toothpaste, toilet paper (I was not going to use that stuff in the C-ration boxes), a couple of handkerchiefs, extra fire pants and fire shirt, extra T-shirt and underwear, a paperback edition of the *Poetic Edda*, which I had never read, a pack of gum left over from the last fire, matches (surprising how often one actually needs matches on a fire), and most important of all, some food.

The Forest Service fed you on a fire, true enough. But not always when you actually needed to eat. On an extended campaign with fire camps, you got excellent food, plus sack lunches to take with you on shift. But on short-notice fires, it was best to load up with C rations from the warehouse (widely reported to be of Korean War vintage), or with whatever you brought yourself. I spread my collection out on the floor and thought about my choices. Small can of beanie-weenies, small can of sliced peaches, small can of green beans. Two packages of hard candy. A cellophane-wrapped spoon. Hmmm . . . obvious deficiencies existed in the cookie department. I left the pack contents on the floor and walked over to the convenience store across the street. The smoke column downriver was "anviling out," flattening on top into the shape of a horseshoer's anvil. Suddenly hungry, I popped a frozen burrito into the store's microwave while I wandered about, harvesting a Coke, two packages of cupcakes, a couple of Paydays (no chocolate to melt), and a small package of Fig Newtons before the microwave dinged and I dropped my choices on the counter.

Back across the street, I stuck my head into the dispatch office again. "Nothing yet," they said. "Still flying around assessing things."

At my desk, I ate the burrito, drank the Coke, and ingested a package of cupcakes and one of the Paydays before stuffing the remainder into my day pack. This was a custom job made up of various army surplus parts: a web belt, shoulder harness, and canvas bag that rode in the middle of my back. Here was room to shove a coat through the shoulder harness, and hooks to hold canteens and even an HT radio, should I be lucky enough to be assigned to carry one. With nothing much left to do, I glanced at the clock. Only four o'clock. The silviculture crew wasn't even back yet, but when they arrived, I'd never get anything else done.

I sat down and began tapping the keyboard on the computer terminal to rearrange my list of thinning units. The Data General system, already outdated when installed a few months ago, opened up a new and exciting world for the district. We could send messages directly to anyone in the Forest Service. We could create data tables and documents. I was deep in composition when Al came into the office and told me, as he scattered some fish food on top of the aquarium, "Go home and have supper and come back at seven."

I did, but by that time the regular fire crews had already gone out. When I was finally assigned to a crew, it was nine o'clock and too dark for the helicopters to fly. Go home, we were told, and come back regular time tomorrow, and we'll send you up to the airport.

So it began.

I got up early to feed the horses as Tom slept. He might have to feed and water alone for days or weeks, so the least I could do was cover for him this morning. The horses saw me and came thundering up the hill toward the barn, all but old Molly, who stood alone, rump turned toward me, under the starveling apple tree in the lower field. "Please don't let it be colic, not now," I muttered as I threw hay into the mangers to keep the others busy, then walked down the hill.

It wasn't colic. Molly nickered at me and tried to turn, hopping awkwardly on three legs, her nostrils pinched back in pain. She held her left foreleg bent, the front of the hoof barely scraping the ground. She could put no weight on it at all. I stroked her shoulder, which seemed out of plumb, and slid my hand down her leg. From long habit she tried to pick up her hoof but immediately flinched and lowered it and hopped a foot or so away from me. And as she did so, something inside her shoulder made a grating sound.

I called the veterinarian in Scott Valley, shook Tom awake and brought him up to speed, and drove in to work. On any other morning, I would have called in to report the emergency and waited beside the horse. Molly was over twenty years old, and this looked like a mortal injury. But I reported to dispatch and then gathered my fire pack and rode up to the airport with the crew.

Happy Camp was smoky. The anvil cloud had collapsed the previous evening, and the smoke poured into the river canyon. Ethan, our crew boss, who disliked fire duty to begin with and disliked sitting around waiting to get it over with even more, gave us the bad news. "They were going to helicopter us in this morning," he said, "but there's too much smoke to fly." He looked disapprovingly out at the helicopters, crouched like grasshoppers on the tarmac. "Maybe the smoke'll lift this evening."

We sat scattered around the dusty interior of a double-wide trailer. I had never been inside this one before, although I had worked in a nearby hangar once, back in my clerical days when I was drafted as a demobilization clerk. I checked off names on crew manifests and noted times of departure as off-Klamath crews filed by our tables.

When Ethan dismissed us, I went outside and wandered around, noting that some of the crew had already staked out spots on what would be the shady side of the building this afternoon. From the east side, I looked over at the hangars and the road that crested the hill behind them. Several winters ago, Paul had assigned Joe and me the task of inspecting a crew of thinners working on the old East Fork Burn. Hundreds of acres of thick Douglas-fir reproduction, with a road running through the middle of it, the burn looked like a lifetime job for the five thinners who carved through the trees at a snail's pace. Joe and I spent most of our time reading and drinking coffee in the truck and looking out at the rain. A few times a day, we put on our rain gear and dragged a tape measure through the slash to throw a plot by counting the number of trees in a circle sixteen and a half feet in radius, which encompassed one-fiftieth of an acre. Sometimes we found too few or too many trees in the circle, or slash insufficiently bucked up, and then we sought out the crew boss and told him about it.

One particularly rainy and dismal morning, we looked at each other and wondered why we had to drive up Indian Creek to East Fork so damn early in the first place, when the crew was often not at work until nine or so. Where, we wondered, could we hide out?

"The airport," Joe said. "I know this place behind the hangars. No one ever goes there, especially this time of year."

The next day we slipped out of the office as if we couldn't wait to get on the road, drove to the airport, slouched down in the cab, and slept for an hour. It was heaven. But on another morning we pushed our luck a little too far. Just as the sun started to burn the fog off the river, I opened my eyes to see Paul and two other men—strangers in too-neat uniforms that screamed "regional office"—standing in front of the far hangar, their backs to us. Paul pointed at something out on the tarmac, and they began to walk toward it. I reached over and poked Joe's shoulder.

"Jesus Christ, wake up!" I said and pointed. Joe shoved in the clutch—we were already headed downhill—and we drifted out of sight behind the buildings, just in time.

"Think he saw us?" Joe said.

I shook my head. "No, but if I'm wrong, we'll sure hear about it this afternoon."

Paul never said anything to us. But after that we took our naps at the job site, safely tucked away on old skid trails out of sight of the main road that ran through the burn. "After all," Joe said, "if you can't trust Paul to be asleep in his office when you need him to be, who can you trust?"

I shook off nostalgia and went back inside the trailer to check the clock. If Dr. Wickse had been able to get on the road quickly, it would still take him two hours to get to my house from Fort Jones. I'll give it another hour, I thought.

The minutes dragged. The building—half trailer house, half slow cooker—grew hotter. We opened all the windows, took turns sitting at the desk and spinning the chair around to stare at the dusty shelves full of fire manuals. I gave up and went outside to sit in the shade and open my paperback. I had stuffed it into my fire pack that spring because it was nice and long, but I hadn't cracked it until now. I was almost through with the introduction when someone stuck his head out of the open door and called my name. "Phone call," he announced.

Dr. Wickse's diagnosis didn't take long. "Shattered shoulder blade," he told Tom and Rawhide Annie, a neighbor with extraordinary radar for horses in need. "She must have been running down the hill and took a bad step. Happens sometimes with old horses." He put her down with the bolt gun and left Tom to deal with a thousand pounds of rapidly bloating horse. But Doc Hall, without even being called, bounced downhill on his backhoe, dug a deep hole, and helped Tom and Annie slide Molly's carcass into it.

"Tell everyone thank you," I said to Tom, "and so sorry you had to deal with this." I went back outside and wondered what else could go wrong. Heather and Helen and Laura, all on the crew, hugged me and offered comforting words.

The smoke hung low all day, and rather than feed us, the fire bosses sent us home. I walked down to look at the new mound of earth. So far, Tom's vacation had included stealing water, digging a trench to nowhere, and finding out more about my septic and water systems than anyone should know. Now he had rolled a dead horse into a pit.

"Let's go get a pizza," I said. It wasn't much, but it was the best I could do.

Another day, another long wait at the airstrip. The smoke lay heavy in town, but around noon it began to lift. Early in the afternoon a helicopter landed on the helispot, and we watched a man being helped out. Tall and bearded, he walked bent over, in obvious pain. "It's Fred!" said Laura and ran over to her husband. We watched as Fred and Laura momentarily bent their heads together before Fred was helped into a vehicle and driven down to the clinic.

We had heard about Fred the previous evening, how he got hurt when someone felled an oak tree, which clipped Fred on the back of the head, knocking off his hard hat and sending him flying down the steep slope. With no way for a helicopter to fly until the smoke lifted, Fred toughed it out and waited.

We clustered around Laura. "What did he say?" we asked. Laura laughed a bit. "He said, 'I'm gonna kill that fucking Michael.'"

We knew how fast Michael could move, how frenetically he tackled any task, often without fully looking around or watching out for other people. But he was strong and eager and so he had been out in front of that crew, armed with a chainsaw. I pictured him on the dance floor at every party, sweating, his arms flailing, so in tune with the music that he seemed out of his body. I pictured Fred, who never danced, who moved slowly and seldom went to parties unless they were at his house.

The sun came out full force, and we retreated to the shade. Trucks pulled up bearing sack lunches and tubs full of soft drinks, and as we ate, yellow jackets demanded their share. I tossed a piece of baloney a few feet away and watched the striped bodies cover it. In the pages of my book, Norse gods were behaving badly. I looked down the line at my companions, one a heavyset young man, a summer volunteer on the trail crew. Ordinarily, he was paid ten dollars a day and allowed to stay in the bunkhouse. Volunteering was not the greatest way to spend a summer unless you were independently wealthy, but some college kids who hadn't been able to hire on for real wages considered it better than nothing. You gained experience and perhaps impressed somebody who'd hire you next year. And the beauty was that if you went on a fire, you were paid AD wages—over six dollars an hour. No hazard pay or overtime, true, but much better than nothing, and just what most volunteers hoped for. Bruce walked like a duck, his feet forever pointed outward. Just now he dozed, and his legs jerked and twitched in his sleep. Later I told myself that I had a bad feeling about him.

Ethan came striding down the line, telling us to make our last calls to the restrooms and to be sure our canteens were full. He called out our names and asked our weights. "Be truthful, now," he grinned at me. "One twenty-eight," I said. Lovesickness had made me want to be thinner. Diet sodas, cantaloupe for lunch, and jogging after work with Ethan and Laura helped. We would take our day packs on the helicopter; our red packs would stay in the hangar for now.

Late in the afternoon, half a dozen at a time, we loaded into a helicopter and flew downriver and then north, deep into unroaded country. When the helicopter set down on a makeshift helispot hastily prepped by the helitackers, I looked around at a strange landscape. The river still ran in a silver thread far, far below us, and a series of knifelike ridges traced their way down toward it. But I had never been here before: atop the world, in what the Karuks called the High Country, where the peaks held spiritual power for shamans and seekers.

Ethan stood on the edge of the helispot and looked down at the fire, map in hand. He pulled a plastic wind gauge from his pocket and held it out at arm's length. At this distance, the Five Fire wasn't particularly impressive, just a smudge of smoke drifting parallel to the river. As I selected a Pulaski from the piles of tools dropped off from the helicopter, I groaned a little. The fire was a long way below us, and we'd be lucky to get there before dark.

We scattered downhill as another helicopter came in and unloaded. Ethan ran to speak to the pilot, and the helicopter shut down while they consulted with someone on the radio. Ethan shook his head. Something about the situation bothered him. Years later, I realized that we were about to enter a situation that had killed firefighters before and would kill them again. We were pointed downhill toward the uncontained flank of a fire that might—should the wind change—burn rapidly uphill toward us. The fire looked quiet now, but it might not stay that way as we made that long downhill hike.

The helicopter took off and we sat alone on the silent mountain, waiting for a decision that might bring the helicopter back. Up here the air was cool, and the wind had started to pick up a little. Ethan strode off just beyond earshot and spoke into the HT set. He returned and made a circling motion with his hand. "Pack it up," he said, "we're going back to town."

Back at the airport, which by now felt like home, we milled around until a bus took us nine miles downriver to the Clear Creek road, then up that road to its end at Five Mile Creek, where a footbridge led onto the old pack trail up Clear Creek. Other buses were parked there ahead of us, so we weren't the first crew to tackle the lower end of the Five Fire.

The terrain and vegetation here were very different from the sparse trees and bare rocks we had recently left. In these steep canyons, the slopes were covered with tan oak, live oak, and Douglas-fir, with occasional pines. Moss hid the boulders, and an understory of young tan oak and poison oak lay in wait. This place had never been logged because it was so close to Clear Creek, and the Douglas-firs, while enormous, were covered with conks, and many had broken tops. They leaned with the unstable ground, rooted in shallow soils. Clear Creek, deep in its prehistoric canyon, threaded through a chasm of smooth blue-green rock. The water was deep and clear and blue green, too, and if you looked closely enough, shadows moved through it: summer steelhead, resting in the cool depths.

We couldn't see much of that now, however, as night came to the canyon and we followed the bouncing headlamps of our leaders, far ahead up the trail. The smell of smoke grew stronger and fresher, and we came around a corner and saw the flames. They hugged the ground, occasionally turning a small tree into a torch, and moved uphill away from us. As we left the main trail, we heard the roar of chainsaws, the rhythmic chink-chink of Pulaskis chopping at the ground, the longer swish of shovels, and the scraping of the humble McLeods (half scraper, half rake), a four-part harmony repeated as each new crew came in behind to widen and improve the fire line.

We were "going direct" now, building fire line right up against an uncontrolled wildfire, only twenty feet or so away from its footprint. We left just enough room so that later, when this section of the line was complete, someone with a drip torch could move along it and burn out the intervening fuel. We moved uphill on a slope so steep that the first Pulaskis chopped little steps into the ground to make it easier to climb, and those who followed improved them. We moved steadily and at least once were "bumped" by a faster-moving crew— hotshots (the cohesive, highly trained fire crews who specialize in the rapid building of fire lines by hand) from off the Klamath, eager to get to the head of the line—and we stood aside as they went by with a whine of chainsaws and a blast of testosterone.

The initial climb out of the bowels of Five Mile Creek seemed endless, but eventually we began to sidehill, tracking the path of the fire. By now, it was full dark and our path marked by a jiggling line of headlamps. Their puny light, multiplied many times and augmented by the glow of fire, was more than enough to see by. Sometimes other lights bobbed down the hill toward us—a sector boss or his scouts— and doled out encouragement, or warnings about snags or drop-offs. Sometimes we stopped entirely and I looked up and up at the fire, its flames like the lights of a great city. I had never seen anything like the sheer expanse of it and was surprised at how cheerful it looked. Not until later did I appreciate all that we did that night by preventing the fire from creeping down into Five Mile Creek. None of us had time to think about larger purposes as we put our heads down and hacked our way into the night.

About midnight, the line stopped and didn't move forward again. We heard a shout from up ahead and then Ethan hurried past us, his long legs moving at speed, and I heard him curse as he went by. In a few minutes he came back. "Take a break," he said. "Someone's fallen up ahead."

He left again, and we sank in our tracks and pulled out canteens and snacks. Ethan soon came back, shaking his head. "Bruce fell off a cliff up around the corner," he said. "Laura, you're an EMT, right?" She stood up and followed him out of sight.

For the rest of that long night, Laura was a voice over the radio that crackled in our ears whenever Ethan walked by. The crews ahead of us who had been blazing uphill, following the line before Bruce fell, kept on without us. We waited—not only because he was our crewmate, but because come morning we would be needed to get him out. He had fallen about forty feet down a very steep slope—not quite a cliff, but not something anyone could stand up on, either—and landed on a flat ledge just above a draw. Laura and another firefighter with an EMT certificate rappelled down to examine him. Laura thought he had a broken hip and perhaps a concussion, and he was in considerable pain. Someone retrieved the big first aid kit, and Ethan radioed to talk to a paramedic back at the airport. Laura gave Bruce a shot of morphine—enough to dull the pain without impairing his breathing. They covered him with their coats and promised not to leave him.

Just as it grew light enough to see, two paramedics strode up the trail, paced by two other men packing ropes and a collapsible gurney. At last the rest of us had something to do. We stood, brushed ourselves off, put on our day packs, and waited. The paramedics examined Bruce, got him onto the basket gurney, and strapped him in.

We reached the place where Bruce had fallen. It was narrow, but it didn't look particularly hazardous unless you happened to walk like a duck and just missed seeing the edge in the dark.

One of the paramedics looked up at us. "We're going to need some of you guys to keep pace with the gurney when we haul him up, and hold your hard hats over his head and face in case rocks come down," he said. This meant cutting footholds in the slope and knocking aside the worst of the rocks where the gurney might hang up. It took over a dozen of us pulling on the ropes, and two more holding hard hats over poor Bruce's face—falling rocks were what terrified him most— until at last he landed safely on the relatively flat ground of the fire line. Taking turns as bearers, we hauled him down the trail, across the bridge to the end of the road where we had started the previous evening. An ambulance waited, and Bruce and the paramedics disappeared inside and drove away.

Ethan, his face pale and pinched, was in no hurry to get us back on the line. We were entitled to breakfast at least, but it looked as though we were on our own for that. Another bus pulled up and disgorged a crew. They hunched into their packs and picked up tools. Some of them, we learned, were assigned to set up a spike camp on a bar on Clear Creek, near the mouth of Five Mile Creek. "Grab some of those paper sleeping bags out of the bus," they said, "and follow us." I clutched the white fluffy bundle to my chest, looking forward to using it. Despite being made out of, well, paper, some miracle of wood fiber technology gave paper sleeping bags an outer covering that managed to be water repellent, and a cozy filling that was padded and warm, yet wicked moisture away from the body.

We followed their leader—our own Robert from silviculture—up the trail and then down a side trail to the bar, which turned out to be big enough for our purposes, but covered with cobbles the size of bowling balls. Nevertheless, it would be home for the foreseeable future, and we made the best of it, rolling rocks around until we excavated clearings that could accommodate our necks and shoulders. A helicopter dropped in close with a sling net, which turned out to have all our big packs in it. We snatched them to our chests like long-lost friends. Laura, Helen, Heather, and I grouped our bags close together, and as the day warmed, we walked down to the creek to brush our teeth and comb out our hair. The canyon walls formed a small cove and hid us from the rest of the crew. We stripped off our clothes and jumped into the creek, and the helicopters flying overhead came in a bit lower after that, but we ignored them.

Back with our packs and sleeping bags, we excavated our foodstuffs. It was lunchtime by now, never mind breakfast. I opened a can of beanie-weenies and chased them with a package of cupcakes. I rather envied one of my fellows, who had lucked into a box of C rations with the cherished pound cake and canned peaches. He had a can of pork, too, which I never found edible, but he was made of sterner stuff and consumed the whole can, plus all the other food in the box. Flat on his sleeping bag later, he moaned, "I'm soooo bloated."

Robert stood above him, a thin thread of smoke rising from his pipe. "Well," he said, "C rations were scientifically designed to provide the entire nutritional needs of one soldier in the field for an entire day. You just ate the whole thing for lunch."

"Oh, Gawd," Calvin groaned. "I'm gonna die." Laura fished a plastic bag full of dried leaves from her pack and advised him to brew some peppermint tea, which reminded someone else that we did indeed need a campfire. We certainly had plenty of rocks to make a fire circle. We heated tin cups of various beverages on flat rocks and said this was all right for hazard pay.

Bruce's fall meant that from now on, we worked the day shift. By the time the sector boss reconnected with us, the assignments for the night shift were complete and the major action on this fire had shifted far from us. We spent the night on the bar and woke to the sight of hundreds of dead steelhead in Clear Creek, their white bellies rippling under the water. "Shit, they dumped a load of retardant in the creek up there," someone said. "Bastards."

As we discussed whether suffocated steelhead were good to eat, we heard a shout from up on the trail. "Hey, if you want breakfast, the mules just brought some. C'mon up!"

We scrambled the hundred yards uphill to the pack trail and found a group of tethered mules dozing while the contents of their packs were arranged for our benefit: square copper containers, designed to fit in pack panniers, and all full of hot food. We tucked into scrambled eggs, ham, and French toast. The copper had turned the scrambled eggs slightly green, but we didn't care. That is, we didn't care until Taylor began to recite from an immortal children's book. "I do not like green eggs and ham," Taylor said. "I do not like them, Sam-I-Am."

"Damn you, Taylor!" we shouted at him later, as we began the long, soul-destroying task of mopping up this lower sector of the Five Fire. "I can't get that fucking verse out of my head!"

"Mopping up" is both absolutely necessary and totally unsexy. A crew splits up and works inward from the fire line, methodically extinguishing any lingering smokes. It's neither fast nor easy and requires considerable skill. Fire clings to roots and must be followed far underground, then drowned with a stream from a piss-pump (a black rubber bladder bag with attached shoulder straps, holding about five gallons of water that can be delivered with great precision via rubber tubing and a hand-operated brass pump assembly). Even a small area can take hours to clear.

Piss-firs using piss-pumps, I thought, remembering the moniker for Forest Service employees that I had first learned in the eighth grade. The thought drove the words of Dr. Seuss out of my head and replaced them with a ditty frequently played at outdoor events by a scratch band of summer crew people, urging mothers not to let their children grow up to be piss-firs. Just why the innocent white fir, a brittle species with sap that smelled remarkably like urine, should have become an insulting name for me and my fellows was lost in the mists of history, but it had a certain ring to it.

Mopping up can be dangerous, too, as I was reminded when our crew came upon a small basin—only a couple of acres in size—on which grew scattered Douglas-firs alive when George Washington was young, and leaning in every direction. I thought I saw smoke coming from beneath a log and walked toward it, my boots sinking into six inches of powdery ash. I grubbed away beneath the log, then heard the uniquely chilling sound of a very large tree starting to fall. I whirled around, trying to pinpoint its location, but couldn't see it. The noise went on and on, so I dove under the log just as a seismic thump raised a cloud of ash so thick that I couldn't even see my hand. If another tree should fall just now . . . I heard my crewmates shouting from uphill. I waited, frozen, until the ash had settled enough that I could see to scramble toward them. As I reached them, still half-blinded, I heard Ethan's voice. "Okay, lunch! Everybody up here!"

We sat on the hillside, chewing and drinking and looking around to make sure we weren't within range of any other tall tree with a death wish. We were surrounded by Douglas-firs gone rotten in the middle and with their roots weakened by fire. Which trees would fall today and which would stand for a hundred years? When the ash cleared enough for me to see the basin again, I saw the fallen tree at last, lying parallel to my log refuge but twenty feet away from it.

Our half-hour lunch ended and no one, including Ethan, made a move to stand. Laura sat cross-legged in her usual after-lunch meditation pose, her chin resting on her chest, her sweatshirt hood pulled over her head, eyes closed. Just below her sat Heather, her face buried in her arms atop bent knees. To my astonishment, I saw that she was quietly crying, her shoulders heaving. I looked away, embarrassed. Why was she crying? I thought of her as the most fortunate of young women. She was beautiful. Her father was rich. The man of my heart loved her. But something was breaking her heart, and I didn't know her well enough to know what it could be.

The next day, a crew of men—most of them black—clad in orange jumpsuits appeared on our line, and we breathed a sigh of relief, for the appearance of the prison work-camp crews meant that we would probably be released soon. We liked them for their lighthearted banter and unaffected delight at simply being out in the woods and making a little money. We felt pretty cocky that evening as we slid back down to our boulder-strewn spike camp, optimistic enough to pile up a tower of the more inedible of the lunch sandwiches and try to set them afire. But damp white bread is surprisingly fire resistant. I was still chuckling at the ridiculousness of the stunt when I slipped and fell while walking in my stocking feet and landed full on my tailbone on a cobble.

I crawled to my sleeping bag and thrashed in sheer agony for a few minutes. When I found a semicomfortable position, I whispered my predicament to Laura. "You think it's broken?" I said.

"Could be," she said, "or maybe bruised. With the coccyx, it doesn't really matter. If it's broken, it's not like they can set it. Can you stand up?" she asked.

I tried. "No," I groaned, falling back on my side.

"Well, try to get some sleep," she said, handing me a couple of aspirin. "See how you feel in the morning."

When dawn came, I looked over at her and shook my head. She walked over and told Ethan. "Can you walk at all?" he said, bending over me.

"Maybe," I said, "if I had a walking stick."

He wandered off and returned with a staff hacked from a bigleaf maple sapling. With it, I could get to my feet and shuffle. "I don't think I'm going to be much good to you today," I said.

"Don't worry about that," he said.

I spent the day beside the creek in sparse company, which didn't bother me, for the helicopter had dropped a net containing our fire packs, and I lay on my side and fished out clean underwear. Slowly, with much yelping, I managed to change my clothes while inside my sleeping bag. Then I pulled out my book and started reading.

I read slowly from a section called the Hávamál, or Sayings of the High One, although they seemed to me like the sayings of someone with a lot of enemies: "All the entrances, before you walk forward, you should look at, you should spy out; for you can't know for certain where enemies are sitting ahead in the hall." Appropriate for Vikings, I thought. These were tough people in a cold tough world, and they didn't expect an afterlife or whine about not having one. They wanted to be remembered, though.

> Cattle die, kinsmen die,
> The self must also die;
> I know one thing which never dies:
> The reputation of each dead man.

That was true. You never knew how things were going to turn out.

At evening should the day be praised, the woman when she is
   cremated,
The blade when it is tested, the girl when she is married,
The ice when it is crossed, the ale when it is drunk.

I thought that was a good philosophy. It would save me a lot of
grief, not to yearn for things I couldn't have, to keep my hopes within
bounds. Painful, but sensible. I tucked the book down into my sleeping
bag, took a couple more aspirin with a swig of water, pulled the grimy
white sleeping bag cover over my head, and fell asleep.

The next day, I managed to stand with the help of Ethan's stick and
was told (to my relief) that the crew could survive without me on the
line. But just as they prepared to head back up the slope for another
jolly day of mopping up, we saw a new crew come sliding down from
the trail. The word spread: we were going home.

The walk to the trailhead was slow and painful, especially on the
uphills, but with Laura carrying my big pack plus her own, I made it.
The hardest part was stepping up onto the bus.

I never learned whether my tailbone was broken. The clinic doctor
palpated it and said it might be cracked, but whatever an X-ray might
show, the treatment was still time and rest. Two days later, I managed
to visit my thinning crew near Slater Butte but had to content myself
with peering down into the unit from the old skid trail at the top.

For others, the damage from the Five Fire was much more lasting.
Bruce recovered from his fractured hip after months in hospitals and
rehab clinics. Fred's injuries were more severe than anyone suspected
at first: the damage to his skull and spine was substantial and ended his
field career. For the next twenty years, he suffered crippling headaches,
back and neck pain, and eventually arthritis.

A couple of months later, when our crew had a chance to reminisce
about what we now called our "Fuck Off and Die Squad" (F.O.D. for
short), we discussed how to commemorate the event. A few of us sat
down with the district geologist's wife, a talented silk-screener, at a
party, and she sketched out a design for a commemorative T-shirt.

"That pile of smoking sandwiches!"

"The footbridge—and we can be whistling 'hi-ho, hi-ho' as we cross it!"

"And poor Bruce falling off the cliff!"

A few weeks later, we all wore our new T-shirts, and I have mine today—a bit too precious to wear, but there to remind me, if I ever forget, of the Five Fire.

The Five's footprint is long gone. Two subsequent fires have burned through the same area—one in 1987, and a much larger one in 2017. Its perimeters long since dwarfed by its successors, it scarcely shows on the fire history maps. Its few thousand acres, which impressed me so much, seem puny now, almost quaint. Firefighters are more cautious now about digging direct fire line at night, about attacking a fire from uphill, about everything. Fires move faster these days, are more unpredictable. In truth, the Five would have burned about as many acres had we never fought it at all, and that cohort of summer steelhead would have lingered in the depths of Clear Creek and spawned under the shade of the wildfire's smoke, as steelhead had been doing for millennia. They would not have been smothered in a red bath of retardant and would have returned in time to the ocean, unmolested.

"At evening should the day be praised . . ."

CHAPTER 13

A Journey to the Coast

Over the rivers to the bitter sea.
—Elizabeth Barrett Browning

One thing that kept the hope alive that one day Matt would turn and see—really see—me was that Heather persisted, so Laura told me, in her devotion to a helitack guy in Oregon. But he was far away, and we both saw how Matt looked at her. "I think she's trying not to encourage him," Laura said.

"Whatever for?" I said, feeling bitter. "Why isn't she shagging his buns off?" How could she pretend not to see those glances that would melt lead? "I would give my eyeteeth," I said, "to have him look at me like that."

Laura shrugged. "Everybody's different."

"Not that different," I said.

So when I encountered Heather in the copy room just after five o'clock one summer day and found her making copies of her SF-171—the government's résumé form—I mentally pumped my fist. YES! She was trying to get a better job; she was really trying to go Somewhere Else. We began to talk as I leaned on the back counter, clutching a pile of contract papers to my chest. "No hurry," I assured her. And indeed, I was glad to just remain stationary for a few minutes.

"I've been revising it," she told me.

"There's a book on how to do a better 171," I said, watching her place the pages one at a time on the glass screen. The light flashed beneath her fingers and the machine hummed and pages shot into the print tray. "I think Linda has it now. It's got some good stuff in it."

"Cool. I'll ask her about it. What's up with you?" she said. "Haven't seen you much lately."

She flashed me the thousand-watt smile that had rocked Matt's world. I wanted to hate her and couldn't, for above the smile were her sad gray eyes. I knew that her mother had died while she was in college, and that she hated her father's new wife and didn't go home much.

I took a deep breath. "Hand spray contract," I said, rattling the papers. "Sure you want to hear about this?" She laughed, and her eyes, which turned up slightly at the corners, crinkled and twinkled and looked a lot like . . . damn.

"Okay, well, we've got another Hart dummy corporation working with Ignacio and his crew. Someone's been writing nasty letters to George about the spray project and taping them to the office door again. Really steep units, so try carrying forty pounds of liquid on your back down there. The crew hasn't done backpack spraying much before and I ended up having them do Luther Gulch B over again. That made them real happy. But the plots were okay after lunch. The contract's a bitch—they have to have ninety-five percent good plots. Anyway, with a little finagling I managed to drag them up to fourteen errors per acre. They're only allowed fifteen."

"What's considered an error?" Heather asked.

So she was paying attention. Most people's eyes glazed over by this point. "Either they miss spraying around a crop tree entirely, or they don't get the full three-foot-by-three-foot coverage. And I'm trying to cut them all the slack I can because that blue dye isn't exactly easy to see, even when it's fresh."

She nodded, and I plowed on. "Anyway, we finished up that unit, then today they did Luther Gulch C before lunch and Eagle 9 after lunch and finished up by four-thirty. And they did a good job, too—I think making them do that one block over again scared them some.

"How do they treat you, being a woman and all?"

I shrugged. "They say 'chingada' a lot," I said. "I don't know whether they're referring to me or the job. But as long as they get it done I don't care."

She laughed again and shook her head. "I really envy you your self-confidence," she said, and I laughed back.

"Good thing you can't see me inside," I said. "Inside I'm a wreck." And she laughed and I laughed, and then she stepped toward me.

"C'mere," she said and hugged me so hard that tears sprang, and I hugged her back and felt beneath my hands her lean ribs, her spine. On top of being beautiful, she was skinny. I wanted to kill myself.

Later, as I left the building, I saw Matt leaning into the doorway of the copy room, talking to her.

That night, becalmed in beer, I tried to be a good sport about it in my diary. "They would make a lovely couple," I wrote, then gave up and told the truth. "But I'd give my eyeteeth to have him give me that melting look he gives her." Eyeteeth, in those days, were a disposable part of my anatomy. That night I started sanding the old putter, bought at an antique shop in Yreka. "That one's from the 1920s," the proprietor told me. "They don't make them with wooden shafts anymore." My plan was to sand it smooth and then treat it with linseed oil and watch the wood come alive again, its old grain popping to the surface. Someday I'd give it to Matt, and he would thank me, and he would keep it in his golf bag, and now and then he would pull it out and tap a ball into a cup with it, and when someone admired it, he'd say, "Yeah, a friend fixed it up and gave it to me," and then he would think of me a little.

We were twenty- and thirty-somethings in a world that had changed forever, and yet in some respects we behaved exactly as our parents once told us to behave: we traveled in groups, chaperoning each other. And in November of that year, we all took a trip to the coast, which meant Eureka and Arcata and the nearby beaches, and we packed our emotional baggage and hoped that taking a trip with these people, including the objects of our unrequited loves, would somehow change things.

Matt lived downriver at a place called the Blue Heron Ranch, a hillside where several cabins were managed as rentals. One Friday morning Laura and Dave and Michael and I drove downriver in Laura's car. I had never seen Matt's house before and was startled at its resemblance to the old houses in Hilt. The same twelve-paned windows, the same wainscoting behind the wood stove, the same doors that didn't quite fit their frames, the same smell of a wood-framed house that has absorbed smoke for fifty years. I handed Matt the putter and he admired it, surprised, and thanked me, then stood it up in a corner as he grabbed his gym bag and headed out behind us. In the driveway, we split up between Matt's car and Laura's, and as luck would have it, Dave and I rode with Matt, and I managed—oh heavenly circumstance!—to sit in the front seat beside him.

Downriver was different. Below Happy Camp, the Klamath dove deep into a world primeval: the mountains steeper, the drop-offs beside the road more dangerous, and the works of the white man— highway and bridges and buildings on occasional flat places—mere ephemera that the canyon would someday sweep away as though they had never been. And today—today was one of those rare November days when the sun shone after the first strong storm of autumn, and the leaves of the bigleaf maples still clung, blazing with yellow fire, against brown trunks. I rolled the window down to smell wet leaves and ferns and creeks foaming down the draws toward the river.

At Weitchpec the highway left the Klamath and followed the Trinity River through the wide Hoopa Valley, where horses roamed the roadsides. We passed the crossroads town of Willow Creek, then followed a canyon up and up toward the last ridge system, and when we broke out on top, we saw far off the flat horizon of the Pacific, a bank of fog that carried with it the smell of the ocean, where all the rivers went at last.

At Arcata, the college town at the head of Humboldt Bay, we went first to the Arcata Plaza, a classic four-sided downtown business district with a park and a statue of William McKinley at its center. Matt found a barber shop, I bought my first-ever pair of Birkenstocks, and then I wandered through a pet store where parrots perched unfettered above the cages and glared at customers. Laura ran into Heather, who had driven down by herself. A quick drive down the freeway and across mudflats bordered by cow pastures, and we were at the Eureka Co-op, where Laura picked up an eight-hundred-pound order, and Michael, Dave, and Matt decided to head for the beach. I tagged along, and with the crashing waves as backdrop, we played Hacky-Sack with a smooth piece of driftwood since Michael had forgotten the real one.

We wandered the edge of the ocean and watched a column of smoke rise from the hills behind us, a slash burn in a redwood clear-cut. We watched the sun go down, carried liberal amounts of sand back to Matt's car, and headed for Lazio's, a dockside seafood restaurant where all the Happy Camp gang gathered: Ned and Cathy, Ned's brother and a friend, Heather, Rilla, Michael, Dave, Matt, me, Jan and Harry, Casey and his wife, and finally Helen and her boyfriend Jake. It was Helen's twenty-eighth birthday, so a cake aflame with candles appeared from the kitchen at the appropriate moment. We all ate too much and drank cocktails sufficient to make us giddy. Out in the parking lot, I took a deep breath and stared up at the glowing fog above the streetlights. The night was young, and so were we.

We headed back to the Arcata plaza and its bars. I rode with Matt and Dave again, and we all gathered at a bar, where I sprang for the first pitcher of beer, as Helen dove for the jukebox and began shoving in quarters. The Steve Miller Band sang "Abracadabra."

Helen danced out onto the floor, dragging Michael with her, and I lip-synched the words, swayed to the music, and kept time with my feet, clad in their new and very cool footwear. I felt simply stunning, and between the mug of beer in front of me, the two margaritas I had inhaled at Lazio's, and the lingering spell of the beach, surely the man of my dreams could see it, too. I looked across the table at Matt and, caught up in the music and the euphoria of Just Enough Alcohol and the soft lights of the bar, I smiled at him. And then the very last thing that I wanted to happen, happened. He saw me, really saw me, and he understood, and he was horrified. His mouth closed, his eyes went flat and black, and he looked away from me.

The shock of his reaction brought with it a clarity that froze the flow of time, and I saw many things, all at once. Dave's eyes, sweeping from me to Matt and back again, and in them understanding and empathy. Helen, dancing before the jukebox, with eyes only for Michael. Michael, twirling in a sweaty frenzy, not seeing her at all. Jake at the end of the table, Jake who didn't dance, looking at Helen with love and pain in his calm, dull, bearded face. I saw, in that frozen moment, all of our futures, and I knew this was going to be a long, long night.

The plaza had many bars—sports bars, logger bars, biker bars— and we hit most of them. Eventually we landed at a nightclub called Jambalaya, where (after some hesitation over the cover charge—a whole three dollars each!) we went in and sat down, in a bunch, and listened to a five-piece reggae band, whose playing caused Ned to say, over and over, "I can't believe it. An all-white reggae band."

I didn't know reggae from a red apple, but I didn't care. I was too wounded even to be flattered when the bouncer carded me—an ancient lass of thirty-three. "Thank you, my son," I said as he handed my license back. We sat, we listened, and then Ned asked me to dance, and then a stranger, then Ned's brother, and finally his brother's friend. All this unaccustomed attention so emboldened me—it's just a dance, right? Nothing personal here—that I leaned across our table toward Matt and shouted an invitation over the music and the noise of a packed house. Matt shot me a baleful look, so that I regretted my temerity instantly, but he stood up, accompanied me onto the floor, and shuffled without enthusiasm for an endless couple of minutes. Halfway through the tune, I held up my hands and released him from any obligation. "It's okay," I said, "you don't have to," and headed for the ladies' lounge, where a pair of Humboldt Honeys sat on the couch, smoking in unison. They looked at me as I sobbed into my handkerchief, and one of them offered me a Kool. "No, thank you," I wailed.

Ten minutes later, having told the Honeys my life story and splashed water on my face, I went back out and saw Matt dancing with Heather. Over the next couple of hours, he danced several times with her, and only her.

We left at last and crammed six people into a Ramada Inn room with two double beds. Laura and Heather took one; I had the other to myself. The men disposed themselves and their sleeping bags on the floor. Matt slept between the two beds, so close to me that when he rolled over in the night, I felt the tug on the bedcovers.

In the morning, he ignored me and I returned the favor. I stared at myself in the bathroom mirror and saw nothing but misery stretching before me, all the days of my life.

We ate breakfast, somewhere, and then Helen and Laura and I drove the six miles into Eureka. As the freeway slipped beneath us, Helen spoke. "I think," she said, "that I've finally kicked the Michael habit."

I looked at her. Doesn't look like it to me, sister, I thought. But we were women, so we said the right things. Congratulations, good for you, that's great. Laura cleared her throat and said with a chuckle in her voice, "Now, if we could just find a way to help Louise forget Matt."

Helen's eyebrows rose, and she looked at me. "Whaa-aat?" and then it all came out, the hurt and embarrassment, and I sobbed all the way into the mall parking lot, for sorrow and stupidity and the waste of what should have been a fun weekend. And both women patted me on the shoulder and murmured kind words that fell hollow on my heart.

In the big indoor mall, I dried my eyes as we wandered about. I drank an Orange Julius and walked out of Walden's with a complete set of Dorothy Sayers murder mysteries in paperback.

We drove to Ned's brother's house, a crazy dwelling behind the Arcata Co-op, with sloping floors that made me feel drunk as I walked in the door. We met the others and drove to Trinidad to another magnificent beach. Deep in *Strong Poison*, I drugged myself with words. Ned and Cathy's Irish setter leaned against me and panted loudly into my ear.

On the beach, the boys played Hacky-Sack, this time with a real one. The sun shone and the wind blew cold from the west. In my pocket I carried the sea-smoothed piece of wood that we had used yesterday. I saved it because Matt had kicked it; his shoes and his hands had touched it. We threw sticks for the setter and made whistles from hollow pieces of kelp, and Cathy and Helen—both botanists—told us the names of the seaweeds. The boys followed us as we walked and walked, on and on down the endless beach, and I drew ahead of the others. I saw Laura turn and let Matt come up even with her, his hands jammed into his jeans pockets, his head down, the toes of his sneakers kicking at the sand. Laura told me later that he had looked up at me, far ahead near a rock cliff, shook his head, and made a noise between a growl and a moan. She didn't pretend not to know what he meant. She patted his arm and said, "It's all right, Matt."

"No, it's not," he said. "I really blew it."

Helen and Laura and I drove back upriver together after sunset and discussed our love lives in the safe dark most of the way. When Laura told me what Matt had said on the beach, I couldn't think of anything to say for several miles.

"Tell him," I finally came up with, "that I love him, but since he doesn't feel the same, could he please mellow out and at least act as if he doesn't hate me." Tolerance seemed the best I could hope for.

We stopped at Blue Heron Ranch to make sure the boys had arrived safely and found them drinking beer on the porch. Matt looked more relaxed and made actual eye contact with me once or twice.

On Monday I headed out to the woods, ostensibly to check on possible thinning units for next year, but really just to be alone. From Frying Pan Ridge, I looked down on a river of fog and watched ribbons of cloud drifting overhead, presaging the first big storm of the season. When I came back in the early dark, the light was still on in Matt's office, and his car and Laura's were still in the parking lot.

The next day after work, Laura came into my office. "We talked for an hour," she said. "He just had no idea you felt so strongly about him. He kept saying, 'What'd I do?'"

"What'd you tell him?" I asked.

"I told him, 'You were just yourself.'"

"What else did he say?"

Laura spoke slowly, remembering. "He said he thinks you're a really neat lady, but although he likes you, he isn't attracted to you, so he just can't see any basis for a relationship. And he wouldn't want to just have casual sex with you. And I told him that I didn't think you'd want that, either." She looked at me.

"Mmmm," I said.

"You mean yes to the casual sex part?"

"I'd take what I could get," I said.

"You know," she said, "he had an affair with Maureen down in Ukonom this past summer?"

"Um, yeah, I heard," I said.

"Apparently that's over," Laura said. "He could see it wasn't going to go anywhere, and so he broke it off."

"Jesus," I said. "He has scruples. Where do we find these guys?"

Laura smiled. "That's what I told him: that you aren't just going to say 'oh well' and go on to the next candidate. I told him that it'll take you a long time to get over him."

"You're right about that," I said.

"He said he wanted to talk to you over on the coast and just couldn't do it, so he just froze you out, trying to discourage you. I don't think he realized until I talked to him how deeply you felt for him."

The smile that rose into his green eyes. The black beard and the black curls around his ears. His beautiful hands with their long fingers. His bouncy walk on the balls of his feet. His lean build, and the funny way he ran the bases. His kindness, and the fact that he liked cats. His voice. In the honest Spanish phrase for love, I wanted him. Te quiero. But for someone whose only useful tool, all her life, had been hard work, love was a maddening puzzle box that no amount of labor or dedication could open.

"I think," Laura said, "that he's the kind of guy who likes lots of excitement in his life . . ."

"And I don't excite him," I finished. Laura nodded.

"I don't think I can unlove him," I said.

"He said he'd talk to you," Laura said. "I made him promise."

I waited a week, then decided I'd have to ambush him. Everyone had to wash clothes, so I took my laundry bag to work every day and was rewarded on Friday afternoon at quitting time when I saw him head for the laundromat across the street. He left quickly, though, so all the machines must be full. I followed him at a discreet distance to the other laundromat and pulled in beside his red Toyota. I went in and shoved my laundry into a couple of machines without looking directly at him, since another woman was there. When I made a trip out to my truck, he leaped into his vehicle and disappeared back toward town. Foiled again, I thought and sat alone, dangling my feet off one of the tables, leafing through a magazine and feeling like an idiot.

He has to come back, I thought. His clothes are here. But maybe he was trying to wait me out. His washing machines stopped. My washing machines stopped. One of the dryers stopped, and the other woman unloaded it and began to fold her clothes. Just as I was about to concede defeat and load my own clothes into the empty dryer, I heard a car and looked up to see Matt coming in. He threw one of his own loads into the dryer, then shoved the other wet load into a basket and walked out again.

In despair, I jumped down and followed him out to his open hatchback. "Hey, Matt," I said, "could I talk to you?"

He held up a hand. "I've been wanting to talk to you, too," he said, "but can I go put my clothes in the dryer up at the other laundromat? There's one free up there."

"Sure," I said. I sat down on the front steps, the sun warm on my jeans. The other woman loaded her folded clothes into her car and drove away. I waited. Matt's red car pulled up in front again, and I walked over to lean on the warm flank of the Toyota, and we talked. We talked for a long time. He said again what he had told Laura, about not realizing what I felt for him.

"So when I asked you to go to the movies with me, that didn't tip you off?"

"What?" he said. "Oh, the *Star Wars* thing? No, not a clue." He laughed. "Would have been better than some of the movies I've been to lately, though."

"Well, I'm sorry if I caused you any grief."

"You don't have anything to be sorry about," he said, twice. "The thing is, you're very nice, and I like you a lot, but that's as far as it goes."

"I like you a lot, too. And I'm glad you like me—I was afraid you thought I was a jerk."

"No, no," he said. "Just the opposite. I just don't think we have that much in common. And you don't know me very well," he added. "I can be a real asshole sometimes."

I shook my head. "Oh, surely not," I said.

"Oh, yeah," he said. "Ask anybody."

We looked at the scuffed dirt beside our shoes.

I started to tell him how it had started for me, when we planted together on the Frying Pan units, "last year, you remember?"

"Well, we have always worked well together and been friends," he said. "I hope we still will be."

"Me, too," I said and felt my voice break.

"Oh, shoot," he said. "I was afraid of this."

I swallowed and took a deep breath. "No," I said and got my voice back. "I'm okay."

"The thing is," I continued, "I don't want you to be afraid of me, because I'm not going to drag you off by the hair, or anything."

"I know," he said. *Like you even could, lady.* "I just got plastered that night as a way of not having to deal with you," he added. "I wanted to say something, but I just couldn't."

"Sure, I understand," I said. A logging truck went by on the highway, heading upriver, fast. We watched it go and looked at each other, eyebrows raised. "Trying to sneak a load in after hours to beat the scaler," he said.

"Yup," I said.

"So," he said with a smile, taking his car keys out of his pocket, "what did you and Helen and Laura talk about on the way home?"

"Men," I said, smiling, and he threw back his head and laughed. "What did you guys talk about?"

"Women," he said.

And the conversation drifted into safer topics: the timber sales he was working on, what a butthead the new GS-11 was. At last, he pushed himself off the car and said he'd better go get his clothes before somebody stole them, and I stuck my hand out to him. "Friends," I said, and he shook it and nodded, and I watched him drive away.

Later, I thought of the perfect comeback to his "we have nothing in common" gambit. "Of course we don't," I should have said. "You're a man, I'm a woman. What could we possibly find to talk about?" That would have made him smile, at least. Or perhaps, since Laura said he enjoyed getting mad, I should have pitched a fit and yelled. That would have brought a little excitement to his life.

But the next day, as I walked down the hall at work and stopped to peer at a newspaper on the mail cart, Matt passed by. "Ha," he said, "reading other people's mail!" I looked up, and he was smiling.

And life went on. I saw him at meetings, his face like water in the desert. I played Hacky-Sack with him and others at breaks during training sessions, and at parties.

That winter, I went to potlucks and parties that included Matt, and often Heather was there too, and I saw the devastated look on Matt's face one night when Heather told us that yet again she was headed for the East Coast to stay with her sister and work as a cocktail waitress. He left the party early and took the light with him.

When spring came, I practiced hitting Wiffle balls around the horse pasture and learned that all but three of the golf clubs I had recently acquired at a yard sale were left-handed. That left me with only a wood and a couple of irons, but they hit the balls straight and true with hardly a hook or slice.

One day as I contemplated which club to use, I realized that I didn't have a putter. You gave it away, you idiot, I remembered. And although Matt could have returned it to me, along with my lacerated heart, could have made up some story about not needing it, or it being too valuable to use, or some such horseshit, he had not. He had kept it, as he would any gift from a friend. So I knew that although he would never love me, he had not lied about liking me, and that would have to do.

CHAPTER 14

Herbicides Redux

Back in 1979, herbicides on the national forests were news, so Robert wasn't surprised when a reporter from the Siskiyou Daily News in Yreka called him to ask about rumors that a Forest Service timber-marking crew had been sprayed with 2,4-D during a recent aerial project. No, Robert told him: the crew had gotten some drift, but only because they panicked at the sound of the helicopter and ran back through the clear-cut instead of just walking up over the ridge. Later, an article about the same incident appeared in the coastal tabloid Eco-News. I read it and scoffed. Heck, I said, I got more of that stuff on me than they did. What wimps.

Spray projects were usually timed to occur in late spring or early summer, but that year we were still trying to spray in the middle of September. This was problematic because in late summer, the leaves of the target species had hardened off so much that they were resistant to the herbicide. It also overlapped with our precommercial thinning contracts. One day, I went out to check on a thinning contract in the Doolittle Creek drainage, this one manned by a crew of Mexicans under the not-too-attentive leadership of Donny and Kenny, a pair of Anglo brothers. But Donny had gone to Canada to persuade his wife to come home. Why the hell, I wrote in my diary, would anyone go after a runaway spouse? But Donny's wife had taken the kids along, and even people who hated their exes seemed to love their children.

I was still married to Chuck then, and I thought I wouldn't mind if Chuck ran off to Canada with whomever he was dating at Oak Knoll. I knew it had to be someone who lived there, judging from the oh-you-poor-kid look that the Oak Knoll receptionist threw in my direction when I stopped by last week on my way out to a contractors' meeting in Yreka. That, plus the brief look of panic on Chuck's face when I entered his office, told me something was going on. I felt mildly flattered that I had the power to scare him a little. Certain knowledge that Chuck was having an affair would have let me off the hook. I would no longer have felt obliged to have sex with him on weekends, for instance.

These happy thoughts distracted me as I crashed down the hillside through knee-deep slash where yellow jackets cruised, drunk on the oozing sap. With a perfunctory wave to the crew, I started measuring distances between the uncut trees on several random plots before hiking back up to the road and driving back to the office. The helicopter spraying was scheduled to start again late that afternoon.

By three-thirty, we had the spraying crew loaded into several vans and were headed out. Michael rode in a green truck with me. We drove to three units in the old Tom Gray Sale to lay out the spray cards in the wet draws, then wait for the helicopter to come over. I was almost to the bottom of unit F, placing the six-inch-square white cards along the stream, when Ilene called on the radio to say everything was off until five in the morning tomorrow. The winds were too high to spray.

I was up at four o'clock and down to the office by five. Ethan buttonholed me in the hall and told me to meet him at the helispot on the East Fork of Indian Creek, and I drove off into the autumn dawn. I took the Kemper Gulch road and soon came upon another green truck, stopped in the road ahead of me. Ilene stood looking down at a fallen snag that blocked the road. Betsy pulled in behind me. We all stood in the road, looked at each other and at the snag, and felt vulnerable in the chill, colorless half light.

"Well," Betsy said. She climbed up the road bank to see whether the snag had just fallen or been felled. "Nope!" she yelled, and we relaxed a little. Just a coincidence, then.

We turned around and drove back down Kemper Gulch, then took an alternate route up Mill Creek. We caught up with the spray convoy, which by now consisted of the batch truck, the decontamination truck, several inspectors, and two federal law enforcement officers in green coveralls that made them look like cable TV installers. Sandwiched in the middle of the parade was a Volkswagen bus carrying several antispray observers/concerned citizens.

At the helispot, I found Ethan, who climbed in my truck and told me to drive down and pick up Hanna, another concerned citizen, who was coming up the road in another vehicle. She rode with us to two other units. Ethan leaped out and galloped down to set out some spray cards. The three of us waited and watched as the helicopter sprayed the unit, just as the sun came up over the ridge. The diesel-like fragrance of fresh 2,4-D engulfed us, and Hanna covered her mouth and nose with a handkerchief.

We drove back down and dropped Hanna off at her car. She had wanted to see the unit sprayed, as she lived about a mile away. Ironically, her husband was driving the decontamination truck, which held the materials to be deployed in case of a spill.

At our next lookout point, below the Cedar Springs unit, we had a long wait before the helicopter at last whump-whumped over the ridge, sprayed, and left. We drove back to the office for lunch, and I choked down a peanut butter sandwich and a root beer. The front desk patched through a call from a woman who lived near the South Fork of Indian Creek and wanted to know what we were spraying and whether it would injure her garden or water. I explained that we weren't spraying anywhere near her place. She seemed slightly mollified but didn't want to leave her name.

That afternoon, with Michael as my partner again, we passed a few protesters as we pulled out of the parking lot. One had a sign that I couldn't quite read but that seemed to have something to do with water. This time, we would watch Tom Gray E. Since I had put out most of the cards yesterday, there wasn't much for us to do but hike down to the bottom of the unit and wait. Betsy waited over on Tom Gray D, which we sprayed first. Our unit was larger, and the helicopter needed seven loads of herbicide to cover the forty acres. When it was done, we walked back up to the road, picking up the spray cards as we went. It was nearly dark when we reached the road, and Michael's shirt was soaked with sweat. On the radio, we heard Bill Jones announcing that Ilene and Betsy and I didn't have to come in early tomorrow: with only a couple of units left to do, it wouldn't take so many people.

I stopped at the post office on my way home to pick up my mail. I ripped three antiherbicide flyers off the bulletin board of the deserted building, went home, and slept the sleep of the self-righteous.

The author about 1982, at the end of a long day.

Helicopters were expensive, so aerial herbicide projects were short-lived and frantic. They were also very controversial, as this one demonstrated. Backpack spraying got less attention, but it took longer and was arduous even on the flatter units. It also involved handling dyes that left virtually permanent stains on clothes and boots. We started backpack spraying crews on the easier units, to break everyone in gradually. Looking back through my 1980 notebooks, I notice that I worked for sixteen straight days without a day off that autumn, zigzagging up and down logging roads to check on both thinners and backpack sprayers. Bill Jones kept assuring me that we had plenty of money for overtime. The important thing, he said, was to get all the contracts done before winter set in.

We chose campsites for the backpack sprayers with care—not near anyone's source of drinking water, and off the main roads yet fairly close to the work sites. One local man who had bid on a small thinning contract was hostile to any kind of herbicide spraying, which was unfortunate since one of our backpack spraying units was near one of his thinning units. When he started taping poorly spelled polemics to the office door, our district law enforcement officer began shadowing him, which only made him more paranoid. I had been inspecting his one-man operation, but after the notes started arriving, Bill Jones sighed and passed that duty off to Howard, whose bearded male presence, Bill thought, made him less likely to get beaten up. Fortunately, the offending unit was rapidly sprayed by a twenty-person crew of Mexicans, who went through all sixteen acres before lunch. They weren't experienced at the work, however, and when I inspected it, I found too many errors for them to pass. The dye in the spray gave them away when they missed spraying around a crop tree. It was, I noted, "a real bitch of a block," but they attacked it again after lunch and finished it up by four-thirty, with me throwing plots right behind them. This time, they passed.

I had yet another contractor ready to start thinning the old Jade Sale units, so I checked on their campsite while also following a smaller spraying crew made up of Anglos from Oregon. Staring at blue circles around crop trees for several hours had given me a vicious headache by afternoon, so I soaked my bandanna in cold water, lay down in the shade of the truck, and slept for a couple of hours. When I woke up, the Anglos were almost finished with their unit. I made it back to the office by eight o'clock, parked the truck, walked down the dark, silent halls, and went home.

The Mexicans usually finished two units a day and passed their inspections; making them repeat that first, horrendously steep unit had concentrated their minds wonderfully.

By 1982, the opposition to spraying made hand grubbing look better and better. Although slower than hand spraying, it was acceptable to everyone. Simply grub the competing grass, brush, and hardwoods away from the little firs and pines. We tried it out in the winter of 1983 on some old Monk Sale units with easy ground and friable soil. Eight of us from silviculture and sale prep put in some hours during the slow season. Neither rain nor even light snow made any difference to the operation (unlike planting, where we looked forward to snow as a nice break—getting snow in the planting holes resulted in air pockets that dried out the fragile tree roots).

We hand grubbed off and on all that winter, knocking off only when the snow made the seedlings hard to see or the roads impassable. Sometimes Matt was one of the "volunteers" from the sale prep department. We talked to each other without constraint now, quite as if I had never been and was not still desperately in love with him. Laura told me that he had a girlfriend in Medford now, the sister of someone who worked on the district, and frequent sex undoubtedly helped his attitude toward life, the universe, and everything.

That spring the silviculture department considered what it had learned from this practice work, and we started writing contracts for hand grubbing. The NEPA requirements were a cinch—just a short environmental assessment that received a few comment letters and no appeals—and we were on our way.

We went back to the Monk units for our first contract, which went to a group of hippies from over on Salmon River. They showed up on a cloudy spring day with Pulaskis and a can-do attitude, and we were all set to get started when a sticking point arose.

"Has this unit ever been sprayed?" one of them asked.

Why yes, yes it had. Several years ago. But the spraying came too late in the year, after the tan-oak leaves had hardened off, and the treatment hadn't done much good. On the other side of the green truck, Matt and Gary pulled on their rain gear. "Uh-oh," I heard one of them say as the tallest hippie asked exactly what we had used and when.

Oh please God no, I begged the cosmos. Not today. Not today a big blow-up that will end with the crew quitting and us slinking back to town with this unit thrown into doubt. Please, not in front of Matt, just before what promised to be a pleasant lunch break. Please, not a round of change orders and work orders and a meeting with Gil Davies, the contracting officer. Where were the Mexicans when you needed them? Maybe they could do this one, too, if the hippies bailed.

I pulled the stand record card out of my folder and showed them the history of the unit, and they pored over it, then asked for time to discuss the matter over lunch. "For myself, I don't care one way or another," said the tall foreman ("Call me Spruce"). He shook his head, and his dreadlocks, tied back with a piece of leather, bounced behind his head. "But a few of them might."

"A few?" There were damn few of them to begin with. But I sighed and said fine, and Gary groaned. "Cabrón!" he said, and Matt laughed, tossing his head back. His eyes flashed and his bright teeth shone in the midst of his black beard. We sat down on the roadside with a patch of sunshine warming our rain gear, ate our sandwiches, and talked. At that moment I really didn't care whether the unit ever got started at all. "It all pays the same, I guess," I said, looking down at the mud that coated Matt's pair of White's, barely a foot away from the mud on my West Coasts.

Half an hour later, lunch over with, the crew emerged from the van and proceeded to grab tools and head for the unit, all but one young man who seemed to be adjusting something over his face. When he turned around to follow the others, I almost choked on my gum. He wore what appeared to be a tuna fish can over his nose and mouth. The bottom of the can had holes punched in it. Two more holes near the rim accommodated a string that passed around his head and held the can in place. His blond beard poked out in all directions around it.

I sidled up to Spruce. "All okay?" I said, lifting my chin in the direction of the tin can.

"Oh, sure," he said. "He stuffed some Kleenex in there. That should do it." He strode off, and I turned around to find my two-man inspection team bent over, gripping each other's shoulders, their faces red and eyes streaming, about to explode with the effort not to laugh out loud. They waved at me and staggered behind a fir thicket. I started to follow the crew but spit out my gum and stuffed my handkerchief into my mouth before exploding into breathless laughter, like no laughter since I was seven years old and gasping on the floor over something Lucy had just done on TV. Just when I thought I could catch my breath, the vision of the tuna fish can set me off again.

"Oh my God, that was wild," Gary said four hours later, as we started back toward town. "Do you suppose he'll do that again tomorrow?"

"Don't talk about it, please," Matt said, holding his coffee cup hand out over the floor mat to avoid the jolt of a pothole. "I'll spew coffee all over the dashboard."

"A tuna fish can, for cripes's sake," I said, gulping and taking a deep breath. "Let's not talk about it, okay? Otherwise I'll drive off the road."

We rode in exhausted silence the rest of the way home, letting loose only once more as we carried our packs up the back stairs.

Years passed before I saw that the protesters who rode in the VW van and tacked posters up at the post office were right, although perhaps not for the reasons they gave. They felt hostility not so much toward the herbicides themselves—although they were against them in principle, as well—but toward the whole paradigm of industrial forestry. Herbicides were a tool to transform an ancient, self-sustaining forest into a sterile tree farm. Harmful to human health or not—and at the time I thought not—they were seen as a means to a bad end. One way to jam a stick into the spokes of the Forest Service old-growth liquidation program was to question the safety of herbicides. The man with the tuna fish can on his face was in no danger, but his paranoia was a reflection of a greater wrong.

CHAPTER 15

The Man in Joe Sino's House

I built a whole social life around a doomed attempt to attract a man who, it turned out, found me undatable. But other people at the parties and barbecues and gatherings became my friends, so I didn't lose hope that out of those connections Something Would Happen.

Hope was in all our minds, or we would have just given up on romance. Helen still loved Michael, still stood up with him at parties and jived sweatily to the Cars. He would never love her, but neither of them found anyone else who danced so well. Matt still looked at Heather with eyes full of worship, and I wondered whether she noticed, even as she began a relationship with a helicopter pilot from Oregon. And Matt—being, after all, just a man—was dating a woman in Medford.

"Well," Laura shrugged when I mentioned this during one of our prolonged telephone conversations, "people have to move on. You can't keep beating your head against a wall."

I could, and did. If I passed Matt in the hall and he smiled and spoke to me, I was set up for the rest of the day, the week. But the social life I had laboriously stitched together against my own inclinations needed constant tending, so I kept track of the parties and went to all of them. One summer evening, I drove up to a party in Seiad Valley at Allan's new house. I told myself that I just wanted to see what he had done with the house, which had once belonged to friends of my parents. Did some trace of the old, safe and happy world still linger, some ghost of our presence remain in the house where we had all gathered to cut up venison so long ago?

Well, no. But the rich smell of a ripening garden, the tang of woodsmoke, and the voices of shrieking children were still there. Maybe you can't go home again, but echoes remain. Allan and Nancy showed off the house and yard, the smokehouse in the back with filleted steelhead on the racks, and the rock-floored patio on the east side.

Tour accomplished, nostalgia sated, I wandered out to the front yard, sat down under an oak tree, and chatted with a young woman from the Netherlands who worked as a summer volunteer on the Oak Knoll District. We sat in a circle with seven or eight other Forest Service employees while a joint made the rounds. I puffed on it and passed it on and realized this was the first joint I had ever tasted. Whatever had I been doing with myself all through the sixties and seventies? It didn't taste as good as it smelled, and it smelled as though someone had thrown celery leaves onto a hot stove. All through college, I was the good girl who never smoked anything and limited herself to two highballs. I waited for a buzz, but there was nothing. After a while I wandered into the backyard, where Allan was showing off his new smoker again. In the center of the stone patio, a fire pit held a snapping fire of madrone chunks that bit into the cool night air.

I circled the fire, avoiding the shifting smoke, sipped at a bottle of beer, and looked over the roof at the Lower Devils silhouetted against the darkening sky. "Hello," someone said.

He was stretched out on a chaise longue, holding the twin of my beverage. He wore chinos, a bright Hawaiian shirt, and aviator sunglasses. Light brown hair flopped down over his forehead. Was he talking to me? For a second, in the near dark, I thought it was Ronald, who lived up Seiad Creek with his long-time girlfriend Ilene. Once Ilene had said to me, "Ronald's the only one who's ever been able to satisfy my lust," a statement that came out of nowhere during a lunch break and made me stare at her.

But a second look told me that although Ronald was also partial to sunglasses and Hawaiian shirts and was one of the few men of my acquaintance who could get away with not wearing socks, this was not him. I said hello back, focusing on the aviator glasses.

He removed them, put them in the pocket of the flowered shirt, and rose to introduce himself. "I'm Keith," he said, and we shook hands. I slid a glance at his feet. Birkenstocks. No socks.

We soon exchanged the details of our jobs. He worked in timber on the Oak Knoll District. "Where do you live?" I asked, and he described the house that he rented a few miles upriver from the district office. I felt tears prickle behind my eyelids. "Oh my," I said, "you're in Joe Sino's house."

The house stands today, beneath a larger one farther up a steep hill. Both look smaller and shabbier than they did when I first saw them at age nine. They belonged to the Gunns, who built the large one as their retirement home. Jim Gunn built logging roads for Fruit Growers Supply, the big company that owned Hilt, so my stepfather knew him in the way of business. One spring day we went to visit them, because that is what people did on Sunday afternoons in the days of twenty-nine-cent gasoline.

I hated going visiting. I had to wear a dress, for one thing, and to be quiet, for another. Much better to pedal around Hilt on my bike, or sit in the cherry tree in Grandmother's backyard. And although these visits were not about us but about the grown-ups, I couldn't see that it was very entertaining for them, either. Dad wore slacks and a shirt with a bolo tie. Mother wore a town dress and high heels. How could that be fun? Liz and I chalked it up to another bizarre adult behavior. But we knew the drill, so we sat decorously, ankles crossed, and listened while four people talked about other people and events about which we knew nothing and cared less. Our hopes were pinned on some refreshments and the chance to wander around the yard by ourselves. After an hour or so, we'd be back in the car. Rinse. Repeat.

The Gunn house was tall and white with a railed porch running its full length, as though a Mississippi riverboat had gone aground on that steep oak-studded hillside. Below the porch, the lawn dropped away like an ocean swell, its velvet surface begging to be rolled down. A white cabin crouched on a bench below the main house, and in it lived a retired merchant marine named Joe Sino. Joe was the local amateur weatherman in those days before weather satellites. One wall of his house was covered with ham radio equipment, on which he talked at night to ships out in the Pacific and learned of approaching storms.

After an eon of staring down at the oak flooring and the stone fireplace and wondering just how long adults could go without eating or drinking, we waved goodbye and detoured to the lower house, where Joe produced store-bought cookies and a jug of iced tea, which we consumed while seated at the dinette set in front of wide windows that overlooked the river. Liz and I petted his black-and-white border collie.

"What's her name?" we asked, as talking seemed to be allowed here.

"I call her Madam," Joe said, flinging a sideways glance at our parents, who both found something chokable in their coffee.

"That's a cute name," we said, "but why call her that?"

"Because she treats me just like a madam," he said. "Kicks me out of the bed." As Mother and Dad continued to cough, he urged us to go outside and play, and in seconds we headed for the top of the lawn and rolled downhill with our arms tucked and Madam running alongside, barking.

As we climbed, spent, back into the Ford, we waved frantically at Joe and Madam as we headed back down the driveway.

"I don't remember ever seeing him again," I said to Keith, "but I remember that house."

"Well, you'll have to come see it, then," he said. "What's your number?"

We spoke on the phone several times after that, and he invited me to stop by if I was passing through, and one Sunday afternoon I did just that, as I drove back downriver after taking Mother to a play in Ashland. We sat in the bright breakfast nook that overlooked the river, and I looked around the narrow kitchen and cozy living room, feeling as if I had come home. Keith invited me to come with him to see another play in Ashland the following week.

I drove back to Happy Camp with my brain singing "I have a date, I have a date!" and realized that it had been ten years since a man had asked me out on an actual date, as opposed to just inviting me over. Even Chuck had never deigned to squire me to a dress-up restaurant, before or after we were married. Before, I didn't think anything about it. Afterward, he said it was because I didn't have a nice coat. "You could buy me one," I remember saying, and he had rolled his eyes.

But this was summer, when the best-laid plans went awry, and two days before D day, a fire broke out near Horse Creek. The Bear Fire took off on a steep hillside on the south side of the river, in heavy timber. We drew the night shift again and cut line uphill until four o'clock in the morning, when we found ourselves clambering onto a midslope road, where another crew filled drip torches and prepared for a burnout along the fire line we had just constructed. We spread out along the line and watched as flames crept toward the main fire. As the air cooled and the humidity rose, the fire quieted. We pulled food from our packs and heated cups of instant coffee on piles of coals. As dawn approached, we switched off our headlamps and listened for the whump-whump-whump of helicopters coming back after the long night. I looked down onto the misty river and saw one rise like a primordial dragonfly. That sight, and the thought of my actual date, made me smile, until I remembered that before that could happen, we had to be demobbed, then I had to get home, shower, find Something to Wear, and beat feet back upriver to meet Keith in time to drive to Ashland.

My social life was rescued by the arrival of several hotshot crews, who sent us off the line and down to fire camp at the Horse Creek School. Our crew boss copped a plea with demobilization, and by two o'clock we were rolling back to Happy Camp. Still a bit damp, I flew back upriver and into Keith's driveway with minutes to spare, and we were off to Ashland.

To drive "over the hill" was always, for me, a trip back in time. In the presence of someone who wasn't raised here and didn't know why my eyes gravitated toward the valley of Cottonwood Creek, the drive was an opportunity to point out landmarks and retail some history. "You should be a tour guide," Keith said.

In Ashland, we watched *What the Butler Saw* in the Angus Bowmer Theater, and our hands found each other. How long since I had sat in a live theater and held hands with a man? Since never, I realized. Two hours later, we strolled down the street and passed the Lithia water fountains, where we dared each other to take a sip of the sulfur-laden liquid. We found a café, ate cheesecake and drank coffee, and talked. By the time we arrived back in Klamath River—Keith was, I was happy to note, a careful driver—it was after midnight and Keith brought out a blanket and pillow. One of us, it appeared, would sleep on the couch. I assured him it would be me. We sat on it and snogged for a while, and when his hands began to roam farther afield, I let them. O tempora, O mores.

"Oh, Louise," he said.

I woke beneath the open window at the head of Keith's double bed. Jays ratcheted in the oak trees, and the smell of the river and green summer vegetation blew over my face. I looked over the top of Keith's ruffled brown hair and into the disapproving eyes of a gray-and-white cat. Keith's arms reached out and pulled me into an embrace. The cat's breakfast would have to wait.

"Whaddya know, Joe?" I smiled to myself.

We showered together, then consumed waffles and maple syrup, lounged in the breakfast nook over coffee, exchanged edited versions of our life stories. We sat on his patio while he smoked a joint. I invited him down to my place the following weekend and at last pled the needs of my own pets, tore myself away, and drove back downriver. Ah, I thought, it's a great feeling to have had sex and to know that one will soon have it again.

But with the prospect of male company in my house, company that I wanted to impress, I needed to hook up my new hot water heater. I spent the days before Keith's first visit crawling around under the house to hook it up. Before that, I'd been heating water on the stove.

For the rest of the summer, Keith and I spent most weekends together, usually at his place. We went to the Britt Music Festival near Medford. We began to talk about the desirability of living together, which in practice would require one or both of us to move. His parents lived near Placerville, and we talked of moving there: his parents had some land—enough for horses—and we could transfer there, perhaps. He had no interest in horses himself but, knowing they were important to me, would figure out a way to accommodate them. I wrote to my friend Joan, who also lived near Placerville. We agreed the move would be great—we could visit, go to horse shows, and go trail riding together.

In the fall, we said "I love you." We went to a jazz club in Ashland, which he appreciated a great deal but which left me bored and wishing I had brought a book. We went deer hunting, and I realized he was much more intense about it than I was. Hunting was mainly an exercise in nostalgia for me. If I got up before dawn to hunt, I headed home before noon to take a nap, then did a short evening hunt. Keith wanted to stay out all day, even when it was hot. He was left-brained enough to think that the object of hunting was actually to shoot something. We hunted up behind his house through the steep oak woodland, which was still and quiet and full of deer, but we never saw a shootable buck.

I learned that Keith's chest freezer was full of very good pot. "Bud" was just then becoming widely available, and he showed me his stash: the unfertilized flowers of Cannabis sativa, on which the crystals of THC stood out like sugar. He also had some hash, and now and then his friends came over and pipes came out and a stronger smoke scented the air. Keith knew a lot about the local marijuana industry; some of his neighbors worked at clipping and bagging it during the harvest season.

Through Keith, I met the young couple who owned the motel and restaurant at Klamath River. They threw potlucks and barbecues at the least excuse and also smoked a lot of pot. We hung out with Oak Knoll people who played a lot of golf and smoked a lot of pot. One Saturday afternoon, a group of these friends met at a house on Walker Creek to help someone move, and I walked into the kitchen to find Keith and another man sucking a white powder up their noses from a plate. "What was that?" I asked him later. "Cocaine?" He looked horrified.

"Shit, no," he said. "Cocaine's too expensive. It was methedrine."

Whatever it was, it kept him up until all hours that night as he talked a mile a minute. "How often do you use that stuff?" I asked.

"Just when I'm tired and need to keep going," he said. "We had to get all that furniture moved today."

"Well, it can't be good for you," I said. I felt his pulse hammering under my hand. He took a breath and opened his mouth, then shut it again. He reached out an arm and hugged me to his shoulder. "Aw, you really care about me," he said. "That's sweet."

In December, we went on the Audubon Christmas Bird Count with another couple. They were birding fiends, able to find even rarer species such as the sora, which we located with a tape recording. We drove all over the Shasta Valley, and my companions lit up another doobie every half hour or so. They seemed nervous whenever a ranch pickup drove by. Perhaps, I thought, they'd be less paranoid if they smoked less dope.

Keith had by then given up trying to teach me to smoke pot. I was willing enough to puff on a joint when it came around, just to be polite, but any sort of buzz eluded me. Keith insisted that this was a waste of the product and I should learn to inhale. He sat me up in bed one Sunday morning, lit a joint, and proceeded to instruct me. I was game to try, but my first go at sucking smoke directly into my lungs merely resulted in a fifteen-minute coughing fit.

"No, I'm sorry," I rasped. "You'll have to make me brownies or something." Keith looked horrified at the very idea and did not press the issue. I got the feeling he was relieved not to have to share the contents of his freezer. My only addiction was to his pantry full of RC Cola, which was considerably cheaper than pot.

We ate Thanksgiving dinner at my mother's house in Montague with my brother and his fiancée, which seemed to make Keith uncomfortable. "Don't worry," I teased him. "I don't expect you to get down on one knee and propose."

"You don't want us to act like those two, do you?" he said. "It's like they're Velcroed together at the hip."

I blinked at him. Tom and Mary were young and in love and engaged. What did he expect?

In January, we watched the 1984 Super Bowl at Allan and Nancy's house and saw the Redskins lose in spectacular fashion to the Raiders. We drove back to his place in silence and for the first time let the night pass without making love. Keith didn't take well to losing, even vicariously. Later I learned that money rode on the contest.

In the spring, we played golf together at the Eagle's Nest, a fine nine-hole course across the river near Keith's house. Its wide fairways were lined with sycamore trees and punctuated by rattlesnake-infested gullies. Back in the days when I was still trying to impress Matt, I played there perhaps four times. Now, I rented a set of clubs and we played around the course. "You're not bad," Keith said.

One weekend he told me that the foursome was already filled and it was boys only that day—Upriver versus Downriver. "That's okay, I can just watch, can't I?" I said.

"No, I'd rather you just wait here," he said, and I watched him drive away, feeling vaguely resentful at being ordered to stay home in Joe Sino's cabin, like a faithful dog. I wondered why he didn't want me along. Matt was one of the Downriver players, I already knew. Well, who cared? I saw Matt all the time at work. I was over him now. Why shouldn't I go down to the course to watch my boyfriend—my boyfriend, what a lovely phrase—play a stupid game? They would, I knew, go around twice. I would give them a couple of hours, then casually stroll onto the course.

I found them at the foot of the precipitous approach to the ninth green, a nearly vertical hill that made this hole a difficult one. Most players either belted the ball over and over again at the green wall of turf until it made it over the lip and onto the green, or hit it far too hard the first time and lost it on the brown hillside beyond the pin, a place full of rocks and poison oak and the occasional rattlesnake. Ronald, Matt, and Kit—Keith's partner—stood staring up the hill at something. "Better not go up there," Ronald said to me.

"Why not?"

"Keith's having a little trouble with this hole," Matt laughed as they started up the slope. I followed.

Keith stood beyond the green with his back to us. He tried to chip his ball out of the oak leaves and cheatgrass, but it seemed to be wedged between a couple of rocks, and the matter had become a contest between him and the ball.

"Just take a mulligan," Kit advised him. Kit looked very mellow, which he had every right to be, since he had retrieved his bag of hash from Keith's freezer the night before.

Keith began to beat the ground with his club, and to swear and scream at the ball. He picked it up and heaved it into the top of an oak, then flung the club uphill toward the fence. I looked around at Matt and Kit and Ronald, who stood mesmerized beside me.

"Huh," Matt said. Ronald giggled. I remembered that Ronald had played golf with Tom Watson in college and wondered whether even the pros had days like this.

Keith hadn't noticed me, and suddenly I wanted this happy state of affairs to continue. I slid back down the slope, out of his line of sight, and waited for the boys to move on. I headed away from them, crawled up a gully and under the fence to the county road, and jogged down to my truck in the parking lot next to the clubhouse. I slid into the cab and gave a good imitation of nonchalance as Keith came around the corner of the building, still red in the face. But he smiled at me and came up to be hugged. "I didn't see your truck come up," he said. He seemed to have forgotten that he hadn't wanted me to be here.

A few weeks later, as we ate supper at a restaurant in Ashland, Keith reached across the table, took my hand, and began to tell me about his relationship with his ex-wife, how it had gone wrong and what they had done together to try to make it work again.

"That's how I took up bird-watching," he said. "We went to a marriage counselor and she said we should find a hobby, something we both enjoyed."

"Did it work?"

"For a while. But then she was laid off at the hospital—she was a nurse—and she just couldn't take waiting around the house with nothing to do." He paused. "Also she had a drinking problem."

I knew there was more to the story—there always is—but I squeezed his hand and felt very close to him. When he was ready, he would tell me the rest. We would move somewhere together, and someday he would ask me to marry him, and I would say yes. By now I had consumed two glasses of wine, so I leaned across the sparkling glasses and the snowy tablecloth and told him an abbreviated version of my unrequited love affair with Matt.

He went silent, his face rigid and blank. I hastened to assure him that he shouldn't be concerned, that my feelings for Matt were in the past and nothing to worry about. Everything was fine, just fine. Then why, his stare demanded, are you telling me about it? For the same reason, my eyes flashed back, that you're telling me about your attempts to make nice with your ex.

Girls, listen to me. Never, ever, tell your boyfriend about your previous boyfriends, even the unrequited ones, even the ones who never kissed you. If he already knows about them, don't talk about them. If you don't believe me, read *Tess of the d'Urbervilles*. Confession on his part does not mean that confession on yours is a good idea. Trust me, he will Not Understand.

The meal stuck in my throat, a well-acted play passed in silence and misery, and later we lay on opposite sides of a queen-sized motel bed, and I wondered why in the world we wasted our time like this. I remembered a look that flickered briefly across his eyes and realized two things: that he did not like Matt to begin with, and that someone had told him about the connection between us. That was why he had told me not to visit the golf course: he was afraid that the rumors were true. And I had just confirmed them. He didn't believe me when I said I no longer felt anything for Matt. And as I lay in the dark under the roar of the air conditioner, I didn't believe me, either. I still loved him and perhaps always would. But I was going to move on and find someone else to love who would love me back. In fact, I thought I had.

In the morning, the silence continued, and Keith slipped out to smoke a joint or two while I showered. Our Sunday brunch—long planned—at the Medford country club was remarkable for the excellence of the eggs Benedict and the incredible amount of them he consumed from the all-you-can-eat brunch bar. We drove back downriver, still in silence, and by the time we arrived at Joe Sino's house, I had reached the conclusion that all my relationships with men were doomed to involve them not talking to me. While Keith ducked into the bathroom, I swept up the few belongings I kept in a drawer and tossed them into my truck. Then I thanked him for a lovely weekend, got a grunt in return, and drove off believing that I'd never see him again.

He called me on Wednesday evening and we talked, without mentioning the weekend. Could he come down to see me? Of course he could, and in two hours he was in my house and soon in my bed, and the sex was better than it had been in weeks. But the next day was a workday, unlike most of our other overnights together, and he faced the real difference between his house and mine: I didn't have a shower, just a bathtub, which he didn't like. On a weekend, this didn't seem to bother him; perhaps he thought it was like camping out. But now that he had to go directly from my house to the Oak Knoll office without detouring to his own shower, he was unhappy.

"I smell like sex," he kept saying. I was puzzled. Who cared? Even if he totally reeked, the other guys would just think he'd gotten lucky and envy him. I slid my arms around his waist and sniffed his neck. "You smell fine," I said. "But take a quick bath if you like, or just sluice off under the faucet." I placed a towel and washcloth on the edge of the tub for him. I was rather proud of the tub, a claw-legged antique that I had plumbed myself.

"It's not the same," he said. "And I can still smell it."

Feeling rather skunky myself by now, I gave up, kissed him on the cheek, then ran a quick bath for myself. When I came out, he was gone.

A week passed without a call from him, then two, then three. On a Sunday afternoon on my way back from Mother's, I stopped by his house and he came out to greet me, trailed by a woman I had never seen before. He introduced her as an old college friend from Portland. We shook hands and smiled at each other, and I thought, You didn't even have the guts to break up with me over the Data General, you bastard.

He didn't ask me for my house key, that not being the sort of thing one brings up to the old girlfriend in front of the new, so I stopped there once more, in a Forest Service truck on my way back from a meeting in Yreka. On that lovely fall afternoon, I walked beneath the trees, sat on the patio, and spoke to Joe Sino one more time. "It didn't work out, Joe," I told him. "But thank you."

The key still worked. I looked around the breakfast nook. I took a cola from the refrigerator, put the key on the table, pushed in the lock, and shut the door behind me.

"Well, I'll tell you what I would have done," my sister said when I called her that night to give her the postmortem. "I'd have held on to that key until I knew he was going out of town for a few days, and then unplugged his damn freezer and ruined all his drugs."

"Huh," I said.

CHAPTER 16

The Red Queen's Race

Now, here, you see, it takes all the running you can do, to keep in the same place. If you want to get somewhere else,
you must run at least twice as fast.
—Lewis Carroll

Looking up the Klamath River from Thompson Ridge, near Slater Butte. In the foreground, young trees planted after the Indian Ridge Burn of 1966.

By the 1980s, all of us on the Klamath knew that we were running the Red Queen's race, and that it was getting harder. Some of us suspected that it would never get easier again. A few who crunched the numbers knew that it had to end soon, one way or another.

And thanks to the introduction of a computerized communications system into the Forest Service in the 1980s, word of this began to spread fairly rapidly.

Not that the Data General—always referred to as "the DG"—was any great shakes as a computing system, even in 1982, when it first hit our district. It was strictly in-house, for one thing. Surfing the internet wasn't possible, and many districts were left out of the initial wave of installations. It was possible to construct database tables, and I found them a great help in planning my thinning contracts. Other applications, like spreadsheets, were not user friendly, but they provided endless entertainment for the few self-taught computer nerds among us. And the clunky monitors and keyboards came in handy when trying to avoid eye contact—or worse—with visitors, such as the contractor who sat in front of my desk one day to discuss camping sites with one ankle crossed over a knee. The crotch of his jeans was torn, and he wore no underwear.

A youth versus age divide was evident in attitudes toward the DG, and not only when it came to the learning curve. Ease of unofficial communication was not something that everyone loved. "The ability to network through e-mail greatly assisted the dysfunctional relationship for employees with the environmental agenda. A message in support of an environmental agenda could be instantly sent to other regions with a simple push of a button," wrote one Forest Service veteran who began his career about 1960. In other words, anyone in the Forest Service could now talk to anyone else quickly and easily and without going through channels. The full force of this would not be felt until the 1990s, but the ability to write down exactly what one thought about anything and then click on "reply all" was a genie that could not be put back into the bottle. Practices that had been conducted under the radar for decades were now revealed. Wildlife and fisheries biologists contacted outside groups to report on efforts to sidestep environmental laws. Women talked about which national forests and districts discriminated against them.

Dissenting voices had spoken before, of course. In the 1970s a stooped old man named Harry sometimes shuffled up and down in front of the office, carrying a hand-lettered sign that read, "A Clean

Forest Doesn't Burn." Ranger Henry rolled his eyes and went out the back door to avoid him. George was more patient and curious: he invited Harry into his office and heard him out one day. "He actually has some good ideas," George said.

One day Jeff leaned on the counter at the front desk and watched Harry's performance. He told me that sometimes in the fall after the first good rains, after the lookouts came down from Pony Peak and Slater Butte and Baldy Mountain, on days when fog hid the peaks, he drove into the forest with a drip torch, walked out on a ridge, and spread a line of fire on top of the duff so it could creep downhill and clean out the small fuels.

"Really?" I said, knowing he could be fired if anyone could prove this.

Jeff looked at me. When I first came to work on the district, Jeff noticed that my rented trailer in Seiad Valley had a stovepipe but no woodpile. He took me out woodcutting; we gathered two truckloads of firewood from a pile of cull logs the loggers had left. I didn't need a wood permit, he assured me. I doubted this, but Jeff had a chainsaw and a truck and I had neither. When we unloaded the wood, he noticed that I didn't have an ax, either, so he presented me with a Pulaski bearing a strip of red paint around the handle, indicating time spent in the district fire warehouse. I said thank you and took it.

But Jeff and his outlaw drip torch could accomplish only so much. For decades, the only form of burning the forest countenanced was slash burning in the fall to clear the ground so the new clear-cuts could be planted with nursery-grown conifers in the spring. Some silviculturists didn't like the cut-burn-plant cycle and thought that leaving a certain amount of woody debris served to recycle nutrients into the soil and shelter young trees. But their opinions were only a whisper, and our cool rainy winters and hot dry summers meant that by July any unburned slash was dangerously flammable.

In the 1970s, timber sale contracts began to require that larger cull logs and hardwoods be hauled up to the landings and stacked in YUM (yarding of unmerchantable material) piles. The practice provided more firewood for the public and made broadcast slash burning less hazardous. Burning was usually done at night when temperatures fell and humidity rose.

As a teenager, I looked forward to the fall nights when Dad went out with the burning crews. Liz and I stayed up late, made popcorn, and played the records he didn't like. But Mother couldn't forget what night burning involved: lines of men, headlamps strapped to their hard hats, spread out across the top of a clear-cut, carrying drip torches. As they crawled downhill through slash up to their armpits, each dripped a line of fire behind him. Other men stood at the edges of the clear-cut, on either a bulldozer track or a four-foot-wide fire line scraped down to dirt. The men with the drip torches tried to watch the men on either side, lest they get too far ahead or fall too far behind. Sometimes men fell into holes between logs and could barely crawl out again. As the fire above began to catch and spread, anyone lagging behind in the jackstrawed logs risked being trapped.

On steep slopes, as the smaller materials burned, the larger cull logs, bucked by the loggers into sixteen-foot lengths, often came loose and began to roll. One day Dad told us that a young forester had been caught this way; a log slammed into him and rolled over his lower body, fracturing his pelvis.

On most nights, though, all the men reached the bottom of the clear-cut with only scrapes and bruises. Then they took up hand tools and stood watch the rest of the night to stop anything rolling out into the forest. When something too big to stop with a boot or a shovel escaped, they chased it down to prevent the "rollout" from starting another fire. Some of the linemen carried piss-pumps to squirt water on smoldering logs.

The fire usually died down by morning, and the firing crew and linemen hiked to the road and went home to get some sleep while a day crew watched the lines. Sometimes, when too many crews lit too many clear-cuts on fire, a rollout sprang to life after a day or two, and then the district had a wildfire on its hands.

By the time I started working on burning crews, night burning was less common, and daytime burning incorporated new tools. The steepest skyline or helicopter logging units were set alight by helicopters dropping Ping-Pong balls filled with napalm, an awe-inspiring sight. But most slash burns were still lit by hand, for helicopter flight time was expensive. With the help of youth crews from the California Conservation Corps, we had plenty of help for mop-up.

Occasionally, however, slash burning still went south:

> Sunday October 12—Ethan pulled some of us off Huckleberry at
> 0100, so we could come in at 0900 & go put line around the slopovers
> on Jackson 30. Drove up there with Pollard & 5 others in a.m.—
> spots all over hell below the unit—we dropped down from top of
> unit & spent all day cutting line from spots down to road below,
> about 1000 feet! In evening, we burned it out, and it just crept around
> on ground—not much fuel, really, just rocks, live-oaks & big old
> Doug-fir. Wind stayed quiet today even though humidity very low.
> Got back to office at 9 p.m. totally exhausted.

Mrs. Dunaway, my great-aunt Frances's old friend, was eighty-five
now and had seen a few things. One autumn day as I took her for a
drive down to Clear Creek, where she had been raised, she told me
some stories. Sixty years before, she and a friend hired a neighbor with
packhorses to take them into the high country northwest of Happy
Camp. They spent several days picking huckleberries and packing
them into kerosene tins, which were just the right size and shape to
fit onto pack saddles. A few days later at the office, I pulled out aerial
photographs and a stereoscope and found the places she had described.
But the huckleberry patches had disappeared, replaced by taller brush
and trees. Years later, a Karuk historian working to bring managed
fire back to the Klamath landscape explained the prehistoric system
to me. "The huckleberries ripened just before the first salmon runs
came up the river," he said. "So the people went to the high country
to gather huckleberries and dry them, and as they headed back down
to their villages on the river to prepare for the fishing season, they lit
fires. And that kept the trails clear and maintained the huckleberry
patches." And the huckleberry patches must have kept at least some
of the bears up higher for longer, out of the way of the salmon netters.

I was used to thick stands of brush and thought them normal. But
Alice was astonished at the changes she saw near the highway at Clear
Creek.

"This is terrible!" she said. "Look at all that tall brush! That wasn't
there when I was a kid."

But some things had changed even since I was in high school. By the 1970s, a market for wood chips developed, and the chip trucks—huge bins on wheels—ran day and night down to the coast, carrying chips to be made into chipboard, which was fast replacing plywood for construction. The prices of all commodities had spiked as oil prices doubled and doubled again, and the first locking gas caps appeared around town.

Even hardwoods could be converted into chips and thrown into the maw of a growing market. We began to hear the words "hardwood conversion" and "reforestation backlog." Money was made available for the Klamath National Forest to clear-cut stands of hardwoods and replant them with conifers. As long as the chip market stayed high, loggers made money doing this. Get paid on a contract basis to cut hardwoods, then sell the hardwood logs for chips. Entirely left out of the conversation was the fact that for the Karuk people, groves of tan oaks were traditional family property, where acorns had been gathered for many generations. But acorn gathering was done out of sight of the Forest Service and didn't enter into its calculations.

To prevent hardwood stumps from sprouting, contractors dabbed them with Tordon. The slash was burned in the fall and the area replanted in the spring. Foresters spent the winter peering through stereoscopes at aerial photos, picking out the stands of hardwoods—tan oaks, madrones, chinquapins, black oaks—next on the chopping block.

In the summer of 1980, my boss discovered that I was the only person in the department with a pesticide applicator's license, which—considering that only a few years ago a district policy had prevented me from working with herbicides at all—I found ironic. This entitled me to a stint as a timber sale administrator in the Bunker Hill area downriver.

Bunker Hill had been one of the last timber sales my stepfather laid out and administered, and I remembered him talking about "the Battle of Bunker Hill," so called because of the long struggle with Ed Jereb, the forest's head engineer. Dad wanted to build a utilitarian logging road to go in, get the timber, and get out. Ed wanted an investment, a high-standard road for the future. This involved massive cuts through decomposed granite, and a road much too high standard for a simple logging operation. Ed got the road he wanted, but in the end Bunker

Hill was the only sale ever done in the area, and his grandiose plans to blast a road down the south side of the river to eventually link up with Ukonom's road system ran out of gas about the same time the country did in 1973.

As the inspector on this hardwood felling project, I gained the perk of my very own truck, a little black Datsun—rented, as the Forest Service was not allowed to purchase foreign-made trucks. Handy on narrow roads, it could climb steep hills surprisingly well, unlike the gutless Ford Courier that had been the district's first attempt at an economy pickup. Couriers got great gas mileage but were apparently made out of flattened tomato cans, and the gear shift had a disconcerting habit of leaping from second into third gear on a steep hill without being asked.

When I went out to check the work and make sure that the dye in the Tordon encircled the entire cambium on a stump, I noticed that ridgetops almost always formed one of the stand boundaries. These were human-made landscapes, created over thousands of years by Karuk people to provide their families with valued tan-oak acorns, and sculpted using fire at the correct times. That had all ended after 1910, when the Forest Service applied a blanket policy against burning. We were in effect now destroying someone else's orchards.

The ridgetops were open and easy to walk, and in the rainy seasons they hosted an incredible array of fungi—coral mushrooms and boletes, chanterelles and melting fairy rings, shelf fungi on trees and fallen logs. Mushrooms always made me think of Doug, nerdiest of all the silviculturists, who covered a table in his office with the fruiting bodies of mycorrhizal fungi—huge ugly things full of brown powdery spores that threatened to engulf the table. He did research on these fungi, which had a symbiotic relationship with tree roots and evolved along with local trees and soils. Trees raised from Klamath seeds, but grown for two years in a nursery in McKinleyville or Mount Shasta City or Medford, didn't have access to these mycorrhizae and lacked something they needed to thrive. Doug started collecting the brown powdery spores from the fruiting bodies and sprinkling them on the roots of some of our seedlings as they were planted. Was it working? He didn't have enough data yet to be sure. Still, he told us, it couldn't hurt.

Some areas with deep soils were successfully converted to conifers, but others, such as live-oak patches on steep, rocky slopes, were impossible, and in the end all we did was annoy the hardwoods for a while. When the chip market—and the entire lumber market—crashed in the early 1980s, the money to destroy hardwoods ran out. The Red Queen's race began again, for the whole enterprise was a balancing act: if anything went wrong, the projects didn't pencil out. And if growth and harvest didn't balance in the long run, the Klamath National Forest would be in no position to ensure sustained yield.

Many things could go wrong. In the late 1970s, quite a few of the seedlings we obtained from the Humboldt Nursery in McKinleyville didn't survive. The nursery ran studies for several years and found that the problem was not with seed quality or planting protocols but with the very short lifting window at the nursery—the trees went into winter dormancy for only a couple of weeks in December. Dormancy caused the roots to stop growing, so that they could be dug up and packaged without damage to the root hairs. But McKinleyville, with its mild coastal weather, was simply too warm. Trees lifted while their roots were actively growing couldn't stand the stress of bagging, storage, and replanting. They looked fine as they went into the ground, and they might even live a year or two, but death followed. By the time we figured out the problem, some plantations had lost almost a decade of growth and been replanted several times.

When Robert and Bert's computerized system for surveying plantations kicked in, our data showed that in many plantations planted to ponderosa pine in the 1950s and 1960s, the pines survived but were stunted and crooked and often had infestations of Comandra rust, an alien-looking growth with Day-Glo orange spores. Off-site, said Bert. The seeds came from trees grown at a much lower elevation or on a different aspect. Planting seeds from a pine grown at two thousand feet elevation on a four-thousand-foot site was a recipe for failure. I didn't need the surveys to tell me this. I'd spent many a delightful summer day crawling through plantations covered in eight-foot-high snowbrush on my hands and knees. Of the original plantation, only occasional twisted bonsai-like pines survived, still trying to find the sun. But beneath my knees was a carpet of white fir seedlings, growing about an inch per year, content to grow slowly in the shade. In some far-off year, they would peek over the snowbrush, then take off and grow to their full height. But white fir was brittle and easily infected through its thin bark by stain-causing fungi. It was worth little to loggers.

White fir had coexisted with snowbrush in old burns for many thousands of years, but for the purposes of the Klamath National Forest's timber program, these failed pine plantations didn't exist. The suffering pines were supposed to grow fast and mature on schedule, ready for a commercial thinning within the next thirty years. They should be putting on board feet the way teenagers put on inches. That assumption led the district to cut other mature trees.

Board feet cut should equal board feet growing—that was how the accounting system worked, but the system didn't take into account many economic realities. The district's annual cut was fifty-five million board feet per year, and year by year more and more roads chewed into the unroaded areas—the RARE II areas that had not been designated as wilderness. The plan was that these uncut areas would supply old-growth timber while the young trees in the oldest clear-cuts—dating from the early 1950s—acquired height and put on board feet. By the time the old growth played out, the second growth would be ready for commercial thinning, at least. Trees as small as six inches in diameter could yield boards. But our local sawmills were designed and built to mill the largest trees, not the smaller ones. When the old growth was gone, would the lumber mills invest the money to retool their operations?

In the case of the largest mill in Happy Camp, I was not optimistic. I thought it would make more sense, when the time came, for the mill to relocate out to Yreka at the railhead, rather than go to the trouble and expense of hauling new equipment seventy miles down a twisting mountain road. The expense of hauling finished lumber back up that same highway was already a challenge. Why not avoid all that?

When I went to a week-long training session in second-growth management in 1983, we toured a new sawmill in northeastern California whose owner was buying second- and even third-growth ponderosa pine, milling it, and selling it in the Japanese market. His mill cut boards to very exacting measurements—he used lasers to achieve this—and in the metric system. No Japanese buyer was interested in buying boards cut in English units. "You have to give the customers what they want," he told us. I was impressed by this, because at the time the dominant philosophy in American manufacturing seemed to be "they'll buy what we make and they'll like it." No, they wouldn't, now that they had a choice. That was how McCulloch and Homelite lost the chainsaw market to Stihl and Husqvarna.

The Forest Service initially didn't understand that building roads into inventoried roadless areas would become so contentious. When environmental groups began to fight the roads program with appeals and court challenges, they learned that the Forest Service often did not fully comply with either NEPA (National Environmental Policy Act) or NFMA (National Forest Management Act), the most important laws regulating timber sales. If the agency obeyed NEPA and confessed in an environmental analysis the effects of all that it planned to do, the project could often be shown not to be in accord with NFMA, and vice versa.

Alice called me one day at the office. "Come up here for dinner tomorrow evening," she said. "Bring a big salad." I dug out my biggest stainless-steel bowl and wrote out a shopping list.

One of the perks—or hazards, depending on your point of view—of being Alice's friend was helping to feed the guests when she had to entertain as Ranger's Wife. This time, the forest supervisor and an assortment of officials from the regional office in San Francisco were in town. We gathered on Alice's porch on a summer evening, while the guests admired her antiques and listened to the evening breeze roar down Elk Creek and through the boughs of the massive Douglas-fir on the lawn. We drank beer, ate Alice's company dinner specialty— chimichangas—and met the honchos from the Bay Area, who looked ecstatic to be out "in the field."

As the light fell away and the mosquitoes came out, I paused between trips to refill the chip bowls to listen to a conversation between forest supervisor Bob Rice and Bill Jones. Bill was shouting at Bob, repeating himself under the influence of strong emotion and several beers.

"We can't do it, we can't do it!" Bill yelled, and as I tuned in to the exchange, I realized he was talking about the difficulty of doing any kind of spray project these days. He also pleaded to get the roadless areas removed from the Klamath's timber inventory so we could justify lowering the annual cut.

Bob sipped at his highball, ice clinking in the glass. "Well," he said calmly, looking over the top of Bill's head, "you'll just have to do it, is all."

Bill wasn't appeased. "We can't! We can't!" he said, and then, to my astonishment, he began jumping up and down, his five feet ten inches no match for Bob's six feet four when it came to making eye contact. At that point, Alice yelled out that hot grease was coming through, and they retreated to the living room, where Bill shifted his pleas to one of the regional people, and Bob leaned on a door jamb and started talking to George about fishing.

Bill was right, and Bob knew that Bill was right. But Bob also knew that the situation was out of his control, and out of even the regional forester's control. No decision on lowering the Klamath's output would ever be made by either of them. Eventually something would constrain the supply, but until then, plans for logging in roadless areas continued, and the annual timber targets remained unchanged. The only way to meet them was to enter the roadless areas—or try to.

By 1986, though, I felt something else changing.

> Saturday, October 11—Huckleberry Fire—Ethan phoned @ 10:45 a.m., said "Get down here, I need you!" Turned out there was a Huckleberry unit (just logged) on fire—road crew left a couple of hand piles burning. Drove out in van—tanker already there—fire both sides of the road. Started cutting line down the NE side— very steep—we were very spread out—not enough people—saw crew out in front of me—I suddenly saw fire right below them; I couldn't remember whether Al Durazo was below or above us—went chugging up the hill to find him—sent the CCC saw crew down to help Arnold & Morehouse, then ran into Bert & somebody else & sent them down—we cut around spot & made record time to the creek. Having fire below us really scared me—worse to come about 9 p.m. when superheated fuel in unit blew up all at once. Bert above me screaming into his radio—he was on Channel 1 & no one else was!—which scared me even though I know B tends to panic.

What scared me was a feeling that something had changed in the forest itself. The way the forest burned that night was qualitatively different from anything I had seen before. I had been on large, uncontained fires. I had seen blow-ups before, too, but nothing scared me the way that slash fire did, roaring to life on a cool autumn evening with the humidity down in the single digits long after sunset—in October. I saw the great trees on the edge of the clear-cut lean in toward the flames, bent at a forty-five-degree angle over our heads. Dead needles and small branches shot free and were sucked into the inferno. I looked at Al Durazo beside me in the brilliant firelight, but he wasn't looking at the blaze. His eyes scanned the tree trunks below us, until I saw what he saw: the dry moss on their bark starting to smoke. Al leaned toward me and jerked his chin at the smoking boles, bracing himself on the steep ground with his shovel.

"There's a road below us," he shouted over the roar, before moving on down the fire line to shout into other ears. He was telling us that if it all went to hell, we shouldn't try to run uphill, but go downhill before the fire got too active below us. Down below us was a road, and presumably safety. And although a few of the trees outside the line were scorched and killed by the fire, the early hours of the morning found us still on the line, and the flames dying down at last.

Within a year, the 1987 fires—a vast lightning-sparked emergency that extended from the southern Sierras to southern Oregon—would burn up many of the plantations that we had thinned in the Independence and Titus Ridge areas. Thinning contracts called for all slash to be cleared for fifty feet from the roads, and I enforced it. The thinners complained, and sometimes the contractor muttered about needing more money, but as I set the slash piles afire in the gentle November rains, I felt virtuous. At least the plantations were safe from cigarette-flippers. But it didn't matter in the end, for the rest of the slash, many acres of snapping branches and red needles, was still there. Even when bucked up to the correct lengths and mashed down by a snowy winter, it all went up like bombs that September and took our carefully spaced crop trees with it.

I was gone from the Klamath by the time I saw photos of that destruction, but I kept in touch with Jon Silvius, the public affairs officer, a good friend and a reliable source. One day, he told me something surprising. "I was talking to one of the new computer people," he said. "They're starting to use computerized GIS— Geographic Information Systems. It's not all digitized yet, a lot of it is still on overlays. And this GIS guy figured out the number of acres that's burned on the Klamath every decade, and the number of acres we've planted, and the number of acres we've logged. And guess what? I go into his office, and he's just staring at a screen, and he says to me, 'You know, Jon, it's amazing, but statistically, it's impossible to bring a plantation to rotation age on the Klamath. It'll burn up before then.'"

We had all the tools—flaming Ping-Pong balls dropped from helicopters, skyline logging, and roads "up the ying-yang," as the foresters said—and it was all very complicated, and every innovation brought with it more and more ways for things to go wrong. And through it all, we never realized what the Karuks knew thousands of years ago: fire is not just a cleanup tool, but a sculptor's chisel. On its own or directed by humans, it had carved out the landscape on which we stood, the landscape that we had torn apart in a generation.

In the late 1980s, more and more research indicated that the Forest Service's timber program was a house of cards about to collapse. By the early 1990s, timber staff officers were panicking. They knew—none better—that their timber budget for next year depended on getting out the cut this year. And every year, that became more difficult. Most of the old growth was already gone, species like salmon and spotted owls in decline, yet the large timber still left outside wilderness areas was vulnerable to being sold and cut. If that timber pipeline was ever cut off, the money that went to the national forests would also end.

Historian Paul Hirt called our dilemma a conspiracy of optimism: optimistic annual cuts based on the assumption that all lands classified as productive could and would grow commercial stands of timber, thanks to replanting, spraying, and thinning. But those assumptions were often wrong. In fact, the timber yield tables for California overestimated growth rates by as much as a third. Bill Jones and many others knew there was no place left to find the big old growth on which most western lumber mills depended, and unless the roadless areas were removed from the timber base and the allowable cut reduced to something feasible, the game was over, and soon.

The timber program was a runaway train about to go over a cliff, and its eventual end was evident to anyone who watched the dancing green letters on a DG screen. And still we worked to stay aboard, long after we knew where it was going.

CHAPTER 17

Klamath Weed

In 1977, the US government joined Mexican authorities to spray the powerful herbicide paraquat on thousands of acres of marijuana plantations in Mexico. According to rumor, some of the pot was hastily harvested and sold in the United States. The resulting scare among pot users started a stampede to domestically grown marijuana. On the northwest coast of California, marijuana cultivation went from a hobby to an industry overnight, complete with divisions of labor, massive financial backing, and takeover attempts. Although the paraquat program lasted for only two years, the effect on the industry was permanent.

My family was no stranger to contact with illegal substances. During Prohibition, Mother often rode with her father in his Model A Ford down to Hornbrook, where they visited Harry, who made excellent moonshine and sold it in quart mason jars. During World War II, Dad poached deer on a western Oregon stump ranch. His father often spoke of the Mexican laborers near San Diego who smoked, in lieu of tobacco, what he called ditchweed.

My sister learned to smoke tobacco by snitching cigarettes from a friend's mother and lighting them up in the alley when she was about eight. I loathed the smell of cigarette smoke, but we both ruined a package of cigarette papers trying to roll cigarettes for Grandfather. I was never tempted to actually stick one in my mouth and set it on fire.

I arrived at college blessed with a low threshold of hedonism. I went to one fraternity kegger during pledge week but was revolted by the feel of grass slick with spilled beer (and, I suspected, vomit) under my shoes and wasn't tempted to go inside the frat house. I sipped a single cup of the free Budweiser-on-tap offered to all the young women and went back to the dorm. I had been allowed wine or beer at dinner with my parents for years but looked forward to it less than tapioca pudding. My idea of a wild Saturday night at Chico State—a notoriously high-ranked party school—was to lug an armful of books back from the library and dip into them during the commercials while watching *The Invaders* and *Star Trek* in the dorm's TV room. New books and television were the substances hard to access at home, not beer.

When Liz joined me at college two years later, it took her about fifteen minutes to turn her cigarette-rolling skills into cash by buying small amounts of pot, rolling joints, then reselling them to a select clientele in the boys' dorm across the quad. I came to know the smell of the stuff but had no desire to try it.

When Chuck and I split up in the waning months of 1980, my half of the bargain included the two fixer-upper cabins half a mile up the road from Chez Chuck. The larger one had renters, so I moved into the smaller one. The renters were a quiet young couple, with quiet friends who visited after dark. Cars idled in the driveway, headlights doused, and brief conversations took place under the back porch light. The rent tended to appear, in cash, after one of these social calls.

I didn't particularly care what my tenants sold from their back door; many Forest Service employees smoked pot, and most bought the herb rather than risk growing it. At one district meeting, after the ranger had delivered his annual thou-shalt-not-smoke-the-pot-or-thou-shalt-surely-be-fired speech, I looked around the room and compared the number of people I had seen smoking the evil weed at parties with the number of attendees: about 60 percent. In those days of large Forest Service summer crews, drawn mostly from the ranks of college students, this wasn't surprising. But my mental list was by no means confined to the lower ranks; it included staff officers with conservative haircuts. "Well," my stepfather commented, "it's probably better than dipping two cans of snoose a day, like some of us used to do."

I knew, too, that the sale administration foresters kept whiskey in the bottom drawers of their desks and lost little time getting wasted before noon on Christmas Eve. But that seemed different, somehow, since most of them were middle aged.

Marijuana cultivation became common in the Klamath River country in a remarkably short time. Unknown when I graduated from high school, appearing as a cultural hobby among hippies from the Bay Area in the 1970s, by the 1980s it was an economic force. The vast forests of northern California and southern Oregon, with their mild climate and dense vegetation, seemed made to grow the crop in secret. We heard lurid tales of eye-level fishhooks and Uzi-toting thugs down in Mendocino and Humboldt Counties, but most local growers preferred camouflage and caution.

Still, those stories made me watchful in the woods. Sometimes I found tiny plots of half a dozen marijuana plants, deep in an old clear-cut surrounded by young conifers. The cannabis plants looked startlingly alien against the Douglas-firs, with their dark purple-green divided leaves growing on six-foot stalks. Painstakingly pruned, they bore long, slightly fuzzy, drooping "buds"—unfertilized flowers—the mark of the good stuff. With enough sunlight for the plants to thrive but enough shade to shield them from too much summer heat, these wounds in the forest made ideal pot nurseries. When I reported my finds, the answer was invariably "Oh yeah, we know about that one. We'll get it in the fall."

I stumbled on these examples of free-market capitalism while confirming the thinnability of plantations between ten and fifteen years old. Much of the calculation about how much timber the district could sell in the future depended on how fast thinned trees would grow into a commercial crop. In this respect, there wasn't that much difference between the Forest Service and the pot-growing entrepreneurs. In neither case were the lives of the laborers easy, for the plantations grew on ground steeper than a staircase, with liberal quantities of brush, hardwoods, ticks, poison oak, rattlesnakes, biting gnats, bald-faced hornets, and yellow jackets.

Once units were located, the silviculture crew mapped them, marked their boundaries, and calculated their acreages. When we had about eight hundred acres mapped, I wrote up a thinning contract. The contracting officer in Yreka added some boilerplate and solicited bids. After the contract was awarded, I followed crews of Mexican nationals up one drainage and down another throughout the summer, inspecting their work. One contract flowed seamlessly into another, and I saw a sort of continuity as we began to thin some of the plantations that had been planted in the wake of the Indian Ridge Burn of 1966. My stepfather had laid out the fire salvage sales that cleared the way for the plantations, and the young trees were growing fast. But one day as I drove out to the east side of Thompson Ridge and hiked downhill toward the sound of chainsaws, I saw a white van cruising by on the road above me. Later, the van returned, and a tall, bearded man with a shaved head leaned out of the van and spoke to the thinners as they ate lunch on the road. "Who the hell was that?" I asked Ollie, who was helping me inspect that day.

"Oh, him? That's Big Max. He's a contractor."

"What kind of a contractor?"

"He contracts to buy pot, so much a pound."

"He doesn't grow it himself?"

"Nah," Ollie said. "Too much work and risk."

"Then what's he doing out here?"

Ollie shrugged. "Guess he has to check on a few of them, make sure the quality stacks up."

Also, I thought, he needs to know where the thinners are going next, so he can let his growers know if they should pull it early. I'll be darned. There are contractors, and then there are contractors. And if they didn't bother me, I wasn't going to bother them.

On a morning like any other, I flung my lunch and thermos into a green pickup truck and drove up the East Fork of Elk Creek to inspect some thinning on Frying Pan Ridge. I took the long way around, for I loved the coolness of shadows cast by the bigleaf maples in the East Fork canyon. I drove slowly, but even so I overtook the Melota brothers in their little blue pickup. They saw me in their rearview mirror and pulled over to let me pass. They raised their hands in the casual salute of the logging road, but their quick smiles were nervous under identical brown eyes and limp mops of black hair. I waved back.

The first time this happened, I mentioned it to Jeff, now doubling as the district's first law enforcement officer. "Oh, yeah," he said. "They've got a bunch of patches up there. We've spotted some with the helicopters, but I don't know why they even try to hide it. Worst dope in the county; it's a wonder they can even sell it. Or so I've been told," he said, the ends of his waxed mustache turning up.

Later, I connected Jeff's story with an odd anecdote I heard from Brenda, a forester who said she'd met Jeff once on a camping trip to Ukonom Lake. They'd smoked a joint around the campfire. "Then he propositioned me," she said. "I guess he figured that women who don't shave their legs are easy."

The long climb out of the head of the East Fork canyon up a steep, narrow logging road brought me to a plantation near the top of Frying Pan Ridge, here so steep that the sidecast material from the road cascaded hundreds of feet downslope. At the top of the ridge, where the crew had worked the day before on a plantation called Frying Pan A—one of the few successful reforestations on that old sale—no vans waited beside the road, no chainsaws screamed below. I sat on the road edge, feet dangling over the lip, drinking coffee and filling in the headings on some contract forms. Hazy green velvet ridges rolled away into the August dreamtime.

I thought about the Melota brothers. I remembered them as small children, one of them in my brother's kindergarten class. Their parents were poor immigrants with ten children, who eventually built up a family business that elevated them into Happy Camp's middle class. Whatever the brothers' horticultural talents or lack thereof, they were raised to know hard work and the value of a dollar. Their pot growing was probably more lucrative than bagging groceries, and less dangerous than setting chokers.

After an hour, tired of waiting, I bailed off the road edge, dirt and rocks pouring over my boots. At the toe of the talus slope, the waist-high thinning slash began. I rolled my long sleeves down to protect my arms from the yellow jackets that swarmed over the sticky jumbles of limbs and needles. Now and then I stopped to check spacing, but if I paused too long, the yellow jackets started to crawl up my pant legs, so I wasted no time getting to the bottom of the unit, next to the cool dimness of the intact forest beyond. Out of the corner of my eye, I saw where the thinners had stopped, and why.

A thousand feet below the road, sixteen cannabis plants had matured in two neat rows, a plantation within a plantation. Not a branch remained, not a leaf, only the cut stems, each as thick as my wrist and still oozing sap. They sat in depressions a couple of feet wide, mulched with lawn clippings. I looked around, heart thudding, then reminded myself that a grower wouldn't approach a patch with a Forest Service truck parked nearby. Besides, I thought I knew where my thinners were: in Medford for a long weekend. "Thank you, boys," I said. A blessed few days away from poison oak and yellow jackets opened before me.

I hiked up the old firebreak at the edge of the plantation, not hurrying. I reached the road and sat down in the hot dust. Two wide-winged black birds soared on the thermals. Below them, the endless ridges of the Klamath Mountains, notched and gouged by so many clear-cuts, marched away, smaller and smaller in the distance; a quilted landscape stitched from remnants of the forest that was. Ridge upon ridge, clear-cut after clear-cut, an endless pattern sewn by money, out to the world's end.

I reached into the truck bed to pull my lunch out of my green pack and found a wide hole ripped into the canvas, and shreds of brown paper poking out of it. Of my sandwich and cookies, only crumbs remained. The robbers had left most of the apple but poked holes in it with their auger-like beaks. I pulled it out and tossed it over the road bank. High above, the soaring ravens croaked at me: Huginn and Muninn, on their way back to Odin with some news.

I sat in the truck with the windows open and drank some tea and read a chapter from my book, wondering what to do next. I hadn't been to Grider Ridge in a long time. I swung my legs into the cab, closed the door, and started the engine.

Grider Ridge ran north and south and formed part of the eastern boundary of the Happy Camp District. Seiad Valley was visible from its summit. The road that followed the ridge switched from east side to west and back again, and at Cold Springs, near the end of the road, I filled my canteen at the pipe that stuck out of the moss-covered roadcut. The air was cooler up here near the old trail that led into the Marble Mountain Wilderness; time seemed to have stopped decades ago, when trails were the only travel routes. The old world lingered here, a world where nothing newer than a Model A existed, where no strangers grew marijuana in my woods.

I drove back down the ridge road, stopping now and then to look at a plantation and mark it on my map for future reference.

Just before the Four Corners intersection, I passed the plantation that held my stepfather's ashes. I stopped to look over the edge, but young trees and thick mats of vines camouflaged the stumps. I turned east down West Grider Creek and passed the places where I once fished, and ran, and lived. At the mouth of Walker Creek, where the county road met the river highway, I picked up an AM radio signal and turned up the volume. "I am woman, hear me roar," Helen Reddy sang.

Change had come to the Klamath, bringing strange ways. But if change hadn't come, if this was still the 1930s or even the 1950s, I wouldn't be here, either. I wouldn't be driving down the highway in a green pickup truck, a woman working for the Forest Service in a field position. I liked the new world, when it suited me.

I walked into Jeff's office holding a cold can of pop to my forehead.

"Damn!" he said when I told him, and pulled a map from a drawer. "We had that one mapped; we were just waiting for them to come try to harvest it."

"The Melotas?" The question made Jeff's eyes narrow. I was probably the only person under forty in the office who hadn't smoked a whole joint, but he'd never believe that.

"No," he said. "Someone else. And no, I can't tell you who, or if there's any more up there."

You mean you won't, I said, but not aloud, and went off to make copies of the contract maps for him. He'd have to content himself with mopping up whatever remained in the area before anyone else found it.

The thinners returned three days later, cheerful, and some with new boots. But the following week, a grim foreman told me that his vans had been broken into, the chainsaws stolen, and the fuel cans mutilated with an ax. Everything comes with a price.

A month later, two of the stolen saws turned up at a local saw repair shop, which had, of course, been given a list of their serial numbers. The county sheriff raided the customer's house and found many pounds of neatly packaged pot, assorted other recreational drugs, and a remarkably detailed set of books. Legal remedies ensued.

Perhaps marijuana does rot the brain after all, or maybe vengeance is best left to older gods than ours, who wait, meditating upon cause and effect, forgetting nothing, and remembering—just possibly—everything.

CHAPTER 18

Crew Boss

The dispatcher stood up and peered over the tall desk at the row of tired firefighters sitting on the floor in front of him.

"We broke a fire up above West Branch," he said. "Who wants to go?" We stirred, scrambled to our feet, untangled our web gear, checked our canteens, dashed down the hall to get water, and hit the restrooms. "Hey, Louise," he called to me. "You want to be crew boss?"

"I've never been one," I said.

"Yeah, but you've been a squad boss for . . ." he consulted a piece of paper, "the past several days."

"Only because we drew straws to see who got to fill out the time sheets, and I lost."

Ten minutes later, I led a scratch crew of ten out to the parking lot, where another crew from the Lassen National Forest waited. Their boss was a lean young man with the glittering eyes of someone subsisting on adrenaline and caffeine. He nodded as I handed him a map and told him to follow our van.

Years ago, I took the required forty-hour basic firefighter course. All employees were encouraged to take it, even the clerks, who might be given fire camp assignments. It meant a week of (mostly) sitting and listening, a nice break after six weeks of late winter tree planting. Since then, I'd been on a number of fires and gained an elementary understanding of fire behavior. But I'd never taken the crew boss training course, a requirement for the assignment I'd just been given. But the district—indeed, the whole Klamath National Forest—was running out of people to chase the dozens of fires sparked by this late July lightning bust. So I drove a van with a map spread out on the dashboard, up Indian Creek toward something called the East Fire, which turned out to be a ten-acre blaze below a ten-year-old clear-cut.

Headlamps on—for by now it was after eleven o'clock at night—we walked out on an old logging road toward the distant glow. The mile-long route was punctuated by washouts, occasional fallen trees, and thickets of head-high deerbrush.

At road's end, we saw a cheerful blaze creeping over the duffy ground, flaring occasionally as it consumed small fir trees at the edge of the old clear-cut. The flames flung shadows on the broad trunks of the Douglas-firs at our backs. Bill, leader of the Lassen crew, spit into a clump of brush. "Looks good," he said. "We could tie it off right here at the road."

The crew gathered around and we explained the plan, then started digging line downhill, the fire on our right. Two men with chainsaws led off, followed by a Pulaski, chopping at roots and swiping at the duff layer. Then came a shovel, scraping and flinging dirt, and finally a McLeod. The order repeated itself until we ran out of people, as we made a start at clearing a fire line four feet wide, down to mineral soil. In very steep places, we cut ditches that angled in toward the fire, to stop and redirect rolling material.

The chilly night had quieted the fire. Earlier in the day, it had burned hot, crowning in the younger trees, scorching the ancient Douglas-firs with fungus conks on their thick gray bark. We cut a long fire line down the slope from the old road, where the ground was steeper. The fire crawled downhill ahead of us, and as hot rocks and burning embers rolled, they started smaller fires below us that made uphill runs to join the main fire.

The fire burned down into the roots of the trees and made its way into the rotten heartwood of the old ones, and I knew they would soon begin to fall. They came down in the dark, a process rather than an event, their fall signaled by a slow, whiny creaking. When we heard it, we swung our headlamps around in the dark, trying to place the source. Usually we couldn't, so we dropped our tools and crashed through the brush away from the line until we heard the final groan and earth-shaking thump. Then we crept back and started digging again.

We had only one radio, which I wore clipped to my belt in a heavy black leather holster. Sometime after midnight, our fire management officer called me. He was also the incident commander for all of these

ABC lightning fires (class A fires are one-quarter acre or less; class B fires more than one-quarter acre but less than ten acres; class C fires more than ten acres but less than one hundred). He had an idea. "We can drop in a portable water tank to you tomorrow morning with a helicopter and leave you a pump and some hose, and you could start getting some water on it before the day gets too hot, okay?"

"Stand by," I said, thinking. Helicopters didn't fly at night, and for one to fill up a portable tank in the morning, using a sling bucket, would take hours. I keyed the radio again.

"Jim, can you wake George Lemos up and have him put the D-8 on the lowboy, and bring it up here and start opening the road we walked in on? If there's an engine available, it could come in behind him, and we could start laying hose tonight."

I let the key up and waited—waited for him to say that he didn't think my idea would work, that he'd rather go with his. Then the radio sputtered. "Ten four," Jim Allen's voice said. "We'll get going on that. Happy Camp clear."

I stared at the radio in my hand. "Oh my God," I shouted at the moaning branches over our heads. "They're going to do it!"

"Of course they are," Bill shouted back at me from up the hill. "You're the crew boss." And I saw his teeth flash white under his headlamp.

This is it, I thought. This is the rush, the joy, the jolt of power that I had never felt before. I was the crew boss. I had spoken into a radio and men who had been asleep were now awake and walking the D-8 up onto a flatbed. Men and machinery were on their way. They hadn't argued or told me it was a stupid idea, for after a moment's thought Jim knew it was a good idea, too, and much faster than waiting till morning.

Two hours later, I heard a faint, far-off screeching—the sound of Caterpillar treads backing and filling, gradually coming closer; the noise of a D-8, blade down, lights on, moving slowly and rebuilding the road as it came. George Lemos was filling washouts, shoving fallen trees aside, blading deerbrush off the old road. And at that moment it was the loveliest sound in the world.

The fire was no more active than it had been when we arrived, but it still outpaced us, falling steadily downhill no matter how fast we dug. As the euphoria of my talk with Jim Allen wore off, as we listened for falling trees and scampered out of their way, a full realization of just how much shit I would be in if someone got killed or injured hit me. I wanted, very much, for dawn to come.

Just as the world turned gray again, the Caterpillar fell silent, and I hiked up the fire line to the road. As I stood there panting, leaning on my Pulaski, I saw the green fire engine, its belly heavy with water, its crew busy setting up a portable water tank and tossing rolls of hose off the engine. I grabbed a Coke out of a cooler and slid back down the slope to send some of the crew uphill to start unrolling the hoses. I joined the rest of the crew below, now cutting line with renewed energy, for we could see the finish line.

At nine o'clock, with the day already getting warm, I looked up to see a fresh crew coming down the slope, a sawyer in the lead, and at last—at last—with the new crew's help, we hooked the bottom of the fire and began working up the far side. By noon, hundreds of feet of canvas hose poured water onto hot spots while firefighters filled their piss-pumps and started mopping up. By early afternoon, our two crews had been relieved, and we sat on the landing beside the portable tank and ate lunch. Then I drove my crew home.

My crew: unhurt by fire or falls or ax blades or killer trees. Covered in soot and dirt and ash, but unhurt. Unhurt, that is, except for the feelings of one member, who never spoke to me again because I insisted on driving the van back myself even though he wanted to do it. Somehow, his pride was tied up in the idea of driving, although he had been content to doze in the back coming out. Later, I thought that perhaps I should have tossed him the keys and gotten some sleep myself, but my pride was involved, too. I wanted to be the one to make sure everyone got back to the station safely. As we unloaded behind the station, Bill shook my hand outside the dispatch office and said, "Good working with you." I felt as though the universe had leaned down and pasted a gold star on my forehead.

No one in authority, then or later, tumbled to the fact that according to Forest Service rules, I shouldn't have been a crew boss at all. In light of all the fatal mistakes made on forest fires since that day in 1985, it amazes me that the mission of putting out what was, after all, a small fire burning in relatively benign weather conditions should have loomed so large that the agency's own protocols were ignored.

Sometimes when rules come in second, people die. But in those days, we tended to get away with it. Forty years later, the odds have changed.

These days, building direct line is done much less often because fires often move faster and more unpredictably, but it has taken fatalities and ruined careers to make incident commanders more cautious. These days, there is less firefighting at night, especially when large unstable trees are involved, and less building line downhill toward the bottom of an uncontained fire. But what still makes me shake, all these years later, is that it never occurred to me or to Bill or to Jim Allen that the wisest thing to do would have been to wait for dawn so that we could see those trees falling. It never occurred to us because we had always attacked fire both by day and by night, even in dangerous situations.

On the first fire I ever fought, our crew boss Al Durazo, who really did know what he was doing, got tired of rocks the size of washing machines thundering past us in the dark. He pulled us back into the timber and we waited for dawn. But he didn't tell the fire boss, back in camp at Seiad Valley, what he had done. Instead he lied on the radio, pretending that we were still out there, still sucking it up and cutting line, though the heavens fell.

I had never known a fire crew to stop working because of a little thing like falling trees. The previous autumn, when a slash fire burned out of its containment lines one evening, the fire gods sent crews out to corral it, again at night. The slop-over burned over a ridge and down into a grove of decadent Douglas-firs, rotten at the heart. As the creeping fire gnawed away at their roots, the trees came down one by one, groaning and protesting. We cut a line around the grove and stayed nearby all night long, improving the line and watching for rollouts. We told each other to be sure to have a big stump picked out to dive behind if we heard a tree fall. And we often heard one.

It would take the unstoppable conflagrations of a new century to teach the Forest Service that containing a wildfire isn't really worth risking anyone's life.

CHAPTER 19

Years of the Ski

As a child, I loved snow. After a rare heavy snowstorm in Hilt, I couldn't wait to get outside with my sled, tromp down the snow on the hill near our house until it was packed down enough to slide, and careen downhill on the sled, faster and faster with every run.

My mother had sledded these same streets and even learned to ski a little as a teenager. But by the time I was old enough to fit her wooden skis, they had long since disappeared into the Well of Lost Recreation Equipment.

We lived within sight of Mount Ashland, where a downhill ski area, built more on hope than on a consistent snowpack, attracted skiers in good winters. I had never been up there, or to the ski area on Mount Shasta to the south. Our stepfather considered downhill skiing a frivolous, expensive, and dangerous waste of time, and cross-country skiing was almost unknown in those days in our area: the complicated business of waxes for different snow conditions discouraged all but serious aficionados, and no-wax skis were twenty years in the future. So I managed to reach my thirties without ever having a pair of skis on my feet.

Keith, however, had taken it upon himself to introduce me to skiing, so we went to Mount Shasta, where he had signed up for a telemarking class. Telemarking had recently been discovered by American cross-country skiers, and for many of them, part of the attraction was to enjoy downhill skiing without the expense of buying lift tickets.

I followed the instructor and a dozen students down the marked trail on the south flank of the mountain. The trails began at the parking lot where the old ski lodge once stood, at the mercy of occasional snowless winters and a relentless sunshine that turned whatever snow there was to glare ice. But it was close to Mount Shasta City, and the city fathers provided unconditional support until it became clear that no one could make money running the place. By the 1980s, the site of the lodge was a hub for snowmobilers, cross-country skiers, and snowshoers. In the summer, teenagers rode their skateboards down the paved access road at frightening speeds.

Climbing Mount Shasta was another thing our family didn't do. Every year, a few people got lost on the mountain and died of exposure, or fell into a crevasse, or were caught in a blizzard. We preferred to admire the county's largest landmark at a distance. But this was a bright, still day on the middle reaches of the mountain, the snow was perfect, and managing my rented skis on flat ground wasn't too hard. By copying the person in front of me, I managed to achieve a sort of kick and was able to follow the others to where the instructor would initiate his pupils into the mysteries of telemarking. On the way, just as I prepared to crash into a boulder, he took pity on me and showed me how to turn the front points of my skis toward each other. "That will slow you down," he said with a German accent.

I watched as pupil after pupil step-climbed the slope into untouched deep powder. The instructor gestured and spoke, then plunged off the top, his hips and knees describing arcs as his students followed him. Often, they crashed halfway down, only to stagger upright and keep going. By the second time he reached the bottom, Keith was covered with snow and fuming—he couldn't seem to master the technique. I had to give him credit for persistence, though. By the time the sun touched the horizon and my sweat-soaked long underwear had grown cold, Keith managed to make a few long, sweeping turns on his own. He stood at the bottom looking like a powdered doughnut, tired but encouraged. "Almost got it," he said.

As I followed the weary class back to the parking lot, I was tired but cheerful. Maybe I can do this, I thought. I could manage flat ground and gentle slopes. Maybe next time. . . . But with Keith, there was no next time. Over the next few weekends, he went skiing with the Oak Knoll crowd to Mount Ashland and left me behind. "You couldn't keep up with us," he said, and of course he was right.

After Keith and I broke up, I might never have attached another pair of skis to my feet if I hadn't still been determined to swim in Matt's social sea. The following winter I found myself in ski shops where I was fitted with skis by incredibly handsome men often younger than me. Somehow, while I was planting trees and running chainsaws and marrying and divorcing and falling in love with a man who didn't, couldn't, wouldn't love me back, I had become a thirty-something. My years made it harder to keep up with the youth of America, but hopeless passion is a stern taskmaster. One winter weekend, I rode once more through Mount Shasta City and up the mountain to the parking lot at Bunny Flat.

This time, however, I had a raging cold that should have kept me home in bed, but I dosed myself with enough daytime cold remedy to medicate the US Olympic Team and carried on.

Everyone else disappeared over the first hill while I still struggled with my boot clips. Laura turned back to help me, then gave me some advice on how to move forward. "You sort of have to kick out sideways," she said over her shoulder as she sped up to catch the others. I pushed on my poles and lurched ahead—too fast, for my skis shot out in front of my hips, and I fell backward. I clawed myself upright again, only to find that one of my skis had popped off. The mountain seemed very quiet now. I stumped back to the station wagon, sat down on the back seat (Ethan and Mary had forgotten to lock up, thank God), and just managed to clip the ski back on.

More careful now, I took small, tentative steps. The waxless rental skis had overlapping plastic scales on the bottom. After several near falls, I achieved a sort of scoot, like someone polishing a hardwood floor with rags tied to their feet, and felt rather proud of myself. Ahead, the trail entered the shade of a clump of silvertip firs, their branches covered with snow like blue frosting. I saw Matt's brother Ted crouched nearby, covered in what looked like red gore. Alarmed, I uttered a squeak, and he looked up at me.

"Have to change waxes," he said, and I realized that what looked like blood was the goo he'd been scraping off the bottom of his skis with a plastic implement. Much of it had ended up on his coat. "This is klister," he said. "Gotta use different stuff now. Snow's old and it's warm."

"Okay," I said. I was glad to stop and catch my breath. Several new muscles in my hips and thighs already hurt. I leaned on my poles and looked at Ted. He was a taller, skinnier, red-headed version of Matt. Although older than Matt by a couple of years, he was the follower in their relationship. "I wish he'd go somewhere on his own and stop following me," I heard Matt grumble once. Now and then, I wondered why I wasn't attracted to Ted—he was, after all, unattached, which made him at least nominally fair game. But, aside from a total lack of attraction on either side, hitting on the brother of my major crush seemed excessively creepy, even for me. I shuddered as I stood in the shade and watched him.

"You cold?" Ted said. "Go ahead, I'll be along in a minute. Better keep moving."

"Okay," I said. This, for me, was easier said than done. Unlike the flat groomed trail with gentle contours that I had navigated on my first ski trip to Mount Shasta, this route plunged down the south side of the mountain and eventually connected with the same highway that brought us up. The idea was to ski down and then catch a ride, either back up to Bunny Flat or down to town if you'd had enough. The trail was ungroomed except by the tracks of skis and snowmobiles, and although it meandered to some extent, it was steeper than I realized. I pushed off and headed down, then tried the "snowplowing" technique I had learned last year. But I couldn't seem to get the hang of it now. When I tried to turn the skis they resisted, and to avoid crashing into a large tree I sat down, which worked. I rose with my skis turned ninety degrees to the slope and contemplated the long, curving trail that descended through the trees. I took a deep breath and slid another twenty yards downhill before again falling back on my butt to avoid another tree. The whole trip was going to be like this. I paused and stared off into the distance, as though posing for a travel brochure. Ted passed me with a wave.

I unwrapped another menthol cough drop from the supply in my coat pocket, felt the cold air assault my inflamed nasal passages, and wondered what the hell I was doing here. To see Matt's face and hear his voice and watch the way his eyes crinkled up when he laughed? I could have stayed home and imagined those things just as well, for they certainly weren't in sight now. If I survived the trip down the mountain to the switchback, where friendly cars and a bonfire waited, I would see him this evening when we went to dinner and then out to a bar with a foosball table and soothing beverages on tap. How many falls until the bottom? I pushed off once more.

Hours later, I sat on the side of the plowed road and removed my skis. I was plastered with snow, soaking wet, and had lost a glove. That night I drank beer and, squinting hard, tried again to imagine Ted as boyfriend material. I learned across the table and asked him to explain waxes to me. A blob of klister still clung to his nose. He launched into an explanation of the theory and practice of waxes, to which I actually listened instead of imagining what kissing him would be like. Later, we played shuffleboard with some bikers, and I wished that I felt as indifferent to all men. Back at the motel, I drank NyQuil straight from the bottle and drifted off to the sounds of snores from my dozen roomies.

I rode back to Happy Camp in a pickup between Matt and Terry without even having to fight for the privilege, and that seemed to make the whole weekend worth it. "Thanks for putting up with me," I croaked between coughs, as my head screamed from last night's alcohol overload, while my cold symptoms retreated under the assault of over-the-counter pharmaceuticals. I blew my nose and the men looked at each other across my head, probably wondering what the hell I was talking about.

"No problem," Matt said.

I had just about recovered from Mount Shasta when I heard of a proposed trip to Oregon's Bachelor Butte. As the end of the season for good downhill skiing approached, a friend of someone's friend lucked into a condo in Bend that could accommodate a dozen or so. Ethan and Mary, like houseparents, commandeered the largest bedroom. The rest of us staked out our places on the floor and headed for the hot tub.

I felt a bit cocky. Severe dieting and a recent bout of stomach flu had removed ten pounds from my frame, and I felt confident enough to wear a yellow two-piece bathing suit that set off my brown hair and hazel eyes. I probably looked like a ripe banana, but I felt gorgeous and was pleased to see Terry's eyes open wider as I stepped into the hot tub out on the deck. I even caught Matt checking out my cleavage. I slid into the steaming water with a sigh of triumph.

"So how do we do this?" I said to Mary, as we drove up the winding road to the ski lodge the next morning. I sat up straight in the middle of the back seat, not daring to let my eyes stray from the middle of the road. I wished I had stopped at two margaritas the night before.

"Simple: you just go down to the rental shop in the basement, get some skis, and sign up for a lesson—you should have at least one to get you started—and you're off." At the parking lot, she and Ethan unloaded their own skis from the roof of their Subaru and shooed me on my way.

In the ski shop, which seemed such a cozy place that I was tempted to hide among the racks of goose down and Gore-Tex all day, I screwed up my courage, asked about lessons, and was rewarded when a gorgeous man approached, spoke to me gently, smiled into my eyes, and told me he'd be my instructor. Twenty minutes later we were out on the bunny slope behind the lodge, where a mob of children seemingly born on skis frolicked in the glaring sunshine. Tiny ice crystals floated in the air. "How cold is it?" I asked.

"Oh, about zero," Eric said, his knitted black cap contrasting nicely with the blond hair escaping from the sides. Avoiding the little monsters, he lined us up on a clear spot and took me through some knee-bending exercises. As we started down the gentle slope, I was delighted to see how easy it all was. I pointed my bent knees in one direction and then another, and the skis simply took me there, as if they could read my mind. I arrived at the bottom of the knoll with a grin on my face. Life was good, and I'd just been introduced to a larger world. After a few more experimental runs and turns, Eric led me over to the lift. "You're doing great," he said. "I'll go up with you for your first run."

I watched the chairs come swinging around and saw confident people position themselves in front and wait to be slapped on the rear and swung off into the sparkling air. Despite the cold, I felt very warm under my jacket. Eric signaled the attendant to halt the next chair and sat down on the right side. I hesitated. "All right?" he said.

"Sure," I said and planted myself on the left while Eric swung the grab bar down in front. I looked ahead at the couple in the next chair laughing and talking, not even hanging on. But as we swung into the air and headed up the mountain, rising higher and higher from the white ground, panic set in.

"How you doing?" Eric said, looking at me with his kind blue eyes.

"I don't know why I didn't see this coming," I said, clutching the grab bar with a death grip. "I really don't like heights." In my eagerness to fit in with the crowd, I realized, I hadn't taken something rather important into account.

The eyes narrowed, with concern or possibly exasperation. I wondered how often a student freaked out on him on the chairlift. "Don't look down," he said. "Look ahead to the next landing."

"Okay," I said, squashing the urge to curl up in a fetal position and bury my head in his armpit. My skis dangled over the yawning chasm, their weight threatening to pull me under the bar like warm spaghetti over the lip of a colander.

"I had a friend," I said, "who was in an accident here at Bachelor a couple of years ago. The lift stopped and then the chairs started to slide backward, and she panicked and jumped off." I stared ahead at the upper slopes of the mountain. That was better, I found. Focusing on something at roughly the same elevation helped.

"Well, that won't happen today," Eric said firmly. After a moment, "Was she all right?"

"Oh, she is now," I said. "She's up there somewhere." I tilted my chin at the top of the mountain and then, seeing the look of alarm on his face, added, "Up on top skiing, I mean. She broke her back, but she's all right now."

"Oh, good," Eric said, staring off at some skiers on a distant run, probably wishing he was with them. We reached the first landing, and Eric lifted the bar and took my elbow. "Off we go!" he said, and I found myself back on my feet on firm ground. He smiled at me. "We'll go back down together," he said, and I felt rather brave again. We pushed off, and I made wide turns down the slope, hoping that the kids I heard yelling upslope wouldn't crash into me. I almost forgot the terror of the lift and the sight of the shadowed ground so far below. Almost.

Back behind the lodge, Eric smiled once more and shook my hand. "You'll do fine," he said. "Enjoy your stay." He headed for the lodge. I stood alone in the midst of the crowd and wondered what to do next. First things first: I took off my skis, planted them in a snowbank near some others (perhaps someone will steal them, I thought), and headed for the lodge's coffee shop and restrooms.

Bladder emptied, I paused at the coffee shop, stuffed full of exhausted parents ignoring the shouting children outside. I wanted to sit down with a cup of cocoa, but what if Eric came by and saw me Not Skiing? Besides, I had rented the skis for the whole day. It seemed like a waste not to be on them. I headed for the lift.

On the other side of the lift turnaround was another gentle slope. It wasn't crowded with children, and as I stood watching, I saw Laura and Heather glide past below me at the end of a long run from much higher up the mountain. They stopped and I headed down toward them. I gave them an edited version of my first flight.

"We're going up again," Laura said. "Want to come with? The chairs can fit three."

"I have to go to the ladies' room," I said and waved to them as they swung away in a chair. I trudged to the lodge again and this time did sit down with a cup of hot chocolate. The marshmallows stuck in my throat. This is ridiculous, I thought. All kinds of people ride the lift, and they're fine. You don't have to go all the way to the top. Just go up to the first landing again. Do that, and you can call it a day.

Back at the lift, I almost chickened out in front of the bored teenage operator, but a voice at my side stopped me. "Want to ride up together?" I turned to see a stocky woman with short silver hair who reminded me of my grandmother. The zipper pull on her jacket bore a season lift ticket. "Sure," I said, and we sat down together.

We chatted. She was a retired schoolteacher, sixty-six years old, who had learned to ski only last winter. "I'm making up for lost time," she said and did not smile as she said it. I felt suddenly ashamed. If she could do it at her age, surely I could. We rode up to the second landing. The sun had dropped close to the mountain now, and the trees beside the runs cast long shadows and looked sinister. At the landing, the woman nodded briefly to me before taking off at a speed I couldn't match, chasing that lost time.

This run was steeper, and I went after her slowly. I heard a scream as someone shot by at warp speed. ". . . outa my fucking way!" I heard.

After that, I hugged the right side of the run and frequently looked back—too frequently, as it turned out, for I failed to notice an icy patch and was suddenly on my back beneath a tree. I crabbed my way out into the middle of the run again and from then on just concentrated on getting down alive.

What are you trying to prove? I asked myself. You're afraid of the lift, you can't keep up with anyone, and they sure wouldn't wait around for you. You're alone up here, and if the purpose of these jaunts is to meet eligible men, well, do you see any around here? Only guy you've met today couldn't wait to get shed of you, and he was getting paid.

Near the first lift landing, I stopped to rest my shaking legs, then set out on the final run with more confidence. I had been here before, after all. I reached the bunny slope at last and pulled up behind the lodge. Down here I felt better, but no way would I get on that lift again. The bunny slope would have to do, although side-stepping my way back up to the top after every run was sweaty work.

Minuscule amount of honor salvaged, I turned the skis in at the rental counter. Three o'clock already. Our group was to meet in the parking lot at four. I headed down the hallway to the bar. What the hell: it's five o'clock somewhere.

Sunday brunch was remarkable for the excellence of the restaurant's food and my desire to eat almost none of it. I sipped on hot peppermint tea and stared across the table at Heather's boyfriend the helicopter pilot. He worked out of Redmond and had come down to be inspected by Heather's friends, which earned him at least a couple of points in my book. His tanned features were straight out of central casting: "Find me a helicopter pilot—think Harrison Ford only blond." He made Eric look like Don Knotts. He held hands with Heather beneath the table. Their shoulders touched. She hadn't been at the condo last night.

Matt sat on my left, cracking ice cubes with his strong white molars, jaw muscles working hard beneath his short black beard. "So, where you from?" he asked Cory. I looked back and forth at them, then across the table at Laura and Mary and Ethan, all of us mesmerized by the tableau. Laura, mother confessor to us all, shone with empathy for everyone: for Matt, as his heart was ripped out before our eyes; for Heather; for Cory, who didn't know what the hell was going on; and possibly even for me, who had never seen anything like this. Didn't

Heather know how Matt felt about her? Ethan sat chin in hand, one side of his mouth lifted. Oh yes, his half smile said. She knows what she's doing. Take the hint, Matt, and move on.

I slept through much of the long drive back to Happy Camp, stretched out on the back seat of the Subaru, the engine noise cutting in and out as I drifted in and out of sleep.

"Well, did you have a good time?" Ethan asked as I yawned and sat up at last. As though you care, I thought, but I knew, in that instant, that he did.

"It was interesting," I said. "Learned a few things."

"There's a bunch of us going to Sunriver for cross-country in a couple of weeks," Mary said.

"Laura's going to ride up with us," Ethan added. "You could come along."

I leaned back in the seat and put an embroidered satin pillow over my hot forehead. "Thanks, I'll think about it," I said.

I spent the next ten days at work trying not to run into Ethan or Mary in the halls, afraid that if Ethan winked at me and tilted his head with his "I dare you" look, I'd give in and go with them again. But they didn't press the invitation, and on Friday afternoon I sighed, picked up a pint of ice cream and an armful of videos, and went home.

"Ethan said he felt bad that he didn't nag you more about coming with us to Sunriver," Laura said to me a few days later. I shrugged and felt ungrateful. Maybe if I'd gone to Sunriver, I'd have met Mr. Wonderful. Or learned how to stop on cross-country skis without falling backward. Or something.

That should have been the end of my skiing career, but the intervening spring and summer and fall dimmed the bad memories, and now the gang was to spend New Year's at a resort called Fish Lake in the southern Cascades. Hope was gone, but the old pull survived, and I was curious, too. Heather had broken up with Cory ("He turned out to be a male chauvinist pig," she explained), and Matt, after a three-season romance with the woman in Medford, was on the loose again. If something was going to happen, I wanted to be there to see it.

The plan for the long weekend was cross-country skiing from several cabins beside a frozen lake. We stopped in Medford to rent skis and arrived at our cabins after dark. We made supper and played Trivial Pursuit, during which it turned out that I alone knew the name of the airplane that dropped the atomic bomb over Hiroshima. "Hey, I want her on our team next time," Terry said, and I laughed and looked at him a little more closely.

The next morning after breakfast, we attached skis to our feet and set off for the woods. Groomed trails wound through a series of steep, rounded hills, and I fell in behind Heather and Laura and three other women. The men went on ahead on a mostly uphill trek, stopping now and then to consult a trail map. "You can't get lost," Heather said. "All the loops end up back at the lodge."

At one trail junction, we saw the men coming toward us and took a break with them. We nibbled on snacks. Joints were lit, and the sweet smoke rose into the dazzling blue sky. When the group broke up, I watched Heather ski away with Matt. I followed Laura and we climbed again, for a long time. When the trail plunged downhill I fell behind, and then just fell, and fell, and fell. When I stopped to look around, I stared down a corridor flanked by ranks of evergreens, with the sun going down fast. I wasn't sure how far away the lodge was, but I felt cold and rather sorry for myself. My woolen long underwear was soaked with sweat. I looked up and saw a figure on skis coming toward me from the bottom of the hill. It looked male, and he was tall and lean and wore a red cap that looked like Matt's. My heart lifted. Maybe it was Matt. Maybe he had come back to check and see whether I was all right. Maybe Laura had met him and maybe she had looked back and said, "I hope Louise is all right," and maybe Matt had said, "I'll go check." Yes, that was it. I smiled to myself and set off to meet him, my skis pointing at each other, trying once more to snowplow. Usually this meant that I just got trapped in the parallel grooves worn by better skiers, then got going too fast, until my skis shot out in front of me, but this time I stayed upright until I reached the foot of the hill. I looked up at him, triumphant, proud that I had stayed on my feet in front of this chivalrous friend who would never love me but who had come back to make sure I was all right. I tried to think of something clever to say as I looked up and smiled into the eyes of . . . a total stranger.

"Hi," said the stranger as he schussed on past me.

"God, I'm an idiot," I said aloud and pushed on through the twilight. When the cabins hove in sight, I headed straight for mine, left my clothes in a soggy pile on the bathroom floor, stepped into a very hot shower, and stood there for a long time. I wrapped myself in my robe and sat down on the couch under the table lamp. It was full dark outside now, and I picked up a paperback edition of *To Kill a Mockingbird* from the end table and began to read under the pool of warm yellow light. I had read the book several times before, but for the first time I really heard the author's voice in my head, saw the precise beauty of a finely honed sentence, and rode on a wave of prose to a faraway world that, for all its faults, was at least warm. I need to stop playing this whole silly game, I thought, as my eyes closed and the book fell open on my chest.

"Aren't you coming to dinner?" Laura's voice shook me out of my nap.

"Oh, yeah, sure." I came awake and sat up. "Just getting dressed."

We walked down to the main cabin, toward food and drink and warmth and company. We made paper hats with funny sayings on them, and mine said "Scum Queen" for some reason having to do with a Steve Martin comedy sketch. Music blared and we danced, and once more I watched Matt dance with Heather, over and over. He seemed relaxed, and something about her was different, too, something that seemed to give Matt's eyes a new gleam. Perhaps she's changing her mind about him, I thought and yelled the idea in Laura's ear as we stood by ourselves in a corner, sipping eggnog and watching the dancers.

"Maybe," Laura shouted back. "But right after this, he's going to that forest engineering course with Ethan for three months, so who knows where they'll be when he comes back?"

"Well, he won't be with me," I said. "I dream about Matt a lot, but we're never in the sack. I've never even dreamed about him kissing me."

"Then it's not going to happen," Laura said.

"I know," I said.

When midnight came, we circled the room and hugged each other into 1986, and I didn't seize the chance, as I might have done once, to embrace Matt just a little longer. I hugged him hard for the space of two heavy heartbeats and then let go.

Ten years later, as the owner of a pair of new cross-country skis, a set of poles, and boots to match, I joined a trek with my husband and two of his friends. In crusty knee-deep snow, I fell down, lost skis, found skis, and remembered events I could tell no one. Five years after that, I followed a friend around a snowy golf course, bobbing along in her wake, most of the time with only one ski. Two years after the golf course fiasco, I spent fifteen minutes trying to attach a ski to a boot while sitting on a truck tailgate in my own driveway. Fuck it, I said at last. Fuck it forever. I went inside, pulled on my snow boots, and came back out again. I headed out across the field, one of the ski poles in my hand. It made, I discovered, a great walking stick.

CHAPTER 20

Nigel

Chuck and Debbie finally married in 1982, but his Forest Service career didn't last much longer. His early-onset glaucoma had grown much worse since we parted, and he managed to use its grim prognosis to obtain a medical disability retirement from the Forest Service. Still, he had his professional forester's license, earned at the cost of weeks of study and a written exam, and with it he began a wandering life as a consultant, as he and Debbie traveled up and down California in their travel trailer, accompanied by a cat.

Boots, the cat I'd adopted as a kitten before I met Chuck, once traveled back down the creek to Chuck's house after I moved out. Chuck called me when he showed up at their back door, and I went down to retrieve him. I saw Chuck and Debbie together for the first and only time and was catty enough to notice that Debbie had grown decidedly chunky since high school. Boots crouched behind Chuck's easy chair and hissed at their cat, which hissed back. I slipped him into a cat carrier and headed for the back door again, pausing to exchange the obligatory pleasantries. They were, Chuck told me, planning to rent the house out soon. Did I know Matt up in sale prep? Did I think he'd be a good tenant? The room whirled and I lost track of my feet. I assured him that Matt was a fine upstanding citizen and would take good care of the house. I sped back to my dwelling, dumped the cat out with a promise to keep him indoors for a week, had hysterics, a beer, and called Laura. "Do you think Matt will ever get together with Heather?" I said.

"Yes, if he has a brain in his head," she answered.

"Or if she does," I said.

A couple of weeks later, I drove down Indian Creek and saw Matt's car parked in Chuck's driveway. For a few seconds, I thought about stopping to offer advice about the quirks of the plumbing system but did not. Several weeks later, however, Chuck called me to announce that the oven element had burned out in his house. Could I get another one from the hardware store and take it up to Matt? Yes, I said into the mouthpiece. Yes, I could. No problem. No problem even if a bed of hot coals or broken glass stood in the way.

The next evening I stopped by, oven element in hand, to find Matt entertaining several friends from Ukonom. "Take a look around," Matt said. "You can tell me how it looks."

I wandered down the narrow hall toward the back bedrooms. Matt had a box spring and mattress, but no bed frame. Almost all of Chuck's furniture was gone except for the Franklin stove, the couch, the kitchen table and chairs, and the appliances. I came back to the kitchen, opened the oven door, pulled out the old element, and inserted the new one. I flipped the dials to turn the oven on. "I'll just turn it on and make sure it works," I said, sinking into a kitchen chair. This, I thought, is about as surreal as it gets. Matt's dog, an indeterminate setter mix named Rufus, plastered himself against my leg, begging to be petted.

"What do you think?" Matt said.

"Be careful about letting him out at night," I said. "The road's pretty close, and every once in a while some drunk runs into that oak tree out front. You could put him in the garden area, that's got a good fence."

"I meant about the oven," Matt said. I jumped up and opened the oven door. A wave of heat gushed out, masking my deep blush, and I looked at the glowing electrical element.

"Looks fine," I said. I flicked off the oven, eager now just to get away. "Lots of memories here," I said, conscious that I was just babbling. "Mostly bad." A ripple of laughter ran around the room, and as I waved hastily and backed out the door, several sets of eyes followed me. I wondered how much they knew. Everything, probably.

"Why the hell did I say that about the bad memories?" I said as I turned the truck around and, for the last time, drove out of Chuck's driveway.

In the early 1980s, the Forest Service in general and the Klamath National Forest in particular discovered that there existed in the world

people unhinged enough to want to work in the woods all summer
for ten dollars a day "subsistence" pay and the opportunity to gain
experience with the Forest Service. In an active fire season, they could
also earn six dollars an hour digging fire line. The volunteer program
meshed nicely with an initiative to bring European forestry students
to the States for the summer. The latter was run by Ernie Weinberg,
who had worked on the old Seiad District when I was in high school.
Born in Germany, then sent to school in England when being Jewish in
Germany grew dangerous, Ernie had retained his accent, which stood
him in good stead when he played Tevye the milkman in community
theater.

Some who lost their entire families in the Holocaust—Ernie never
saw his parents again—didn't want to go near Germany, but Ernie
maintained a lively contact with the forestry school at the University
of Freiburg, a connection that enabled a series of German forestry
students to spend a summer on the Klamath. In 1985, a young British
forester joined them. After secondary school, Nigel had gone not to a
university but to a forestry training course, after which he went to work
for the sponsoring company. His father, like Ernie a Kindertransport
refugee, had been at school with Ernie. Nigel's father remained in
England, anglicized his last name, married an Englishwoman, and
became a rather renowned scientist. He did not understand his son's
desire to work in the forest with a chainsaw.

I learned all this over the course of the summer. But in the
beginning, when two Germans and a Brit walked into the silviculture
office, I pegged Friedrich as a smartass and Dirck as a nerd, and my
jaw dropped at the sight of Nigel. I still carried a heavy torch for Matt,
but I also had a pulse. With his square jaw, curly black hair, lively
brown eyes, olive skin, blinding teeth, and nicely muscled arms poking
out of a sleeveless T-shirt, Nigel was built to make the heart of any
woman not in a coma beat a tad faster.

"Yikes," Laura said as we watched the group continue down the
hall.

"Oh, yeah," I said. "This should be a fun summer."

The boys moved from one department to another over the course
of the summer, and between work and barbecues, I started to learn
more about them. Friedrich had grown up near Mannheim Airbase in

the Frankfurt area, and his English was very good. A natural mimic, he could drop into a flawless midwestern twang in midsentence. His haircut gave him away as a European, but that changed once he started to visit the Happy Camp barber. Dirck, a child of divorce, was born in South Africa of a British mother and a German father and raised on two continents. Gangly and talkative, he had a more artistic and verbal temperament than an analytic one, but he was eager to learn the American trees, and he could keep up with anyone in the woods. Nigel was quiet but possessed of a sarcastic wit, and nothing about the work seemed to surprise him. All of them were alternately amused and appalled by the habits of Americans.

Eating in the truck, for example. Our habit of constantly sipping at a cup of coffee or tea in the truck in the mornings, and driving with a can of soda clenched between our thighs in the afternoons, made them shake their heads, as did stopping for a bag of chips and a burrito at the store before heading out to the woods. "In Germany," Dirck said primly one day, "people don't eat in their autos."

At the time, I was driving up Cade Mountain and shoving handfuls of Doritos into my mouth. Shamed, I slipped the bag down beside the door, took a final swig of my Coke—dammit, now it'd be warm by the time we reached the thinning units—and placed both hands on the steering wheel. I caught Nigel's grin out of the corner of my eye and started to explain the plan for the afternoon.

The tools and practices of American silviculture didn't differ much from the British varieties, although at home Nigel's job entailed working alongside the company crews after also planning the work. His company was hired to manage plantations of conifers in private ownership, and as he showed me some photos, I realized that most of the trees were Douglas-firs: American immigrants.

"The only native conifers in the UK are Scotch pine and yew," he said. "And a lot of the first Douglas-firs brought in were from ornamental stock and didn't have good timber genetics. That's why the big trees in this picture are so lumpy at the base. It's better now."

"Well, they should grow fast over there, with all that rain," I said.

Nigel was soon going out on small lightning fires—which didn't faze him although he had never seen one before—and running chainsaws. Nor did it seem to bother him that trees larger than any he had ever seen might fall on his head. With the sangfroid of a Dick Francis hero, he had the skills to make bravery seem ordinary. Nothing bothered him out there, his bunkhouse mates told me—nothing. They were clearly impressed.

Now and then, however, I caught a glimpse of something that told me he came from a very different place. Once, as a group of us ate lunch near Sulfur Springs at the head of Elk Creek, someone asked him how it felt to be in such a big country after growing up in a small one. Nigel looked up, and his eyes flashed below his long black lashes. "Actually," he said in a quiet-but-deadly tone, "England's a big country. It's just that this place is so bloody ridiculous."

Utter silence descended on the lunch group, until Gary started to laugh. "Well, at least we don't name any of our kids 'Nigel'!" he said as we threw fir cones at him.

A couple of events over the summer made me realize how life in an intensely class-conscious polity had shaped him. One day the sound of an English accent from the front desk area drew me out of the hall to peek at a couple of middle-aged tourists. The man spoke in a voice straight out of Masterpiece Theatre as he told all and sundry that he owned a considerable amount of woodland in Dorset. I knew that was near Nigel's stomping grounds. He was talking to Robert, who had suddenly gone all I-went-to-Purdue-and-have-been-to-Europe, as the two of them exchanged names and credentials.

Later that day, when Nigel came in with the sale prep crew, I mentioned the visitor's name to him and asked whether his company had done any work for him. "Oh, yes, we know him," Nigel said. "Pompous ass. Doesn't know a lot but thinks he does," and I laughed all the way down the hall.

A few days later, at a barbecue at the lower station, Nigel met a young Englishwoman traveling with a group of kayakers. I watched as she and Nigel exchanged pleasantries. They seemed to know a great deal about one another. I asked him about this a couple of beers later, and he laughed. "It's true," he said. "We can tell, just from the way the other person speaks, where they're from, where they went to school, and how much money their parents have." And he told me all about the stranger's antecedents, region, education, and money.

"Can't you tell that about other Americans?" he said.

"Not exactly," I said. "At least, not with that much precision. I can tell whether someone's from the South or the Northeast, but usually not exactly where. And so many Americans have this flat midwestern accent, it can be hard to tell. A person's car tells you more about how much money they have, but not always." I told him about a young forester who spent a few years in Happy Camp. "He went to Andover—a fancy prep school in the Northeast—but I didn't know that till later. He lived in the barracks and sounded like everybody else. He drove a dented Chevy pickup. One day someone sneaked a peek in his top drawer and found a huge stack of uncashed government paychecks. The kid's parents were stinking rich and he had a trust fund." I took another swig of beer. "Like you said, it's just that this place is so bloody ridiculous."

Throughout the summer, many of us tried to give the boys a crash course in Americana. I taught them how to shoot a revolver, introduced them to horseback riding, and chauffeured them over Grayback Road to the drive-in movies in Cave Junction. They went swimming in Clear Creek and fishing in the river. They went out on river patrols with Dave and learned about rubber rafts and canoes and kayaks. George and Alice had them over for dinner. Nigel attended the Wednesday night poker games. Dirck and Nigel accompanied me to the county fair in Yreka one evening after work, where we hit all the rides and ate all the food, then closed down the Rex Club before driving back downriver. We all made it to work by seven that morning.

"Strange," Nigel said to me as I navigated the river road. "Petrol here costs half what it does in the UK, but the beer is twice as expensive and half as good. Why is that?"

I had no answer. I thought Coors was good beer.

One evening, as Nigel and I arrived at the lower station from a stint on separate crews during a lightning bust, he seemed so glad to see me and stood so close that I had a moment of soaring hope. Was it possible that he wanted to spend some time with me alone? I asked him whether he wanted to go fishing that evening. He looked at me, then away. "No," he said. "I'm pretty tired."

"Oh, okay," I said. I picked up my backpack and headed for my truck. Stupid, stupid, stupid. When would I learn not to actually invite rebuffs? Still, summer was ending, and a great-looking guy who had not yet turned me down was just about to leave for his home country. What did I have to lose? He'd be gone soon, and I'd never see him again.

"How about tomorrow after work?" he called out, and I turned around.

"Sure," I said. "I'll pick you up at the station."

Just in case, I plucked my eyebrows, shaved my legs, wore deodorant and new undies. But he made no advance as we drove downriver to the mouth of Clear Creek. Maybe it's just British reserve, I thought. Whatever the hell that is. We split up and worked up and down the river with our fishing poles, casting out into the riffles and letting the wet flies drift down into the eddies. We didn't catch anything, although both of us got strikes. As visibility waned and evening came on with its mosquitoes and croaking frogs, we met back at the truck and began to take our poles apart. I took a deep breath and informed Nigel that he'd be welcome to come home with me. He said nothing for a bit, just looked down at the sand between his feet, watching so as not to crush the hatchling toads that hopped everywhere this time of year. "I really appreciate the offer," he finally began, "but I'll have to say no. I promised Jocelyn . . ."

"Jocelyn?" I said.

"My girlfriend," he said.

"That you'd behave yourself in the States?"

"Yes."

"Okay." I exhaled. "Well, better get you back to the bunkhouse," I said. And that, I thought, must be that. I knew how these things went. Once you propositioned a guy and he turned you down, he never wanted to see you again. So I'd better say something now. Hands clutching the steering wheel as we passed Wingate Bar, I spoke.

"I apologize for that," I said. "I'm really sorry."

"You don't need to apologize," he said, and his slight laugh sounded genuinely surprised.

I dropped Nigel off at the lower station, went home, drank two stiff gin and tonics just the way he had taught me to make them ("always keep gin in the freezer compartment," he told me), and fell asleep on the couch listening to the soundtrack to *The Empire Strikes Back*.

At seven o'clock the next morning a pounding on the front door woke me, and when I flung it open, Nigel and Dirck stood on the front porch. Nigel wore a wide grin. Is it my jammies? I wondered—and as Dirck began to speak, I knew that he and Nigel had cooked something up between them.

"Would you like to drive up to the Oregon coast with us?" Dirck asked. Nigel added, as he saw my mouth hanging open, "He means, would you be so kind as to haul us around in your truck for a few days and show us the sights?"

And that, I realized, was the real difference between American men and their cousins across the pond. I had propositioned Nigel and he had said no, but far from being insulted, he had evidently been both mildly flattered and unafraid, as if I had tried to hand him a cookie. And at that moment, my feelings for him escalated from attraction and admiration to genuine affection. Damn Jocelyn anyway, I thought. I could fall in love with this guy.

"Come on in," I said.

I made a pot of Earl Grey and set out cups, milk, and sugar. Nigel looked at it all with something akin to wonder. I set the pot on the table and started to toast some English muffins. Hesitantly, Nigel poured a mugful of tea, added milk and sugar, took a tentative sip, then practically drained the cup.

"Is it okay?" I asked.

He nodded, his eyes wide. If I had known this would be on the menu . . . they seemed to say. I laughed and tilted my head at him. He looked at the toasted muffins. "What are those?" Nigel asked. I showed him the package.

"English muffins?" he read.

"You don't have these in England?"

"Definitely not. Whatever they are, they aren't English. However," he added hastily, "they are good, whatever they are."

I left the boys slurping up tea and scraping the last of the strawberry jam out of a jar while I fled to the bedroom and dressed, then started packing.

We spent four days roaming the tourist meccas of Oregon: Oregon Caves, Crater Lake, Bend, the coast. Thanks to Oregon's excellent system of state parks, good camping spots were easy to find. The canopy on my Chevy LUV had a raised plywood platform where I slept while the boys bunked down below. Dirck, sliding clever looks from one to the other of us, tried to convince Nigel to move upstairs, but we both shook our heads and threw things at him. A deal was a deal. Jocelyn, you would have been proud of us.

Toward the end of Matt's time in Chuck's house, something tragic nearly happened to him, and when I heard about it years later, I tried to imagine what it must have been like for him.

Matt woke in the night, shivering on the rug in front of the Franklin stove, which had gone out. Rain hammered the roof, and he realized what—besides the cold—had awakened him: the frantic barking of a dog. He stood up and walked to the back door, flipped on the porch light, and yelled out into the wet night, "Rufus! Rufus!" From farther away now, he heard the barking again. Grumbling at the troublesome mutt, Matt found a flashlight, shrugged into a hooded sweatshirt, and walked out into the rain, pausing now and again to try to pinpoint the barking. It came, he realized, from Indian Creek. Away from the house, the noise of rain was muted, but the creek louder than ever. Not surprising, he thought, it's been raining all day; we must have gotten a couple of inches. He swung the beam of the flashlight around, yelling again and again for the dog as he walked through wet grass toward the lip of the gorge and the rising creek. He squatted on the edge and played the beam across the creek, and now he saw the lousy mongrel—running back and forth on a rock ledge, across the creek.

"How the hell did you get over there?" he shouted. "Come on, boy, come on!" But Rufus just kept barking and barking and making little running starts at the slapping waves, too scared to jump in and swim.

Maybe if I wade out a little bit, Matt thought. He worked his way down the rock face with the aid of the flashlight and the memory of summer swims. He stuck a sneakered foot into the water. The current was strong, but not right by the shore. He knew a gravel bar reached far out into the streambed. If I can just encourage Rufus to jump in and swim, he thought, I can snag him and get him over here. But Rufus, the cowardly bugger, refused. He got his toes into the water, but that was about it. Matt felt ahead with one foot, inching farther out. Suddenly the current caught him and swept his feet out from under him, and he flailed against the water, trying not to be swept downstream. Something long and dark flashed by, riding the first high water of winter: a log with limbs attached, ready to bash anything in its path.

I could die out here, he thought. I could die, and no one—not my parents, not Heather—would ever know where I went or what happened to me, and it would all be for nothing, all those endless days cutting brush in the rain, all the arguing about timber volumes and sale boundaries, all the waiting and hoping for that promotion to GS-9, all those years of commuting from Somes Bar. It would all come down to a guy who goes missing and drowns trying to retrieve a worthless dog. He thought of the people who drowned in the Klamath or its tributaries and were never found. With all his strength he thrust himself backward and twisted, lunging for the rocks behind him, bashing the flashlight against the rocks in the process. The beam went out. He clung to the slick rock, shivering, while Rufus barked on and on across the creek. Smart dog, Matt thought.

He saw the shine of the porch light, hazy in the rain. He drew in his breath and gave one final encouraging yell across Indian Creek, then crawled, dripping, up toward the fuzzy glow and made his way back to the house. He shed his sopping clothes on the kitchen linoleum, padded naked into the living room, and built up the fire. He navigated the hallway, shivering so violently his hands could barely grab a blanket off the bed. He lay down again before the stove, wrapped in the blanket, and at last his chattering teeth stilled and he fell asleep.

Hours later, a scratching at the back door woke him. Rufus came in wet, but from rain, not swimming. The dog, he realized, had gone downstream, crossed the Doolittle Bridge, then run back up the road. "Asshole," he said to the dog and went to get a towel.

I've got to get out of here, Matt thought. I almost drowned tonight, and Happy Camp sucks. This isn't home. I've got to get out of here.

Farther upstream, a woman who had lived beneath Klamath skies almost all her life woke briefly to the hammer of rain on the roof and the roar of Indian Creek below. She listened to their rhythms for a few minutes before she fell back asleep. You need to go, they seemed to say. You need to go.

CHAPTER 21

Getting Out

Several months before I began to work for the Forest Service, a sociologist named Gene Bernardi, at the Southwest Forest and Range Experiment Station in Berkeley, filed a discrimination complaint, charging that she had been denied a promotion because of her sex. (In the early 1970s, women made up only 2 percent of full-time professionals in the Forest Service.) The case wound its slow way through the courts and finally landed before Judge Samuel Conti, who expanded the case to a class action suit encompassing all the women who worked for the Forest Service in region 5 (California and Hawaii). The court found that women were severely underrepresented in many jobs and pay grades.

The experiment stations were the research arm of the Forest Service, and we didn't think about them much unless we read the scientific papers they produced, which most of us didn't. Each region had one—region 5's was headquartered in Berkeley, across the bay from the regional office in San Francisco. Both might as well have been on a distant planet as far as we were concerned.

But in 1981, Bernardi's almost-forgotten case vomited up something called a consent decree, which gave the region five years to bring the number of women employees in those underrepresented grades and job series up to 43 percent—a number based on the percentage of women in California's civilian workforce. Out on the national forests, agency leaders were both livid and mystified. How was such a thing to be done? The Forest Service already labored under severe constraints as to how many people it could hire, and from where it could hire them. The Reagan administration had placed a freeze on hiring and promotions.

202

When the ramifications of the consent decree began filtering down to district rangers, I was serving a term as the Federal Women's Program representative for our district. My duties consisted chiefly of holding a monthly lunch meeting, where a handful of women complained about the Forest Service's hidebound bureaucracy and wondered whether a woman would ever become a district ranger. At the monthly safety meetings, I updated a captive audience on FWP news (chiefly national) after all the department heads spoke. But one day the ranger gave me custody of a flip chart and a felt pen and charged me with explaining the entire consent decree to the slack-jawed masses.

I didn't look forward to it. Most of my women colleagues were proud of what they had accomplished. We had made progress, without a great deal of overt hostility from the men. We feared that anything called a decree would upend all that. We all wanted promotions for women, but not at the expense of the males we worked with, some of whom were our friends, and all of whom were colleagues that I, at least, felt I could depend on. Jim and I, for instance, had been promoted in lockstep with one another under Bill Jones's tutelage; I didn't want to jump ahead of him simply because I was a woman.

My audience was friendly that day. Most seemed puzzled as to how such a thing would work given the current constraints on hiring. The Forest Service was known far and wide as a "can-do outfit," which was true up to a point. But given a mission that many believed to be unattainable, some line officers simply wouldn't try very hard. I also didn't discount the effect of plain old misogyny, since I had experienced it myself. The Klamath was better than many other national forests, and field-going women already on board found it fairer. Yet our own engineering department, judging from what Helen told me, was rife with discrimination. Engineers didn't work for the district but for the forest supervisor. For women clerical workers, as always, the glass ceiling was both low and thick.

What I heard at that meeting was dismay from women who wanted fairness in promotions but didn't want to be seen as some sort of quota. Some men feared surviving the lean years only to lose out on a permanent job or a promotion to a woman. "If I'm the best candidate, why shouldn't I get the job?" one asked. "It's not my fault they weren't fair to that woman in Berkeley."

With the consent decree, I knew, it would be harder for a district or department to promote a good male candidate. Yet hiring "off the street" directly into a job in a professional series remained virtually impossible, too.

Five years later, the attorneys for the plaintiff went back to court: the Forest Service, they said, hadn't held up its end of the bargain. Government attorneys retorted that the agency didn't have the tools to bring new people into the agency, so that temporary employees could apply for the professional jobs for which they were qualified by education. Forest Service line officers blamed the Department of Agriculture. The Department of Agriculture blamed the Justice Department. The judge was not amused and extended the consent decree.

The Justice Department agreed to the penalties assigned by a magistrate judge for missing the deadline. She recommended that a fund be set up to ensure compliance, do monitoring, and extend the decree for another three years.

That brought the deadline out to 1989, but the numbers hadn't changed much by then, so the class attorneys filed a motion alleging contempt, since the Forest Service hadn't complied with the decree. The decree was extended to 1991, and at last the Forest Service started to get creative, but only after Judge Conti threatened to appoint a personnel administrator to take over all Forest Service hiring.

Achieving 43 percent women in each of the many pay grades and job series in the Forest Service was a stern challenge. Simply dumping some male employees to make room was against civil service regulations. The clerical and administrative series remained overrepresented, but even there, the numbers of women dropped off sharply in the higher grades.

One of the practical hurdles to hiring more professional women was the difficulty of bringing in professionals from outside the agency. I had been hired that way: I drove into Sacramento and took a written clerical examination (they took my word for my typing speed, thank God), passed it with a high score, and was placed on a civil service roster for all the federal agencies in California. This was how new clerical people were hired, and once hired, after the year-long probationary period, they became career-conditional employees, then career employees after three years. But foresters and other professionals had to wait for a roster for their specific profession to open and then apply to get on it. Back in the 1960s, the forester roster was almost always open, but starting in the late 1970s it opened only rarely, and for such brief periods that an applicant without an SF-171 (the federal employment application form) ready to go was left at the starting gate.

Many forestry school graduates looking for a career position signed on as seasonals or took a term appointment lasting from one to three years as they waited for a roster to open. Some languished for years, cobbling together a living, with marriage and children often complicating their lives in the meantime.

In my case, once classified as a career-conditional employee, I could apply for any job for which I met the X-118s, the requirements listed in the Forest Service's job classification handbook. But seasonal and term employees couldn't apply for a professional position unless the roster for that position was opened.

Sometimes the consent decree did work in favor of a male employee. One case on the district involved a seasonal employee, injured on the job and unable to work in the woods anymore. He was hired on as a GS-1 clerk. Clerks could be hired without taking the clerical exam if they started at the GS-1 level. After a year, they could be promoted to GS-2, then GS-3 after another year. As a permanent employee, they could then apply for any job for which they were qualified.

But this didn't help women or men without a degree, or with a degree in the humanities, even if they had years of experience in forestry. So region 5 and the University of California at Santa Cruz came up with another idea. "What if," they said, "we set up a program to push students through a four-year forestry program in two years? Many of these people already have some college credits. What if we paid tuition for others to go to college in the off-season? We could get more women who already work for the agency into the higher grades."

"And what if we allow anyone who meets the X-118s to apply for any job that we fly?"

Wow, what a concept. And that, boys and girls, is what happens when an agency is left with no option except to do the right thing.

Some Happy Camp employees carpooled down to Santa Cruz every two weeks, while Laura and I attended the winter sessions over on the coast at Humboldt State, with our tuition paid, starting in the fall of 1985. I was also able to work part time at the Arcata station of the Pacific Southwest Forest and Range Experiment Station, a branch of the very outfit that had gotten the whole consent decree rolling in the first place. Laura studied for her degree in forest management, which meant forestry and calculus and statistics. I picked up enough credits to qualify in the range conservationist series, taking less math but more botany.

Why range conservation? you ask. Why not forestry? Why not build on the knowledge of silviculture I already had, the profession that I had worked so hard to learn? It boiled down, as many things did in those days, to Matt.

Four years after that horrid weekend on the coast, he still lived rent-free in my head, every day. All his flaws, the ones that Laura had helpfully pointed out to me, remained just as true as ever, and as time went on I recognized them more fully. But over those years I also saw him work and sometimes worked with him. And Matt was simply one of the best foresters I had ever seen. He might shout and wave his arms when he thought something wasn't right with the way a proposed timber sale was coming together. But all the people he worked with upstairs either liked or respected him or both. He took pride in his hard-won knowledge and resented it when he or his coworkers were second-guessed by line officers who outranked him.

"There's two kinds of district rangers," he said once. "There's the kind who realize that they're really administrators, and they give their employees what they need to do their jobs and get out of the way. Then there's the kind who has a hobby, and God help you if that hobby is your department."

That Matt wasn't in it just for the paycheck, that he cared about the work, everyone knew. Whether you called it dedication or a work ethic or a mind that created its own excitement, it told me that Matt would go quite far in the Forest Service. The men and women who worked with Matt listened to him. Their eyes swiveled toward him when a decision had to be made. I saw him for what he was—not just a pretty face, or a fellow Red Sox fan, or someone who had actually seen those haunting New England landscapes—but a combination of mental agility and toughness and love of the game of life that would take him beyond Happy Camp.

When we love someone, we want them to love us back. Why? Shouldn't just sending love out be enough for us? But it seldom is. We want something in return. We want vindication—approval, if you like—from another human being. We want our existence to be valued by someone we value. In our childhoods, we link that desire for approval to our parents; in adulthood, we seek out a living representation of the love we got—or didn't get—from them. We couch it in the language of sex or romance, but what we really seek is recognition of ourselves as worthy, from someone we see as worthy. Raised to believe that I could have anything I wanted if I was just willing to work hard enough, I crashed headlong in my thirties into something I could not work for, earn, or win. Unlike the fox in the fable, I didn't conclude, therefore, that the grapes were sour. I decided that I had to leave the vineyard, even though I loved it, too, beyond all reason.

I knew that Matt would not stay in Happy Camp forever. He was a journeyman now and could go anywhere. He had made a good impression on several more-senior timber beasts who had moved on from the Klamath and were now in management positions on other national forests in other regions. Matt would be gone before long, but whether he was here or not, I wanted to move on to a place where no memories dwelt and, most importantly, where our paths would never cross. The trick was how to do that.

I'd been working in the silviculture department for ten years. I was a GS-7 forestry technician and had the secondary title of contracting officer's representative. I wrote contracts for planting and thinning and spraying and hand grubbing, laid out units on the ground, and administered the contracts. I met with contractors and the contracting officer in Yreka. I waded through wet brush in the rain with a partner, dragging a measuring tape as we mapped units with compass, clinometer, and Redy-Mapper.

I argued with foremen and was once threatened with mayhem by a three-hundred-pound Tongan thinner wielding a chainsaw. I broadened my knowledge of silviculture and learned more about keeping baby trees alive. I was a licensed pesticide applicator. Thanks to supervisors who thought any training was good, I attended short courses on logging methods and second-growth management. And now, after all my initial struggles, after all the learning and broadening of experience and achievement awards and praise from people I respected, and with the promise of a job for as long as I wanted one, I wanted to leave silviculture behind and do something else that didn't involve trees. That turned out to be range management, simply because when I was out on a forest range allotment measuring grass and looking at cows, I didn't think about Matt at all, and the sadness with which I had grappled for several years began to lift.

Sadness was a very old acquaintance of mine, but it had never before been so lengthy and intractable. It vanished, though, whenever I rode a horse in the meadows near Mount Eddy or in the Trinity Alps, watching cattle that belonged to Alice's old friend Ethel. Up in those alpine meadows, I didn't think about Matt. The sights and sounds and smells of horses and cattle and cowbells and wild meadow vegetation washed over me and I lived in older rhythms, no faster than a horse could travel. Time was marked by sunrise and sunset; distance in the hours it took to ride from Bear Creek Cabin to Toad Lake, or to follow the trails from Big Flat to the Dorleska Mine and Battle Creek. Weather was more important than sadness, a missing heifer more noteworthy than heartbreak. And after a few days of saddles and hobbles and deciphering cow tracks, I forgot about everything else. It might as well have been 1930, and I not even born yet. And even after all the cows were moved to new pastures or corralled and shipped back to the valley at the end of the October roundup, I carried with me, for days on end, a sense of calm and freedom. I could do at least some of this for a living, but first I needed more range management courses and more range experience.

Hence, Humboldt State. Hence (since Happy Camp had virtually no range allotments), a detail to the Oak Knoll Ranger District, where the range specialist was a woman who needed help doing range analysis and writing allotment management plans.

Moving Ethel's cows near Mount Eddy, Shasta-Trinity National Forest, October 1985.

Whenever I saw Matt again, especially after an absence, the jolt of the heart was as strong as ever, although I flattered myself that I appeared perfectly indifferent to him. One spring day in 1986—it was spring break at Humboldt, and I was home for a week—some trees needed to be hauled out to a planting site, and I found myself in a green pickup truck with Matt. He backed the Dodge up to the tree cooler, and we packed the bed full of the big heavy paper bags. We scrambled back into the truck, he turned the key, and the engine labored and refused to catch. He cranked the key again. Nothing. He slammed his hands against the steering wheel over and over, uttering howls of utter anguish and frustration. "Aaaauuuugh! No, no, no, no!" he yelled. I sat staring at him, coffee cup in hand, frozen in place. I knew what was wrong—with the truck—and pulled the mechanical pencil from my shirt pocket. "It's okay, it's okay," I said. "I know what it is. Pop the hood." I slid out of the cab and ran around to the front of the truck, reached under the green hood, and worked the latch open the rest of the way.

I spun the wing nut atop the air cleaner lid, lifted it off, and stuck the mechanical pencil into the metal flap in the middle. "Okay, now try it," I said and stepped around to the driver's side. I knew better than to stand in front of the truck. Once, Chuck had tried the same trick on his Ford when it stalled in front of the post office, but he left his head under the hood, the better to see the result. I cranked the engine per his instructions and was rewarded by a gout of flame that leaped out and singed his beard and eyebrows. But today, the engine played nice and merely turned over and purred. Matt looked at me, his arm resting on the open window frame. "Thanks," he muttered.

"This one does that sometimes," I said. I slammed down the hood, climbed back in, and rescued my coffee cup from the dashboard.

Shortly after that, Matt and Heather—to the general rejoicing of the multitudes—became an item at last. Laura and I were finishing up the term at Humboldt when the event occurred, so we didn't hear about it immediately. I learned of it one summer evening after Heather had invited me to go with her to the Britt Music Festival in Jacksonville. As she drove us over the Grayback Road into Oregon, she told me how Matt had finally confessed to her how he felt, and how she had at last told him that she felt much the same. As she talked, I leaned against the passenger side door and looked at her flowing skirt and her smooth tanned legs, her bare foot on the gas pedal. I found myself laughing as she told me a few details, even as tears pricked my eyes. But to my own surprise, what I felt was a reasonable approximation of happiness and relief for them. I looked at her and smiled and said, "I'm so happy for you both—it's about time!" and I meant it. It was over.

Late in the fall, Heather became pregnant, but I didn't figure it out until most of her other friends already knew. For me, the penny dropped one day shortly after Bert put together a crew to do some gopher baiting on a couple of high-elevation clear-cuts near Grayback Mountain. Gopher baiting involved inserting a few pellets of cyanide-laced grain into active gopher tunnels to minimize rodent damage to the conifer seedlings. In winter, gophers often tunneled under the snow and chewed on them. Bert had done this work often in eastern Idaho, but it was new to us. He taught us how to home in on a fresh gopher mound, locate the tunnel on one side of it, insert a special tube into the tunnel, and press a lever that dropped in the poisoned grain. The trick then was to block the hole made by the tube with a rock or chunk of wood so that no light entered the tunnel. If the little rodent saw light, he would immediately push dirt into the tunnel to close it off, without eating the grain.

Bert was nothing if not thorough, so he also encouraged us to drop poison into the burrows of the mountain beavers that lived in these high-elevation habitats. Mountain beavers—*Aplodontia rufa*—are not beavers but are from an ancient line of rodents that has survived in these mountains for millions of years. But for Bert, they were just something that might chew on a baby tree, so they must die, too.

"I guess you must have had a lot of experience doing this," Taylor said to him one day as we moved in catatonic lockstep across the damaged landscape.

"Yes, yes, I have," Bert said and proceeded to tell a few stories about baiting gophers in the immense lodgepole pine clear-cuts near Yellowstone National Park.

"Huh," Taylor said, sounding impressed. "I guess by now you must be a real master baiter."

As laughter rippled across the hillside, Bert cleared his throat and moved deliberately away from us. The only one not laughing was Heather, sleeping in the last green pickup to arrive. She had ridden up with Taylor. "I hated to wake her up," he said. Her cheek was plastered against the window, her mouth open in a gentle snore. Somehow, she managed to make even that look attractive.

When we broke for lunch and pulled our packs out of the back of the trucks, she came awake to the noise and emerged, grinning apologetically and sipping ginger ale from a half-empty plastic bottle. I think she would have been all right, but then the lid of a sardine can popped open and was peeled back. Her cheeks went from a postsleep flush to dead white, and she lurched to her feet and fled behind a truck. The unmistakable sound of vomiting reached us. I put down my container of tapioca pudding, suddenly not hungry.

"Why didn't you tell me?" I said to Laura over the phone that evening.

"I was afraid it might upset you," she said.

"Oh, that ship sailed a long time ago," I said.

Despite what my grandmother would have termed her interesting condition, Heather and Matt did not cohabit for some time. "When are you guys going to get married?" someone asked Matt one day. He laughed and shrugged. "I don't know," he said. "I can't even get her to move in with me." Once more, I was astounded at the sheer feisty independence of the woman. "She's been with other guys and never got knocked up," I said to Laura. "She must be sure he's the one. Why hesitate?" And we agreed that we did not know.

Late in October 1986, the Red Sox lost a heartbreaker of a World Series in classic Red Sox fashion. After several hours of catatonic thumb sucking, I searched my baseball library for quotes about the Sox. I found a sentence by Thomas Boswell that I scribbled on a notepad. "The Red Sox," Boswell wrote, "have long memories. It is their curse. They are an imaginative team—more's the pity—susceptible to hauntings and collective nervous breakdowns. They prove that those who cannot forget the past are also condemned to repeat it."

It wasn't a quote designed to cheer anyone up, but I took an odd comfort in the words and carried them with me as I stuck my head into Matt's office the next day to commiserate. He sat at his desk, face buried in the crook of an elbow, but lifted his head when I spoke.

"But why," Matt said, "couldn't McNamara have put Clemens in, instead of all those losers? It's not like there was going to be a tomorrow. What was wrong with him?"

I had no answers, so I slid the Boswell quote across the desk at him, clucked sympathetically, and left. But that week, one of the Forest Service houses across the river came vacant. George made it clear that this time, the house was reserved for Matt and Heather. And so they began their real life together.

That winter, my mission at Arcata completed, I started haunting the printer that spit out the daily vacancy notices for Forest Service jobs across the country, my eyes looking for that magical series number: 454—range conservationist.

CHAPTER 22

Looking Back

Cattle die, kinsmen die,
Even you yourself will leave this world.
But one thing I know that never dies:
The judgement on a dead man.
—Hávamál

In the fall of 1968, my stepfather was promoted to timber management officer on the Happy Camp District, and my parents sold their house in Seiad Valley and moved into a government house on Curly Jack Road, across the river from Happy Camp. The place was dark with the shade of tall firs all around, wedged in between the road and a steep hillside. On winter nights the river roared below. I came home from college in the midst of my sophomore year to Christmas vacation in a house I didn't know. Very early on Christmas Eve, I awoke to the peculiar silence of heavy snow and the absolute darkness of a power outage. I heard a muffled thump behind the house and followed Mother's flashlight beam to stand beside her at the kitchen window.

"A little tree fell over on the garbage cans," Mother said, and then we heard the front door open and saw another flashlight beam swing up through the cottony flakes. Dad came back inside and met four pairs of eyes clustered in the living room.

"Better get dressed and go next door to Hamilton's," he said. "There's two big trees leaning over the house."

Marian Hamilton clutched her robe against her chest and looked at us with wild eyes as we stood on her back porch, then beckoned us into her kitchen while Wes, the district ranger, built a fire in the brick fireplace. The clock on the mantelpiece ticked away and pointed toward four o'clock. We sat in the firelight and dozed while the black sky turned gray. Tom and the three Hamilton kids—a boy and two girls—surrounded themselves with toys in a corner of the room.

Mother and Marian cooked breakfast on the propane stove while Dad and Wes stomped around the yard and peered up at the danger: two Douglas-firs, four feet across at the base, crossed like swords above our roof, and weighed down by mounds of fresh wet snow. While we ate bacon and scrambled eggs, they discussed what to do. "Any way to cut them down?" Wes said, deferring to Dad's years as a timber faller.

Dad shook his head. "Not until we get the snow load off—they'd barber chair on us," he said, referring to an accident in which the butt of a tree splits lengthwise, sweeps up and out, and can strike the faller a fatal blow.

"If we could knock the snow off . . ." Wes said, then grinned. "I'll get my shotgun."

While Liz and I retrieved our sleds from the toolshed and dragged Tom and the Hamilton kids around the driveway, Dad fetched his deer rifle, two boxes of shells, and a blanket. He placed them on the picnic table under the carport behind the Hamilton back door and sat down on the bench. With the blanket folded to make a rest for the barrel of the .284, he lowered his head to sight through the scope and dry-fired a couple of times. The green and brown cap I knitted for him at college sat above his ears, which were stuffed full of Kleenex. He worked the bolt, slid one of the shiny shells into the chamber, and we heard the clean metallic slide and click as he closed the bolt again. We gathered behind him and watched with our hands over our ears as he aimed up through the falling snow. The report bounced across the river and rolled back. The lowest fir branch fell with a silent swoop, dark and feathery beneath its load of snow.

"Yeah, John!" Wes clapped him on the back, then shoved two shells into his own double-barreled twelve-gauge, stepped out to the side of the carport, and pointed it at a mound of snow on another branch. White powder exploded. Tom and the Hamilton boy started to run toward the fallen branch, but Dad called them back. "All you kids keep behind us," he said. "This is going to take a while."

He pulled several shells from one of the boxes and packed the rifle's magazine, then bent his head to the scope again. One by one, the branches fell from the burdened trees, alternately from one groaning giant and the other. He never missed. Whorls of severed branches marched up the trunks. When his first box of ammunition was empty, he set the rifle down to allow the barrel to cool. Wes rummaged in his closets for more shotgun shells.

The snow stopped at noon, and as Mother and Marian broiled hamburgers over a grill in the fireplace, we heard the swish of tire chains as a Forest Service truck churned up into the driveway. Bill Cadola, the fire control officer, stomped the snow off his boots and stepped through the back door. "People keep coming by and asking who those crazy guys shooting at trees are," he said. A few minutes later, he drove away shaking his head. "I'll get the crew over here next week and get those trees out of your way," he called as he backed down the driveway.

"Meaning he'll get the crew to rebuild his woodpile," Dad said to Wes.

By midafternoon, the trees stood scalped but vertical, two dark spears on either side of the house. The power was still off, but we spent that night in our own beds, bundled up and with extra blankets on top. "No more electric heat," Dad said to Mother. "As soon as we can get out to town, we're getting a wood stove."

The next morning, as soon as Tom discovered what Santa Claus had left for him, we gathered up the rest of the presents from under the tree and scuttled over to Hamilton's to warm up.

I was lost in the South Pacific with Mr. Roberts when I heard the grumble of a chainsaw and knew that Dad and Wes wouldn't surrender the fun of a little timber falling to Cadola and his minions. I ran out in time to see a cloud of sawdust under Dad's knees as he carved a back cut into the tree below the house. A few minutes later, he dropped it parallel to the driveway, where it settled with a heavy thud. The tree behind the house was trickier, as it stood at the apex of a triangle formed by the house, the propane tank, and the toolshed. He solved the problem by falling it uphill into a tangle of poison oak. "Gotta make Bill earn it," Dad said, laughing as he lifted his hard hat and scratched at his thin wet hair.

In years to come, I came back to those long white days on the river, to the sharp mingled smells of exhaust and sawdust, the background roar of high water, and the grace of those final chainsaw cuts as the two trees arced toward the ground. I watched Dad step back from the falling giants, his eyes watching their tops, the chainsaw idling beneath his right hand, his booted feet balanced with a dancer's grace. Once more I heard the crack of his rifle as he blew away those laden branches and made the whole world stand straight again, and for the last time.

Six months later, Dad experienced the first of a series of seizures, as the long-dormant cancer in his brain stirred to life. Once more, the mind and destiny of John Brannon changed all our lives.

I told the story to Alice the first time I visited her in "the ranger's house." I pointed the stumps out to her as we stood in the driveway, and with the telling, that world of snow and groaning trees and a boundless future returned. On New Year's Eve 1986, I told the tale to Matt and Heather as they stood before the fireplace in that same living room. Matt was not a ranger, and he was not even married to Heather yet, but times had changed.

I drank a beer, looked at the punch bowl of eggnog on the kitchen table, and knew I was going to drink too much tonight. I hadn't been to a party in this house since George and Alice had lived here, back in the days when Chuck believed having his wife become Alice's friend would help his career. He never thought it would lead me away from him.

I looked around at my audience. Chad and Nell, Laura and Fred, Terry and Yvonne, Ethan and Mary, Helen and Jake and baby Sam. Matt and Heather looked happy. She was beautiful in a red maternity blouse. Matt's beard had grown back, and I felt the old magic. His green eyes flashed, ringlets of black hair curled around his ears, he tossed his head when he laughed, and his eyes crinkled. His shoulders were broader now but retained the looseness of youth, and when he turned to talk to someone, his buttock muscles did interesting things to his jeans. "He does have cute buns," Heather admitted once.

He was Heather's now, entirely, and with his child in her womb, she was his, too. He had never been mine and never would be. But he still made my knees shake as he entered a room.

We drank eggnog, and more beer, and champagne. I tried to figure out what was going on between Terry and Yvonne. None of my business, of course, but the scuttlebutt was that she had a husband in Scott Valley and had taken a permanent job in Happy Camp to give him a hint that it was over. I wondered whether she and Terry were sleeping together yet. Terry hosted the weekly poker games, and several months ago I attempted a hint that I was available, but it turned out that when Terry invited someone over to watch a movie, he really did just want to watch the movie, at least in my case.

As the clock neared midnight, Heather turned on the television, and we watched the countdown from Times Square, cheered and hugged all around the room, and drank more champagne. I made my way out into the night and looked into the black sky. The rain had stopped. I felt my way to my truck and pulled the .357 out from beneath the seat. I could just barely make out the spiked skyline of trees on the ridge south of town. I pointed the revolver toward them and fired two shots: one for the old year and one for the new. The porch light came on and the whole crew appeared on the back porch. They stared at me under the pool of yellow light, and I shrugged and smiled at them. The women shook their heads and laughed. The men's mouths hung open. Chad let out a whoop. "Wish I'd thought of that!"

"Hacky-Sack!" someone yelled, and we formed a circle and kicked the leather-covered ball around and almost lost it in the dark, until finally Matt looked back at the house and saw Laura and Heather and Helen framed in the kitchen window. "Anybody want to finish up the eggnog?" he asked, and we drifted back inside to drink around the fireplace as the rain fell in earnest once more.

We started drinking coffee at two o'clock, and the party broke up at three. I drove home and fell into bed, to wake feeling lost and hungover. I crawled out of bed at ten o'clock, let the dogs out, and drank several cups of Earl Grey with milk and sugar and thought of Nigel. In the afternoon I drove up to Laura's house. We cut wood at her chopping block and talked and later watched football games and then movies on the VCR, and my hangover lifted. A strange sense of resignation settled on me, and I tossed my head back and laughed silently at the thought of firing the revolver last night. *Good God, Louise*, I said to myself. *No wonder you don't have a boyfriend.*

CHAPTER 23

Burning Tom Martin's

One hundred and five degrees on the airport tarmac, and it had been an hour since our crew boss forbade us to move. My bladder screamed from the Coke I had drunk on the bus ride into Stockton. Any shade that the Evergreen Airlines 727 might provide, any relief in the toilet inside it, were equally out of reach.

We sat, twenty firefighters in a line, a few feet away from a file of Apache women firefighters from Arizona. One of the women loosened her black hair from its braid and began to comb it. A breeze carried the shimmering mass out past her ear as she tilted her head and drew the comb through it. She looked cool and serene. I felt hot and sticky, with my green Nomex trousers stuck to my legs and damp gray underwear to my buttocks. We had all spent two weeks digging fire line on several Sierra Nevada fires collectively known as the Paper Complex.

Since I was the only Californian on our crew, my companions assumed I always knew where we were. On our way to the Paper Complex, with our bus stopped between Stockton and Sonora, someone asked me, "Where are we?"

I stood in the blackness with gravel under my boots and inhaled the flat warm smell of soil, fertilizer, irrigation water, and smoke. "We're still in the valley," I said. Later, I saw lights ahead of us in the Sierra foothills and guessed aloud that we were headed for Sonora. This greatly bolstered the crew's faith in my geographical knowledge.

I was the only woman on our crew, and a minority in more ways than one, for only three of us were Anglos: a bearded carpenter from Grants, and two Forest Service range specialists—Frank and me. Frank worked on a district south of Albuquerque, I on a national grassland in western Oklahoma. The rest were Hispanics and Native Americans from New Mexico, seasonal firefighters all, from several different towns and tribes. Ricardo, our crew boss, was a career Forest Service fire specialist. He paid little attention to us Anglos, beyond a single roll of the eyes at being saddled with both a hippie carpenter and a woman. He was far more concerned that his crew included Hopis, Pueblos, and Navajos, all three. This was not done except in the gravest fire emergencies, which the California/Oregon fires of 1987 certainly were.

Our collective journey to California began at an airfield in Albuquerque, where firefighters from all over the Southwest were assigned to crews, fed, then jammed onto 727s in which harried stewardesses with runs in their stockings handed us cans of juice and apologized for the nonworking coffeemakers. Before we boarded the plane, Ricardo gathered us in a circle and ordered us, in Spanish and English, to work hard and not to get into any disagreements or the culprits would be sent home, pronto. The three Anglos nodded understanding along with the rest.

My own journey had begun four hundred miles farther east, when Winona knocked on my trailer door in Cheyenne, Oklahoma, early on a September morning. I wasn't on the best of terms with our office manager, but for once she was in a good mood. She smiled at me. "You have a red card, don't you?" she said.

"Yes," I said.

"Albuquerque's sending a plane for you in two hours," she said. "They're putting together crews to go out to California."

I knew about the massive lightning bust that had lit wildfires from the southern Sierras to Oregon, and thanks to a phone call from Alice the night before, I knew about one fire that had rolled down Thompson Ridge and almost engulfed Happy Camp. I just didn't think that the Forest Service would be so hard up for help that it would reach out and snag one lone woman in Roger Mills County. But by noon I was buckled into a single-engine Cessna as the pilot lifted off the local airstrip.

Twelve hours later, packed into the 727, I flew west with nineteen new best friends into the night. In the small hours, as we unloaded from the bus at the fire camp near Sonora, we saw news about the fires posted on bulletin boards. "Plenty to choose from," said the carpenter as we looked at the maps. My eyes went up to the Klamath. I had left there only five months before, and most of the time I didn't think about it, but now I longed to see home. That was beyond my control, however, and for the next two weeks, as buses ferried us into strange woods, our world became a maze of strange logging roads, smoke, falling snags, and the glow of approaching fire.

We arrived at the Paper Camp in the dark, so we ate and slept—or tried to—most of the next day. Our sleeping area was near the electric generators. I got used to them eventually, but not to the heat that became unbearable by ten o'clock, just as we came off our night shifts and tried to sleep.

Now, on the tarmac at Stockton, I saw Ricardo coming back, paperwork fluttering in his hands as he led us toward yet another airplane. We threw our backpacks up toward the baggage compartment before we climbed aboard. Once in the air, I noticed our heading: north. Half an hour later, Mount Shasta rose above the horizon, floating like a scoop of ice cream in a sea of maple syrup. A faint hope grew in me, but I tamped it down. North could mean anywhere: Oregon, the Trinity Alps, even the Modoc.

We landed at Redding with a thump that brought the oxygen masks down in our faces. As we deplaned into the heat and caught our packs again, I noticed that the plane had stopped only a dozen feet from the end of the pavement. The pilot stood beneath the nose of the plane, gesturing at the weeds beyond as he shouted at one of the ground crew. "They never told me the runway was so short!" he bellowed.

Another bus, another freeway, and then the long climb out of Redding and up the canyon of the Sacramento River. Now we're getting somewhere, I thought. We could have turned off to go to Weaverville, or east to the Lassen National Forest. But we're still headed north. As we drew near Mount Shasta, I held my breath and waited for the bus to turn right toward McCloud. But we passed that exit, and the town of Mount Shasta City, too, where the dark skirts of the mountain were just visible through the smoke. As we barreled through the town of Weed without taking the highway to Klamath Falls, I knew where our dinner stop must be. "We're going to Yreka," I said to Frank, my seatmate. I may have bounced a little.

The sun had set by the time we pulled into the fairgrounds at Yreka.

I stepped off the bus and saw Alice holding a clipboard beside a check-in table. I ran to her and we hugged and sobbed. "I had to come to town today," she said, "but I couldn't stand it, so I came out here and asked them to give me something to do." Her house in Happy Camp had almost burned while I was still on the Paper Complex, but the neighborhood was safe for the time being. "And did you hear? Matt finally got his transfer—he's going up to region 1. At least, he'll go as soon as this nonsense is over with."

"That's great," I said and meant it. Region 1 was huge and far away from anywhere I was likely to go.

Our crew lined up to eat while the smoky hills blurred into darkness. We boarded another bus, which took us over a pass and down into Scott Valley. We passed through Fort Jones and descended into the Scott River canyon just as the door to the bus toilet decided not to stay closed anymore. Worse, a trickle of brown liquid flowed under the door and down the aisle. The carpenter stretched out his long legs and braced them against the door. We opened all the windows, fighting to keep our balance as the road twisted beneath us.

Twenty miles later, we reached the fire camp at Kelsey Creek. We bolted outside and into the anteroom of Hell. Lights glowed yellow in thick smoke, and the ever-present generators roared. Ricardo had to shout at us. He marched us over to the supply tent to pick up paper sleeping bags, then led us off to the quieter sleeping area, spread thickly with wood chips as a cushion. We unrolled our bags and collapsed, grateful just to be still.

Dawn arrived as cold gray claustrophobia, but the Scott River murmured nearby, and I walked over to the edge and looked at the clear green water framed by pines and firs, madrones and oaks. "Where are we?" Frank asked over my shoulder.

"In the Scott River canyon." I gestured around us. "This is home," I said, gobsmacked by the series of chances that had landed me here.

We ate breakfast, drank coffee, napped, played volleyball, picked up new Nomex shirts and pants at the supply tent. I wandered through camp and talked to people I knew. The smoke was so heavy that I couldn't see more than fifty yards in any direction. At six o'clock that evening, we loaded our tools and ourselves into the back of an open National Guard deuce-and-a-half truck.

Deuces are slow and rough. We sat on benches mounted on the olive-drab steel beds. Our driver, an urban lad from Sacramento, was nervous on the narrow dirt logging roads. Sometimes the outer rear duals hung out into space as we rounded a curve. I didn't mind. I knew these roads, or ones very like them, despite the smoke that reduced our world to a small circle. When we walked up a ridge, I knew the drainages on either side, and when I heard a stream below, I knew its name.

We spent our nights cutting line uphill with other crews, often bumped by aggressive hotshot crews, their chainsaws nipping at our heels. You guys go right ahead, I thought. Sometimes morning found us beside a firing crew attempting a daytime burnout, and we stayed with them for a double shift. A persistent inversion held cold air near the ground and blocked the sunlight, so that fires lit by drip torches often failed to carry even in what should have been the hottest part of the day.

Only at night did the smoke lift and the humidity fall. Then the fire ate at the dry duff, and we waited behind ridges to watch a burnout creep up the slope to meet the main fire as it approached with a roar. Sometimes the burnouts worked and deprived the main fire of fuel on that section of fire line. Then we moved in with hand tools to widen the four-foot line scraped down to mineral soil. By morning, we started mop-up, extinguishing remnants of fire in stumps and logs as we waited for our relief crew to show up. Sometimes the wind changed and blew embers over our line, started spot fires behind us, and sent us scurrying to put them out.

One night the burnout operations moved so far and so fast that morning found us beyond the Scott River drainage entirely, cutting line down toward Grider Creek. We slid down a road bank and onto a logging road where an engine crew sat eating sandwiches beside their hose-draped truck, next to a plantation of ten-foot-high Douglas-firs and deerbrush. Deerbrush, I had noticed on this trip, seemed resistant to fire, and its presence seemed to protect the young conifers. Since none of these plantations had been thinned, no flammable slash was about.

We rested awhile, then flagged down another deuce-and-a-half and rode the few miles into Seiad Valley and its main fire camp. By noon, we were lined up for lunch at the old Seiad Ranger Station. After working eighteen hours straight, I was exhausted but smiling. I had won the lottery.

We ate lunch on the lawn while I pointed at invisible peaks. Lower Devils. Slinkard Peak. Blue Mountain. Grider Ridge. The camp crew gave us more paper sleeping bags, and we begged extras to use as pads. We dragged them into corners around the green-and-white Forest Service houses. I spread mine out near some discouraged-looking hydrangeas beside the house where I used to babysit the ranger's kids. I took off my boots, slid into the bag, wriggled out of my filthy socks and trousers, unhooked my bra, and fell asleep in the embrace of a large paper product.

Ricardo let us sleep until six o'clock that evening. We woke, coughed, ate supper, and nursed cups of coffee while he wandered off with other yellow-shirted men to the nightly tactics meeting, where a man with a pointer slapped at a map clipped to an easel.

Ricardo came back to fetch us at nine o'clock, and we dragged our sleeping bags over to the deuce so as to have something to spread over our cold knees on the ride up to the fire. The crew looked at me as we turned onto the river highway and drove eastward. "Dónde?" someone asked.

"Quién sabe?" I said, but after a mile and a half I knew. "Walker Creek," I shouted as we turned off the highway. The lights were on in my parents' old house, the house beside the garden where I had pulled pigweed from rows of corn.

We drove up Walker Creek in low gear as the trees closed in over our heads. Switchbacks took us back and forth across the main creek, then its tributaries. We stopped at intersections while Ricardo—in the cab—consulted the map beneath his headlamp. I hunched deeper into my blackened Nomex coat, turned up the corduroy collar, and caught the smiling eyes of one of the Hopis. I shrugged. I didn't know where we were going, either.

Again and again, the truck swung right, only to back up after a few yards. Once, Ricardo climbed out of the cab and walked ahead, his headlamp lost in the soup. The old spur roads were grown up in brush that scraped the belly of the truck. Pine saplings crowded around us. Ahead, a glow appeared high on a ridge, and we heard the distant roar of fire. Ricardo waved the truck back to the main road again. After another mile, we came to a main road junction. The faces around me were pinched with cold. I stood up and peered over the cab at a wooden sign in the headlights. Enough of this shit. I climbed over the tailgate and walked up to read it, then stepped up on the running board and looked across the driver to Ricardo. "Where are you trying to go?" I said.

"Lake Mountain," he said.

Thank God. "You're on the wrong road," I said, and he opened the passenger door.

"Get up here," he said.

We made it to Lake Mountain at five o'clock in the morning. On the way, while the driver steered the truck under steep slopes thick with flaming snags, Ricardo shot anxious glances in my direction as he tried to follow the lines on his map, but I was on a roll, and we arrived at last at the very spot marked on his grimy blue-line copy.

The night air was beyond cold here at over six thousand feet, at the end of September. We piled out of the truck, grabbed our tools, and headed at a run for a welcoming orange glow fifty yards from the road. Catching up to us, Ricardo pulled a paper from his shirt pocket and consulted it. "We're supposed to improve the line here on the east side of Lake Mountain," he said. We looked at him and then at the bulldozer gouge beneath our feet, cut deep into the subsoil. Ricardo sighed, said something in Spanish, and looked at his watch. "Well, just do some mop-up and we'll see what it looks like come daylight." Tactfully, he disappeared into the darkness.

We dug camp cups out of our packs and brewed instant coffee on the coals beneath a smoldering log. The night sky—somewhere far above us in a world without smoke—turned from black to gray. Lake Mountain appeared, solid and very close, and we saw the lookout tower on its summit, wrapped in foil to protect the old landmark.

The next night, as we headed up Walker Creek again, we came across a van parked at an intersection on the east side of Slinkard Peak. Several men leaned over a map spread out on the hood, and Ricardo climbed down to talk to them. Headlamps semaphored into the darkness.

Ricardo looked back at the deuce, caught my eye, and waved me down. I rested my cold hands on the still-warm hood of the van and with a borrowed pen traced the wanderings of one of the spaghetti strands of road on the blue-line map. The men were a firing crew from Arizona, and they sought the location of a basin below Tom Martin Peak. Their crew boss removed his hard hat, and his forehead gleamed bone white in the darkness. He looked at me and then at Ricardo. "Can we borrow her?" he asked.

In a few minutes I was in the van's front seat, pointing the way. Left, right, straight ahead, until I pointed out at the dark and then at the map and said, "This is the basin, I think—and that's Tom Martin Peak straight ahead of us."

The crew boss rolled down the driver's side window and spat into the night. A faraway liquid roar that was not the roar of fire floated up through the dark and the smoke, and time stood still and rolled backward. Far below, the Klamath talked to me once more.

Drip torches and fuel cans emerged from the back of the van; I slid over into the driver's seat as Steve stepped out. He hoisted on his day pack and tested the squelch button on the radio strapped to his chest. "Keep even with the crew," he said, "and drop off a fuel can every hundred yards or so. Meet you at the saddle in the morning."

The six crewmen filled their drip torches and disappeared below the road, their paths marked by bobbing headlamp beams. I leaned my arm on the open window and listened to the river.

Tom Martin and a partner came north from San Francisco in 1850 to look for gold. They settled in to spend the winter at a Karuk village on the Klamath River. In December, heavy snows came, and they grew hungry. Two Karuk men came to visit and asked to borrow a rifle. At first the partners refused, fearing treachery, but finally starvation seemed the greater problem, and they loaned out the weapon. The Karuks left but returned the next day with a deer carcass. In the fall, they told Tom and partner, they used dogs to chase elk into the bluffs below the high peak above the village. But guns, they said, would make the hunt much easier.

The next year, thousands more white men came to the Klamath. They built wing dams to turn the river out of its bed and mined the gravel for gold. Elk and deer alike soon grew scarce. Most of the miners left in a year or two, but Tom stayed, married the daughter of a medicine woman, and died an old man, with his name attached to the peak where his wife's brothers killed the deer. One of his descendants, rosy cheeked and green eyed, rode the school bus with me. She was eager to leave the river and go "where no one knows I'm an Indian."

I traced the progress of the firing crew by the liquid fire falling from their drip torches. Thin lines of flame flowed among the slash piles left from last year's logging. No lightning fires had burned free in this place for eighty years, and duff and branches lay thick on the ground. I revved the van's engine, crawled ahead a few yards, dragged a plastic fuel container out of the back, and placed it on the roadside. Shapes of men, backlit, moved through the sparse conifers below. Tom Martin Peak, once just a faint dark presence against the sky, popped into view as the inversion layer broke up at last. Smoke rose and dissipated, stars burst out of the night, and the world I had left was all there once more.

The road wound between the basin and the peak, on its way to the saddle. I watched the fire below and followed it as it grew. Trees torched out with a hiss. Rising air created a wind that swept through the walls of fir and pine above me and drew them down toward the heat. Now and then I set the brake and stepped out into the dark, one ear cocked for the crackle of the radio. By now the basin was a circle of fire, pulling everything in toward its center, the flames rising higher and higher. Branches tossed and roared and drowned out the river's voice.

I reached the saddle just as the stars started to fade and the workaday world began to return. The burners straggled up to the road and set down their drip torches. I stood in the saddle at the intersection of three roads and looked out toward the east. For a little while, before the inversion came back, I saw Mount Shasta, my old friend, floating there still, lost in time but steady of place, right where she should be.

A few days later, yet another bus trip took our crew back to Yreka on the first leg of the trip back to Albuquerque. I had time while we rested and ate a meal at the fairgrounds to touch base with old friends from the Klamath. "How do you like Oklahoma?" Jon Silvius asked me.

"It's different, but fun in a lot of ways," I said. "I miss the Klamath, though."

He nodded. "Well, when this is all over"—he waved his arm at the pall of smoke and the mania of the great fire camp—"there'll be jobs here again, and the black money will flow for a while. If you want to come back then, I'll bet you can."

I had not thought of that, about the "black money," the funds for reforestation and repair that always followed a big fire. All the national forests in California and southern Oregon would be hiring new people in the following years, and anyone with silvicultural experience could probably write their own ticket. It was something to think about, and I did, all the way back to Albuquerque and then all the way back to Oklahoma. It was good to have options.

CHAPTER 24

Moving On

With a great sum bought I this freedom.
—Acts 22:28, King James Version

I went back to Cheyenne, Oklahoma, where my escape plan had worked
to perfection. On the Black Kettle National Grassland, I explored a
land of buffalo grass and little bluestem, of bobwhite quail and wild
turkey and white-tailed deer. A land of gas drilling rigs glowing on
the horizons at night, and tornado warnings, and murky streams
full of catfish. A land of scissor-tailed flycatchers and roadrunners,
the full spectrum of poisonous snakes, and windmills. A land full of
ghosts—of bison, and Cheyenne warriors, and Custer's soldiers, and
all the white farmers who abandoned the dusty land in droves in the
1930s. A land of people strange to me, who recognized a newcomer
on the street and stopped to tell her the story of their lives. But of the
man who got me off the Klamath, I did not think at all. The voices of
pain and regret went silent, and with that silence came a relief that
abolished even homesickness.

"I want you to go to level two law enforcement," said my boss. "I
need somebody else here who can write tickets."

"Where's the class?" I said.

"Santa Fe," he said and grinned around his pipe. "A week-long
course."

I wasn't excited about driving over four hundred miles to go to a
training session on how to tell Texans not to trash our campgrounds,
but I had heard good things about the old tricultural town, and it all
paid the same. Besides, a week away from Roy and Winona wasn't the
worst thing in the world. Now that Susan, the recreation technician,

228

had left, I was the only other permanent employee on the grassland, and the full brunt of their suspicions fell on me.

Not that they were unwarranted. We didn't even have the Data General on the district yet, so for me, Forest Service social networks didn't exist. If I wanted to talk to someone in the supervisor's office in Albuquerque, I had to write a letter or telephone them. And our office was so small that I couldn't phone without tipping off the boss. Luckily, Oklahoma was on Central Time and New Mexico on Mountain Time; I could go home for lunch or after work and still call people I knew, especially a couple of former grassland employees who knew the lay of the land.

Eventually, word of my communications reached the forest supervisor, but instead of being displeased, he mused, "You know, she's the third person out there who has said the same things about Roy. I think it's time for a change."

But that was in the future as I drove across the Texas Panhandle and into New Mexico. At Albuquerque I turned north and drove the fifty-odd miles to Santa Fe. I checked in to my motel and took a nap. The sun had just set when I awoke, and I stood at the patio doors of my room and looked west, mesmerized by the turquoise blue of the sky against the dark mountains. I had never seen a sky that color. Perhaps it was the scattered pink clouds near the horizon, perhaps the seven thousand feet of elevation, but I never knew until that moment that such a sky existed. I stared at it for a long time, until the color faded.

The class met in a room at the Santa Fe National Forest headquarters, and as I looked around the room at the other students, a man caught my eye. I didn't know him, but he looked familiar somehow, and I threw an occasional glance his way. Blue eyes, prominent cheekbones, short reddish beard, high forehead, reddish-blond hair going gray and pulled back into a ponytail. When the instructor had us introduce ourselves, I listened for his name, but it wasn't familiar.

Three days into the class, I counted the cash in my wallet and realized that meals and incidentals in Santa Fe were more expensive than I had bargained for, and businesses didn't want to take Oklahoma checks. My government credit card was good only for gasoline. At this rate, I would have to live on the doughnuts from morning coffee break.

"Um," I said, approaching a knot of students during a break, "I'm out of cash. If I wrote a check, could someone cash it for me?"

The man with the ponytail lifted a hand. "I have to go to my credit union at lunch," he said. "I could do that."

"Oh, thank you," I said, and we shook hands and exchanged names. Bob was the lands officer on the Pecos Ranger District, a short drive east of Santa Fe.

At lunchtime, we rode in his small blue car to the credit union, and he went inside while I checked out his cassette tapes. He seemed to like Blondie. He came out and counted out five twenties into my hand.

Business over, we sat and talked. He had been on the Pecos District for only about a year and had worked in Montana for a decade before that. I told him about the Klamath, and he told me that he was born and raised in western Oregon.

"What do you find to do around here?" I asked him.

"Well, I hike, and I visit the museums, of course. And right now I read a lot," he said. "It's the rainy season, and by the time I get home the daily thunderstorm usually rolls in. That's why they have such beautiful sunsets here—it rains all the time."

"That makes sense," I said. "What are you reading now?"

"I just finished a novel by Isabel Allende," he said. "*The House of the Spirits*. Have you read any magic realism?"

"No," I said, suspecting that this was a conversation I wouldn't have had with any other man in that room.

"And I'm starting a book I've always wanted to read—the *Elder Edda*. Great stuff. There's one verse I really like," he said. "Praise not the day before evening, nor the woman before she is burnt, nor the blade before it's tested, the girl before she's married, the ice before it's crossed . . ."

"Nor the ale before it is drunk," I finished. "That's the Hávamál."

"You know it?"

"I read it a few years ago. On a fire," I said. "Are you Swedish?" I asked suddenly.

"Well, part," he said. "On my mother's side."

"Me, too," I said. "On my father's."

We looked at each other. "Would you like to go have lunch with me?" he said.

"Yes," I said. "Yes, I would."

CHAPTER 25

Epilogue

So we beat on, boats against the current,
borne back ceaselessly into the past.
—F. Scott Fitzgerald

Some paths open all at once and take us in unexpected directions: to another job in Idaho, to marriage, to bosses good and bad, to a realization that a world of stories exists, waiting to be told.

In 1999 I went to a writing seminar in Montana, taught by Bill Kittredge. During a break, he reminisced about a boy he had known when he was eight years old in eastern Oregon. "We went to the county fair one day with our folks," he said, "and somehow the two of us got hold of some beer, and we drank it all, sitting in the back of a pickup truck. We fell asleep, and when we woke up we were so sick!"

"What happened to that kid?" someone asked.

"He grew up," said Bill, "and his family moved to Nevada, and the last I heard he was ranching in Idaho someplace."

Something clicked in my head. "What was his name?" I asked.

"Powers," he said. "Jack Powers."

"That's our neighbor," I said. "He ranches a couple miles down the road from us."

"I don't believe this," said a woman across the table, a professor from Georgetown. "You two have never met before," she moved her finger back and forth between Bill and me, "and you live hundreds of miles away from each other, but you both know this man?"

Bill laughed. "Well," he said, "the West is a small town with a very long main street."

As is the Forest Service. After we left Happy Camp, Heather and I kept in vicarious touch through Laura's visits, which brought each of us news of the other, but it would be twenty years before we saw each other again. During that time, she and Matt raised a son and she ran her own business, then launched a second Forest Service career.

Matt rose in the timber management ranks, and now and then I saw his name in Forest Service news reports. Sometimes I met people who had worked with him, especially after 2000, when the big fires of a new century brought fire teams from all over the country to the national forest where I worked. But not until one late October day, seventeen years after I left Happy Camp, did we exchange a sentence again.

In the office that morning, the talk was all of that final World Series game, the one that vanquished at last the memories and the hauntings and the collective nervous breakdowns, the first time in eighty-six years that the Red Sox won the last game of the season. We could breathe again, uncross our fingers, launder our filthy lucky shirts. At the computer, I typed Matt's last name into the search box and double-clicked.

Curse? What curse? Yesssss!! The keys clicked under my fingers. I looked at the words, the first in so many years, floating on the screen, then moved my hand over the mouse, shifting it. The arrow pointed to "send." My finger reached, and the mouse clicked. I whirled my chair around and rejoined the celebration.

Later that day as I sat alone with the autumn sun drifting south, I checked my in-box one more time. "It doesn't matter, it doesn't matter," I said to myself as the messages winked onto the screen. "It doesn't matter."

Then I saw his name, and the words, new and fresh as thunder.

UNBELIEVABLE! I only wish my parents could have lived to see it.

And then the tears came, joy and sorrow rising through my throat and out into the thin mountain air, decades of grief and memories turning loose, not gone at all, only waiting to be poked to live again.

Bob and I bought a house on eight acres of rocks and raised sheep and hauled hay and irrigated and fixed fence. I counted cows and measured grass and wrote allotment management plans. I wrote essays and then a book. I retired. We sold all the ewes and ate our last wether. I started writing another book. Bob cut wood and coaxed greenery from the rocky ground, built a sun wheel, and welcomed the ravens back every winter. And one day Heather phoned to tell me she had accepted a job only a few miles away. "Six months on and six months off," she said, and did I know any places to rent?

"I could probably retire now myself," she said, "but a few more years will bring more of a nest egg." It seemed like a good time to leave her current job. When it came to promoting women, that national forest hadn't gotten the memo.

"I'll stay for two or three years," she said, "then maybe I'll go to Alaska. I've always wanted to see it."

She came and we had lunch, and when Matt came to visit her I saw them both. And if they had changed at all, it was in the happiest possible way, for they were still charming and kind and funny, but with any coltishness replaced with a mature beauty and strength that spoke of outdoor exercise and self-confidence and wisdom about what was really important. I picked Matt's brains about timber markets and mill closures and log exports, fodder for the essays and opinion pieces I wrote for regional newspapers.

Heather and I met and talked often while she was nearby. And I learned that her life with Matt had not been all beer and skittles. Ten years into the marriage she had moved out on him, an experience that floored him, coinciding as it did with the death of both his mother and Rufus.

"He'd lost his mother and his dog, and then his wife and son moved out, all in the same week," she said. "I think he realized then he had to make some compromises. Also," she added, "I simply couldn't afford to raise a child by myself."

"So you worked it out," I said.

We sat silent for a few minutes. Over the years we had both learned, often painfully, that some things were common to almost all men, and to expect more from them was like expecting our cats to read.

Later, walking down the sidewalk, I understood at last the reason that I could still carry a little splinter of a torch for Matt, after all those years: I had never had to live with him.

Matt was part of a time in which anything seemed possible, because all of us were young and a decade and more of balls-to-the-wall logging and planting and thinning rolled out before us. We thought we had this ancient place figured out, that what our professional forebears had stumbled into during the postwar boom was permanent and would support us and a town forever. We worked hard at doing what we thought were the right things. We thought that the green world around us would forgive our mistakes and let us start over. We did not know that it was already on its way out, driven by hubris, greed, and a warming and drying climate ever more hostile to conifers.

In 1988, the black money that Jon Silvius predicted arrived, and new people came to the Happy Camp District and drove on the logging roads and walked the halls where I had walked, and for several years, an orgy of salvage sales kept the mills humming. The runaway train kept running, until 1993.

In that year, a switch, in the form of the northern spotted owl, was thrown on the Klamath and over the whole Pacific Northwest. In the vast Snake River drainage, the lever was not an owl, but several species of salmon. All the trains careened onto sidings and coasted to a halt. Throughout the West, the needs of species that required old-growth trees and clear streams and undisturbed soils overcame, for once, the desire of the timber industry to skim off the last stands of ancient trees, carve up the last roadless lands. In Happy Camp, those needs couldn't be reconciled with an annual timber cut of fifty-five million board feet.

The fact that the train never quite reached the cliff led to a kind of cognitive dissonance among those most affected when their way of life came to a sudden stop. Because that last 10 percent of old-growth timber was never logged as originally planned, the people who had seen the cliff approaching couldn't say, "I told you so," and the loggers and mill workers could say, "The spotted owl took our jobs." Because we didn't eat all the cake, the notion that the cake could have lasted forever was too attractive not to gain a following.

In 1994, the only surviving lumber mill in Happy Camp closed down forever after the big timber sales stopped. Its corporate owners might have retooled to process smaller amounts of smaller trees from thinning sales, but they had long since run the numbers and decided against it. The mills that survived in Siskiyou County were near railroad tracks and designed to process smaller logs, but even they would struggle. In Happy Camp, the local economy crashed and many businesses closed. The town reverted to its Depression-era base: the Forest Service, the state highway department, and the schools, with the addition of an organized Karuk Tribe, recreational floating on the river, and marijuana cultivation.

In the twenty-first century, a series of droughts set the stage for massive forest fires. My frame of reference for big fires was 1987, when fires burned for months over both logged and unlogged, roaded and unroaded lands, so I didn't buy a connection between lack of logging and big fires. But for many, especially after 2010, as fuel moisture ratings reached new lows, fuel loads in tons per acre became a worry in the inland West. On the coast, with its rain and fog, no one cared about ladder fuels or big chunks of wood on the forest floor.

The Happy Camp Complex began in August 2014 near Frying Pan Ridge. Wind from the west drove the fire upriver, primed by record heat in Happy Camp that summer—over five degrees above average in July. The fire crossed Grider Ridge, followed the river corridor, and tore up through the Walker Creek drainage, reburning all of the 1987 fire footprint and then some, and more severely. Lake Mountain Lookout was wrapped in foil once more. The fire headed east to leap the Scott River and even jumped the Klamath at one point, before the autumn rains at last slowed it down.

Three years later, scars of salvage logging stretched for miles across the river from Seiad Valley and up into the Walker Creek drainage. I read the NEPA documents for this Westside Fire Recovery Project and learned that at least a few lessons had been learned since 1987. Although the prescription was still to log and replant, the advice was to leave space next to green hardwoods, to mimic natural groupings of trees, and aim for a sharply reduced number of trees per acre, compared to our old eight-by-eight plantings. "There is," said the final environmental impact statement, "no intention to create densely stocked plantations of continuous fuels." And most remarkable to someone with my memories: "Growth of existing hardwoods will be encouraged; hardwoods will be included in the target stocking for units in areas where they exist."

Somehow, that prediction from three decades ago—"It's impossible to bring a plantation to rotation age on the Klamath"—had survived and made its way into institutional memory.

Some of the big new fires were not wind driven; although they covered tens of thousands of acres, they often burned in a mosaic pattern that left patches of green, cleared out the understory, and probably did more good than harm. Dead trees are havens for woodpeckers and other wildlife, and some plant species need severe fires to reproduce. But their sheer size was like nothing anyone had ever seen before, and they were part of a procession: Panther, 2008; Beaver and Happy Camp Complex, 2014; Gap, 2016; Abney and Eclipse Complex, 2017; Natchez, 2018. This was not the old Klamath.

Even knowing this, I was startled by the stark words of a scientific article: "In the Klamath, the influence of a reduction in severe fire during the Little Ice Age, or a period of frequent but lower-severity fire in 1700–1900 may have increased the dominance of conifer forests. That legacy may increase the vulnerability to higher fire activity today in a remarkably warmer climate."

The article went on to conclude that much of the Klamath ecoregion seems likely to revert, under the pressures of heat and drought and fire, to a shrubland-hardwood ecosystem in which conifers will no longer dominate. Forget the future: the Klamath is already out of balance with the present, a situation known as disequilibrium.

Late in May 2018, I hiked with Laura up the East Fork of Indian Creek, where a trail now followed the route of the obliterated main logging road, and the streams ran clear beside mossy logs and banks of ferns under the enormous Douglas-firs that had survived the logging years. After thirty years in a high desert, it seemed to me a fresh green marvel. For despite droughts and summer heat and low snowpacks, plants kept growing: bigleaf maple and hazel, yew and dogwood and poison oak, and above it all the leaning giants.

When the Natchez Fire came that summer, it burned a large chunk of the northwest quarter of the district, but widespread underburning ahead of the fire helped keep it out of the main Indian Creek drainage, while the footprint of the Eclipse Complex stopped it from progressing to the southwest. Happy Camp itself was untouched, as was the main drainage of Indian Creek.

Later, Laura wondered whether that success in protecting Indian Creek might have made everyone too optimistic about handling a fire in that canyon, especially a wind-driven fire on the west flank of Thompson Ridge, below Slater Butte.

Twice before—in September 1966 and September 1987—fires had consumed that area, but they moved slowly enough that burnouts kept them away from the many houses along the thirteen-mile stretch of county road that paralleled Indian Creek. But early on September 8, 2020, a tree fell onto a power line near the Slater Butte Lookout and started a fire. A fifty-mile-an-hour wind out of the east did the rest. Within a couple of hours, the Slater Fire ran down from the ridge and over the twice-burned slopes, blew across draws, threw rains of embers onto the houses on Indian Creek Road, then jumped the creek and raced up both sides.

Flames cascaded downhill, growing ever hotter as superheated air descended into the canyon, the wind ripping big trees out by their roots. With fire blocking the road into Happy Camp, Indian Creek residents fled north over the Grayback Road, and the fire followed, spilling over the divide. By evening it was far into Oregon. More than 150 houses burned on Indian Creek and its tributaries that day, and— in what is becoming a familiar pattern in the West—the trees beside them were scorched and often killed, but not consumed. Laura and Fred and their cats got out with minutes to spare. Two people were killed, but the fire hit when many Indian Creek people were already at work in town, and their children in school. Their homes burned, but they were safe and watched in disbelief as the towering pyrocumulus clouds rose into the sky.

The Slater Fire would burn over one hundred thousand acres in its first forty-eight hours. The scar of the 2018 Natchez Fire prevented the rolling flames from advancing very far up the South Fork of Indian Creek, but as the fire struck the East Fork, it moved under the influence of both wind and terrain and leaped into that vast drainage faster than a human could run. By nightfall, virtually every tree in the East Fork was dead, all the vegetation on the steep upper slopes utterly consumed, and fifty years of sugar pine research at the outplant site gone forever.

I know that in the spring, millions of dormant deerbrush seeds will come alive and grow and begin to heal the burned and naked soil with their roots and leaves and ability to pull nitrogen from the air. A few more Junes, and a blanket of their white and pink and blue blossoms will clothe the mountainsides, and hardwood sprouts will grow around charred trunks. Woodpeckers will drum and call and raise their young in holes in the dead conifers amid a cacophony of scavenging insects. Deer and elk will come back and grow fat on the new growth. All the places where we walked in hope or sadness will be there still, with or without us: the steep slopes and the draws and the long fingers of the ridges, and floating just above them, the lost voices of the trees, trying to tell us something we never understood.

Sources

Davies, Gilbert W., and Florice M. Frank, eds. *Memories from the Land of Siskiyou: Past Lives and Times in Siskiyou County*. Hat Creek, CA: HiStory ink Books, 1997.

Doron, Dr. William, Russell W. Bower, and Al Groncki. *Chronological History of the Klamath National Forest*. Vol. 6, The 1950s, Parts 1–3 (Yreka, CA: USDA Forest Service, 1990).

Hirt, Paul W. *A Conspiracy of Optimism: Management of the National Forests since World War Two*. Lincoln: University of Nebraska Press, 1996.

Limerick, Patricia. *The Legacy of Conquest: The Unbroken Past of the American West*. New York: W. W. Norton, 1987.

Pence, Ned N., and F. Carl. *Lost in the Forest: A Story about the Forest Service*. Privately printed, 2008.

For those who want to learn more about the fire ecology of the Klamath bioregion, the following materials may be of interest:

2014 Klamath National Forest Fire Season Review. Yreka, CA: USDA Forest Service, Klamath National Forest, 2015. fs.usda.gov/Internet/FSE_DOCUMENTS/stelprd3841893.pdf.

Bushy, Judy. "Fire Siege of 1987 Remembered." *Happy Camp News*, August 28, 2007. http://happycampnews.com/fire-siege-of-1987-remembered.

Frost, Evan J., and Rob Sweeney. *Fire Regimes, Fire History and Forest Conditions in the Klamath-Siskiyou Region: An Overview and*

Synthesis of Knowledge. World Wildlife Fund, 2000. sipnuuk. karuk.us/system/files/atoms/file/AFRIFoodSecurity_UCB_ ArielleHalpern_002_001.pdf.

Mann, Charles C. "There's Good Fire and Bad Fire. An Indigenous Practice May be Key to Preventing Wildfires." *National Geographic,* December 15, 2020. http://www.nationalgeographic. com/history/2020/12/good-fire-bad-fire-indigenous-practice- may-key-preventing-wildfires/.

Ruediger, Luke. *The Eclipse Fire Report.* Klamath Forest Alliance, 2017. https://www.klamathforestalliance.org/documents/2017_ Eclipse_Fire_Report.pdf.

Serra-Diaz, Josep M., Charles Maxwell, Melissa S. Lucash, Robert M. Scheller, Danelle M. Laflower, Adam D. Miller, Alan J. Tepley, Howard E. Epstein, Kristina J. Anderson-Teixeira, and Jonathan R. Thompson. "Disequilibrium of Fire-Prone Forests Sets the Stage for a Rapid Decline in Conifer Dominance during the 21st Century." *Science Report* 8, no. 6749 (2018). https://doi. org/10.1038/s41598-018-24642-2.

Slater/Devil Post-Fire BAER Assessment Report. Yreka, CA: USDA Forest Service, Klamath National Forest, 2020. https://inciweb. nwcg.gov/incident/article/7237/58811/.

Taylor, Alan H., and Carl N. Skinner. "Spatial Patterns and Controls on Historical Fire Regimes and Forest Structure in the Klamath Mountains." *Ecological Applications* 13 (2003): 704–19.

Westside Fire Recovery Project. Yreka, CA: USDA Forest Service, Klamath National Forest, 2016. fs.usda.gov/ project/?project=45579.